D1643640

CHRONOLOGY

OF

MUSIC COMPOSERS.

In two Volumes

Volume 2
1810 to 1937.

Compiled by
JOSEPH DETHERIDGE.

Copyright 1937.

PUBLISHED BY
J. DETHERIDGE.
26, BELL END, ROWLEY REGIS, BIRMINGHAM,
ENGLAND.

CONTENTS OF VOLUME II.

PLATES, ILLUSTRATIONS.

INTRODUCTORY REMARKS TO VOL II.

This work is intended to serve as a guide, not only to the musician and music student, but to the general reader and ordinary listener.

It may be expedient here to remark, as concisely as possible, on a few points which have presented themselves during the compiling of the work.

The idea of a chronology was conceived from a personal desire to see the composers' names in that order, realising that *Period is of the utmost importance with regard to musical composition and its performance.*

Names were first arranged in chronological order; afterwards, biographies were read several times.

By this method many facts were observed which hitherto had passed unnoticed and statements either verified themselves or called for further research.

Every effort has been made to include accurate information.

The number of composers stated in Volume I as about 2,500 has been greatly exceeded.

Pictures herewith included serve the purpose of marking the various periods.

The Chart of Vol. II should be compared with the map of Vol. I.

Although it may not be of musical importance, it will be noticed that performers on a particular instrument often follow each other closely by date of birth. This appears to happen in periodic cycles.

It is possible to trace through these pages the succession of persons engaged in certain important musical posts: such as principals of academies, chapel masters and organists of cathedrals, etc.

A more practical use of the book may be made by musicians who may desire to project a system of study of the works of the masters in chronological order. In any branch of the Art this seems a sound and thorough method. The growth of instrumental technique together with musical development would be easily followed.

The Author feels that his labours will be amply rewarded if these books (Vol. I and II) will in any way assist the reader to arrive at a better understanding of the works of the various composers.

He wishes to thank most heartily the people to whom he is indebted for suggestions and in matters of research ; also the living composers for information concerning themselves, and especially the printers for their unerring care and attention, and who by keen interest and observation have averted what may have been serious errors.

APRIL, 1937.

THE GREAT MASTERS.

VOLUME I.

These have portraits included.

		Born			Born
JOSQUIN.	Netherlander.	1445	HANDEL.	German.	1685
DR. TYE.	English.	1498	BACH.*	German.	1685
TALLIS.	English.	1515	TARTINI.	Italian.	1692
PALESTRINA*	Italian.	1525	GLUCK.	German.	1714
LASSUS.	Netherlander.	1530	HAYDN.	Austrian.	1732
VITTORIA.	Spanish.	1540	MOZART.	Austrian.	1756
BYRD.	English.	1542	BEETHOVEN.*	German.	1770
MONTEVERDE.	Italian.	1567	SPOHR.	German.	1784
GIBBONS,	English.	1583	WEBER.	German.	1786
SCHÜTZ.	German.	1585	ROSSINI.	Italian.	1792
			SCHUBERT.	German.	1797
LULLY,	French.	1633	BERLIOZ	French.	1803
CORELLI	Italian.	1653	MENDELSSOHN.	German.	1809
PURCELL.	English.	1658	CHOPIN.	Polish.	1810

VOLUME 2.

		Born			Born
SCHUMANN*	German.	1810	BRUCH.	German.	1838
LISZT.	Hungarian.	1811	TCHAIKOVSKY.	Russian.	1840
WAGNER.	German.	1813	GRIEG.	Norwegian.	1843
VERDI.	Italian.	1813	PARRY.	English.	1848
FRANCK.	Belgian.	1822	ELGAR.*	English.	1857
BRAHMS*	German.	1833	DEBUSSY.	French.	1862
			DELIUS.	English.	1862
SAINT-SAËNS.	French.	1835	STRAUSS, R.*	German.	1864

EXACT CONTEMPORARIES.

	Born
SWEELINCK—BULL	1562
CORELLI—STEFFANI	1653
PURCELL—SCARLATTI	1658
HANDEL—BACH—SCARLATTI, G.D.—VERACINI	1685
ARNE—BOYCE	1710
BACH, C. P. E.—JOMMELLI—GLUCK	1714
SPOHR—PAGANINI	1784
GLINKA—BERLIOZ	1803
CHOPIN—SCHUMANN	1810
WAGNER—WALLACE—VERDI	1813
BRUNEAU—ELGAR	1857
DELIUS—DEBUSSY	1862

This page reproduced from Vol. 1 for convenience of readers.

ROBERT SCHUMANN.

Chronology of Music Composers.

VOLUME II.

Born	Died	Name	Nationality.
1810 8 June. Zwickau.	1856 29 July. Endenich, n'r Bonn.	**SCHUMANN,** Robert Alexander. Pupil of Wieck for piano and Dorn for composition. Husband of Clara Schumann, the pianist (1819). Studied law until 1830, then became writer and critic. Met Mendelssohn first at Leipzig in 1835. Professor of composition and piano at the Dresden Conservatorium. Succeeded Hiller as conductor at Dresden in '49, and was director at Düsseldorf in '50. Symphonies, overtures, concertos (for piano, 'cello, violin and horn respectively), string quartets, quintets, trios, cantatas, choruses, opera, dramatics, songs, and every kind of piano piece. All kinds of works to Opus 148, and 9 without opus numbers. His songs and pianoforte and orchestral music reach the highest poetical ideals, and are classified as " modern music."	German.
1810 19 June. Hamburg.	1873 18 July. Klosters.	**DAVID,** Ferdinand. Born in the same house as Mendelssohn. Violinist: pupil of Spohr and Hauptmann at Cassel. Teacher of Joachim and Wilhelmj. Leader of the orchestra of the Gewandhaus Concerts at Leipzig under the conductorship of Mendelssohn, where he gave the first performance of the master's violin concerto in 1845. Became professor of the violin on the opening of the Leipzig Conservatorium in 1843. Made frequent visits to Russia. 6 Violin concertos, solos, a school, chamber music, 2 symphonies, and an opera.	German.
1810 Shrewsbury	1882 4 February. London.	**HILES,** John. Brother of Henry (1826). Organist at Shrewsbury, Portsmouth, Brighton and London. Pianoforte pieces ; songs, etc., and didactic works.	English.
1810 9 July. Königsberg.	1849 11 May. Berlin.	**NICOLAI,** Carl Otto Ehrenfried. Pupil of Zelter and Klein in Berlin and Baini in Rome. Organist to the chapel of the Prussian Embassy in Rome in 1833 to '37. Chapel-master of the Court opera in Vienna in 1841, and that at Berlin in 1847. Founded the Philharmonic Concerts in Vienna in 1842. Italian and German operas, including the " Merry Wives of Windsor," also orchestral and choral works.	German.
1810 14 August. London.	1876 19 April. Gloucester.	**WESLEY,** Samuel Sebastian (Mus.D.). Son of Samuel (1766). Enriched the music of the English Church. Chorister of the Chapel Royal in 1820. Organist of three London churches from '26, of the Cathedrals of Hereford in '32, Exeter in '35, Winchester in '49, and of Gloucester in '65. Professor of the organ at the Royal Academy in '50. Conducted the Three-Choir Festivals at Gloucester once in 3 years. English church music, anthems, services, glees, songs, organ, and pianoforte works.	English.

Born	Died	Name	Nationality
1810 7 November. Békés.	1893 15 June. Budapest.	**ERKEL, Franz.** Pianist. Conductor of the National Opera at Budapest from 1838. Several operas (the most popular being " Hunyady László "), and national songs including the Hungarian National Anthem.	Hungarian.
1810 16 November. Bleckade.	1882 3 April. Schwerin.	**KÜCKEN, Friedrich Wilhelm.** Studied counterpoint under Birnbach at Berlin ; composition under Sechter at Vienna, and Halévy and Bordogni in Paris. Chapel-master at Stuttgart, 1851-61, succeeding Lindpaintner. Operas ; sonatas for pianoforte, violin and 'cello ; songs and duets.	German.
1810 1 December Zsàmbèk.	1889 31 January. Weimar.	**GUNG'L, Joseph.** Uncle of Johann (1828-83). Bandmaster of an Austrian regimental band, and of his own band at Berlin, with which he toured, visiting nearly every capital on the Continent. Music-director to the King of Prussia in '49, and chapel-master to the Emperor of Austria in '58. 300 Dance tunes and marches.	Hungarian.
1811 23 February. Namur.	1840 27 February. Paris.	**GODEFROID, Jules Joseph** Brother of D. J. (1818). Harpist. Harp music, and 2 comic operas.	Belgian.
1811 23 March. Berlin.	1891 7 January. Berlin.	**TAUBERT, Karl Gottfried Wilhelm.** Pupil of Berger for piano and Klein for composition. Music-director of the Royal Opera in Berlin in 1841, and Court-chapel-master in '45. 6 Operas, 4 dramas, 4 cantatas, 3 symphonies, sonatas for piano and violin and piano, chamber music and songs (294 in number), and vocal duets.	German.
1811 23 March. Rome.	1870 19 April. Paris.	**STAMATY, Camille Marie.** Pupil of Fessy and Kalkbrenner, and later of Mendelssohn at Leipsic. Teacher of Gottschalk and Saint-Saëns. Chevalier of the Legion of Honour in 1862. Many books of piano studies, concerto, sonatas, a trio, and variations.	Italian.
1811 14 April. Paris.	1887 5 July. Paris.	**LE COUPPEY, Félix.** Pupil at the Paris Conservatoire, assistant teacher of harmony in '27, and succeeded his master, Dourlens, as regular teacher of harmony in '43, and succeeded Herzas as pianoforte teacher in '48. Pianoforte works.	French.
1811 17 April. London.	1891 24 June. London.	**MOUNSEY, Ann Sheppard.** Sister of Elizabeth (1819). Pupil of Logier. Organist at 3 London churches. Gave classical concerts in London, for one of which Mendelssohn composed " Hear my prayer," first performed 8th January, 1845. 100 Songs, 40 part-songs, piano and organ works, and an oratorio, " The Nativity."	English.
1811 9 June. Rotterdam.	1884 15 May. Rotterdam.	**LANGE, Samuel de.** Father of Samuel (1840) and Daniel (1841). Organist of the church of St. Lawrence, Rotterdam. Organ works.	Dutch.

Born	Died	Name	Nationality
1811 28 June. Boston.	1872 14 June. London.	**FLOWERS, George French (Mus.D.).** Pupil of Rinck and Wartensee in Germany. Organist in Paris and London. Organ fugues, ode on the " Death of Wellington," vocal pieces and didactic works.	English.
1811 5 August. Metz.	1896 12 February. Paris.	**THOMAS, Charles Louis Ambroise.** Pupil of Lesueur, Kalkbrenner and Barbereau at the Paris Conservatoire. Professor of composition at the Conservatoire in '52, and was Director in '71, succeeding Auber. Received the Grand Cross in '94, on the occasion of the thousandth performance of " Mignon." Many French operas, cantatas, motets, part-songs, chamber music, orchestral and piano works.	French.
1811 22 October. Raiding.	1886 31 July. Bayreuth.	**LISZT**, Franz. Abbé. The greatest combined pianist and composer. *Inventor of the " Symphonic Poem."* Pupil of Czerny, Salieri, Randhartinger, Reicha and Paër. Teacher of Bülow, D'Albert, Tausig and W. Bache. Toured as virtuoso pianist, first visiting England in 1824. Stayed some years in Paris. Conductor at the Court Theatre, Weimar (where he produced some of Wagner's operas) until 1861, thence to Rome and Budapest. Orchestral works, oratorios, cantatas, vocal pieces, and the difficult piano works, on which his fame chiefly rests ; also literary works ; over 200 in all.	Hungarian
1811 24 October Frankfort-on-the-Main.	1885 10 May. Cologne.	**HILLER, Ferdinand.** Pupil of Hummel ; teacher of Max Bruch. Municipal chapel-master at Düsseldorf in '47, and the same at Cologne in '50, becoming director of the Conservatoire there. Conducted the Rhine Festival from '50. Visited England first in '52. 5 Operas, oratorios, cantatas, motets, 3 symphonies, 4 overtures, much chamber music, and literary works.	German. (Jewish parents.)
1811 25 October. Dublin.	1899 28 June. Dublin.	**LEVEY, Richard Michael.** Pupil of Barton ; teacher of Stewart and Stanford. Leader, and afterwards conductor at the "Royal" Theatre, Dublin. One of the founders of the Royal Irish Academy. 50 Overtures, 44 pantomimes, and 2 volumes of old Irish airs.	Irish.
1811 15 November. Guntrams-dorf.	1887 12 January. Boulogne.	**BLAHETKA, Marie Leopoldine.** Pupil of Jos. Czerny, Kalkbrenner, Moscheles, and Sechter. Toured as a concert pianist. Dramatic, pianoforte and pianoforte with orchestra.	Austrian.
1811 1 December. Paris.	1879 7 February. Paris.	**VARNEY, Pierre Joseph Alphonse.** Father of Louis (1850). Pupil of Reicha at the Paris Conservatoire. Conductor at several French Theatres. Short operas, operettas, etc.	French.
1811 8 December. Königsberg.	1864 30 March. Darmstadt.	**SCHINDELMEISSER, Louis.** Educated at the Gymnasium at Berlin, and played the clarinet. Chapel-master at Salzburg, Innsbruck, Graz, Berlin (Königstadt Theatre), Pesth, and finally became Court-chapel-master at Darmstadt. 6 Operas, cantata, orchestral, overture, clarinet concerto, pianoforte, and songs.	German.

Born	Died	Name	Nationality
1812 7 January ? Geneva.	**1871** 27 April. Posilipo, Brazil.	**THALBERG, Sigismund.** Pupil of Sechter and Hummel in Vienna, and Pixis and Kalkbrenner in Paris. Chamber-virtuoso to the Emperor of Austria in 1834. Compared with Liszt as a pianist. Toured the capitals, visiting London for the first time in 1836. About 70 pianoforte works, 2 operas, trio, German songs, and a duet with De Bériot.	Swiss.
1812 8 January. Sudbury, Derbyshire.	**1885** 23 April. London.	**HOLMES, William Henry.** Student, and later, professor of the piano, at the Royal Academy. Teacher of Sterndale Bennett, the Macfarrens, etc. Symphonies, concertos, sonatas, songs, and an opera.	English.
1812 14 January. Rostock.	**1883** 10 June. Hamburg.	**GRÄDENER, Carl Georg Peter.** Father of H. T. O. (1844). Musikdirector at the University of Kiel until '51, when he founded an academy for vocal music at Hamburg, and became teacher of singing and theory in the Vienna Conservatorium. 2 Symphonies, oratorio, overture, pieces and a concerto for piano, and much chamber music.	German.
1812 9 February. Exeter.	**1901** 22 September Exmouth.	**PYE, Kellow John.** Pupil of Potter and Crotch : the first pupil to receive a lesson in the Royal Academy, London, in 1823. Anthems, songs, etc.	English.
1812 27 April. Mecklenburg.	**1883** 24 January. Darmstadt.	**FLOTOW, Friedrich, Freiherr von.** Pupil of Reicha in Paris. Intendant of the Court Theatre at Schwerin in '56 to '63. Many operas (French, German and English), including " Martha " and " Stradella " ; ballets, overtures, songs and chamber-music, of but little musical importance.	German.
1812 27 June. Worcester.	**1884** 21 February. London.	**HULLAH, John Pyke, LL.D.** Pupil of Horsley and, for singing, Crivelli. Instituted a system of class-singing instruction, whereby 25,000 persons passed through his hands. Organist at Croydon in '37 and at the Charter House in '58. Teacher of singing in various institutions. Operas, madrigals, and songs, including " O that we two were Maying," " Three Fishers," etc. Also numerous essays and didactic works.	English.
1812 London.	**1870** 7 December. London.	**GLOVER, Stephen Ralph.** Songs, ballads, including " What are the Wild Waves saying ? " pianoforte pieces, a chamber opera, and sacred songs ; numbering in all from 1,200 to 1,500.	English.
1812 22 July. Lavenham. Suffolk.	**1879** 23 September London.	**WESTROP, Henry.** Pianist, violinist and singer. Organist at Norwich, and later in London. Conductor of the Choral Harmonists' Society, etc. 2 Operas ; symphony ; string quintets, quartets and trios ; sonatas for piano, viola, and flute ; anthem, orchestral, and songs.	English.
1812 26 July. Bradford- on-Avon.	**1887** 2 June. Great Yarmouth.	**KNIGHT, Rev. Joseph Philipp.** Pupil of Corfe, and was a good organist. 200 Songs, duets and trios ; including " Rocked in the Cradle of the Deep," " She wore a wreath of Roses," etc.	English

Born	Died	Name	Nationality.
1812 28 November. Trondhjem.	**1887** 23 May. Christiania.	**LINDEMAN, Ludvig Mathias.** Established the school which developed into the Conservatory at Christiania. Organist of Our Saviour's, Christiania, in 1840. Collected 600 Norwegian Melodies from which Grieg and Svendsen benefited. Organ works and much church music. The hymn tune to " The Church is it an ancient house " belongs to him.	Norwegian.
1812 24 December Sheerness.	**1900** 8 December. London.	**RUSSELL, Henry.** Father of Landon Ronald (1873). Studied under Rossini at Naples. Organist in America. Over 800 songs, including " Life on the Ocean Wave," " Cheer, boys, cheer," etc.	English.
1812 28 December Berlin.	**1877** 12 September Dresden.	**RIETZ, Julius.** Pupil of Romberg and Ganz for 'cello, and Zelta for composition. Conductor at Düsseldorf 1834-47, succeeding Mendelssohn, and preceding Hiller. Conductor of the opera and the Gewandhaus orchestra at Leipsic, also teacher of composition at the Conservatorium. From 1860 held similar appointments at Dresden, where he was entitled General-Musikdirector. Operas, symphonies, violin concertos, chamber-music, songs, and a Mass.	German.
1813 23 January. Cologne.	**1887** 17 August.	**COMMER, Franz.** Pupil of Klein, Leibl, A. W. Bach, and Marx. Organist at Cologne, and later choir-master of St. Hedwig, Berlin. Best known as collector and editor of church and organ works. Church music, lieder, dances for pianoforte, and dramatic works.	German.
1813 14 February. Toula.	**1869** January.	**DARGOMIJSKY, Alexander Sergeivich.** Followed the style of Glinka, who instructed him. Took an active part in establishing the Russian National School. Russian operas (one of which was finished by Rimsky-Korsakov) ; orchestral works ; vocal duets, trios, and quartets ; songs and pianoforte pieces. The opera " The Stone Guest " is his most important work.	Russian.
1813 22 February. Weston-super-Mare.		**GREATHEED, Rev. Samuel Stephenson, M.A.** Studied under Schwarz at Berlin. Anthems, Te Deum and other church music, a short oratorio, organ fugue, and literary works on church music.	English.
1813 2 March. London.	**1887** 31 October. London.	**MACFARREN, Sir George Alexander.** Brother of Walter (1826). Pupil of Lucas and of the Royal Academy of Music, where he became professor in 1834 and Principal in '76, succeeding Bennett. Professor at Cambridge, succeeding Sterndale Bennett, in '75. Became gradually blind. Operas, oratorios, cantatas, symphonies, overtures, string quartets and quintets ; piano sonatas, violin concerto, a cathedral service, anthems, songs, and didactic works,	English.

Born	Died	Name	Nationality.
1813 22 May. Leipzig.	1883 13 February. Venice.	**WAGNER, Wilhelm Richard.** The greatest grand-opera writer and poet. Advanced the opera, harmony, and instrumentation. Musik-director at Magdeburg Theatre, Leipzig '34, Konigsberg '36, Riga '37, Paris in '39, and became Hofcapellmeister at Dresden in '42. Conducted first in London in '55. At Paris in '59, Germany in '61, and settled in Munich in '64, becoming a naturalised Bavarian, thence to Bayreuth in '72. 16 Operas (including " The Flying Dutchman," " Tannhäuser," " Lohengrin," " Tristan," " The Mastersingers," " Parsifal," and " The Ring.") 6 overtures, symphony and other orchestral works, cantata, pianoforte pieces, songs and many literary works.	German.
1813 5 June. Toulouse.	1890 17 October. London.	**SAINTON, Prosper Philippe Catherine.** Violinist, pupil of Habeneck at the Paris Conservatoire. Played first in London in 1844, under Mendelssohn. Became professor of the violin at the Royal Academy in '45, and was leader of the Royal Italian Opera at Covent Garden, the Philharmonic Band, the Birmingham Festivals, etc. From 1848 to '55 was conductor of the State Band and solo-violinist to the Queen. Violin concertos, romances, variations, fantasias, etc.	French.
1813 June. Manchester.	1832 19 August. Leamington.	**ASPULL, George.** Pianist; played to Clementi in 1822, and before George IV at Windsor in '24. Pianoforte works, published posthumously.	English.
1813 Bath.	1865 5 April. Manchester.	**LODER, Edward James.** Pupil of Ries at Frankfort. Conductor at the Princess's Theatre, London, and later at Manchester. Operas, cantata, string quartets, and sacred and secular songs, of which " The Diver " and " The brave old Oak " are the best-known.	English.
1813 1 July. Waterford.	1865 12 October. Château de Bagen.	**WALLACE, William Vincent.** Studied the violin in early life. Lived in Australia, North and South America, Germany, and London. Operas, i.e. " Maritana " 1845, " Lurline " 1860, " The Amber Witch " 1861," Love's Triumph " 1862, etc. ; pianoforte works, a violin concerto, etc.	Irish.
1813 5 October. Königsberg.	1869 12 March. Bergen.	**HABERBIER, Ernst.** Concert pianist and teacher. Court pianist at Petrograd in 1847. Ephemeral piano works.	German.
1813 5 October. London.	1885 24 March. Margate.	**DAVISON, James William.** Pupil of W. H. Holmes and G. A. Macfarren. Friend of Mendelssohn, Bennett and Smart. Critic to the " Graphic " and " Times." Promoter of classical performances. Orchestral, piano, and vocal works, on words by Keats, Shelley, etc.	English.
1813 26 October. London.	1879 6 July. London.	**SMART, Henry Thomas.** Grandson of Sir George Thomas (1776). Pupil of Kearns. Organist at Blackburn in '31, and at St. Philip's, London, from '36. Became too blind to write in 1865. Operas, cantatas; anthems for solos, chorus and organ ; organ works, and part-songs.	English.

Born	Died	Name	Nationality
1813 10 November Roncole.	1901 27 January Busseto.	**VERDI, Giuseppe.** The most popular Italian opera composer of the 19th century. Pupil of Provesi and Lavigna. Lived chiefly at Milan during his active career. Visited England in 1847, '55, '62, and '75. 30 Operas, including " Rigoletto," Venice, 1851 ; " Il Trovatore," Rome, '53 ; " La Traviata," Venice, '53 ; " Sicilian Vespers," Paris, '55 ; " La Forza del Destino," Petrograd, '62 ; " Aida," Cairo, '71 ; " Othello," Milan, '87 ; " Falstaff," '93 ; also sacred works, chamber-music, cantata, and early works in the form of symphonies, concertos and church music.	Italian.
1813 30 November Paris.	1888 29 March. Paris.	**ALKAN, Charles Henri Valentin. Morhange.** Pupil of the Paris Conservatoire. Pianist and teacher. Pianoforte concertos, sonatas, duets, trios, works for " piano with pedals," songs ; though best known by his difficult studies for pianoforte—to opus 72.	French.
1813 1 December. Palermo.	1877 7 April. Genoa.	**PETRELLA, Enrico.** Pupil of Zingarelli, Bellini and Ruggi. 19 Operas, including " Ione," " Giovanni II di Napoli " and " Manfredo." They are works of but little musical quality.	Sicilian.
1813 2 December. Mannheim.	1894 21 March. Baden-Baden.	**ROSENHAIN, Jacob.** Pianist ; pupil of J. Schmitt, Kalliwoda and Wartensee. First appeared in London at the Philharmonic in 1837. Afterwards lived in Paris and carried on a school in conjunction with J. B. Cramer. Operas ; cantata ; symphonies, quartets ; trios ; piano concerto, sonatas, studies and pieces ; songs, etc.	German.
1813 31 December Berlin.	1870 16 March.	**OESTEN, Theodor.** Pupil of Rungenhagen, Schneider and A. W. Bach. Teacher of piano, clarinet, violin, etc. Dance music and attractive pieces for P.F.	German.
1814 21 January London.	1856 17 January. Hastings.	**WALMISLEY, Thomas Attwood (Mus.D.).** Son of T. F. (1783). Pupil of Thomas Attwood. Friend of Mendelssohn. Organist of Trinity and St. John's Colleges, Cambridge, in '33, and succeeded Pratt at King's College Chapel and St. Mary's. Professor of Music at Cambridge University in 1836 *vice* Clarke. Odes, anthems, cathedral music, madrigals, services, chants and songs.	English.
1814 20 April. Naples.	1856 21 February. Florence.	**DÖHLER, Theodor.** Pupil of Benedict in Naples and Czerny in Vienna. Travelled as a virtuoso pianist. Many "salon" pieces, variations, fantasias, etc. for piano, and an opera, reaching to opus 75, but they are of no musical value.	Italian.
1814 22 April. Birmingham.	1900 30 December London.	**POLE, William, Mus.D., F.R.S.** Professor of Civil Engineering at London University. Organist in London. Writer on music and science. Psalms and motets.	English.

Born	Died	Name	Nationality.
1814 6 May. Brünn.	1865 8 October. Nice.	**ERNST, Heinrich Wilhelm.** Pupil of Böhm and Mayseder for violin, and Seyfried for composition. Toured as a virtuoso violinist, appearing first in London in 1843, afterwards settling there for some years. Violin concerto, studies, 2 string quartets, brilliant solos and other solos which are well-known to violinists, being, perhaps, the best works of that particular style.	Moravian.
1814 12 May. Schwabach.	1889 10 October. Warmbrünn.	**HENSELT, Adolf von.** Pianist: pupil of Sechter for composition and Hummel for pianoforte. His playing combined the style of Hummel with that of Liszt. Court pianist, and teacher of the Imperial children at Petrograd. Pianoforte concerto, studies, salon pieces, and arrangements; 54 works in all.	German.
1815 9 January. Masham.	1866 15 April.	**JACKSON, William.** Self-taught. Organist of St. John's Church, Bradford, and conductor of the Festivals and the Choral Society in that town. 2 Oratorios, cantata, anthems, glees, part-songs, Psalms, a singing manual, and harmonised the "Bradford tune book."	English.
1815 22 January Leipzig.	1891 2 September London.	**PRAEGER, Ferdinand Christian Wilhelm.** Pianist: pupil of Hummel. Played in Paris, Leipzig, Berlin and Hamburg. Teacher in London from 1834. Was intimate with Schumann and Wagner. Orchestral, chamber music and pianoforte pieces; he also wrote a book on the life of Wagner.	German.
1815 25 January. Brussels.	1845 20 July. Paris.	**ARTÔT, Alexandre Joseph Montagney.** Pupil of Ries, Snel, and Kreutzer at Paris. Toured as a solo-violinist, as far as America and Cuba. Appeared first in London in 1839 at a Philharmonic concert. Violin concerto, fantasias, airs with variations, etc.	Belgian.
1815 2 March. Vienna.	1888 17 November. Vienna.	**DONT, Jacob.** Pupil of Böhm and Hellmesberger at the Vienna Conservatorium, where he afterwards became professor. His pupils include Auer and Gregorowitsch. 50 Violin works, the studies being the best-known.	Austrian.
1815 8 March. Bayonne.	1888 22 February. Paris.	**ALARD, Delphin Jean.** The first representative of the "Modern" French school of violin-playing. Pupil of Habeneck. Succeeded Baillot as professor of the violin at the Conservatoire in 1843. Violin concertos, concertantes for 2 violins, fantasias and a "School."	French.
1815 14 March. Munich.	1880 2 December. Tübingen.	**LANG, Josephine (Frau Köstlin).** A pianist who attracted the notice of Mendelssohn. Songs in several books, up to the opus number of 38.	German.

Born	Died	Name	Nationality
1815 6 April. Lommatzcsh	**1883** 30 October. Pesth.	**VOLKMANN, Friedrich Robert.** Resided and taught in Prague, Vienna, and Pesth, where he became professor of composition at the Landes-musik-akademie. Symphonies ; overture ; string quartets and trios ; sonatas for violin and piano ; 'cello concerto, songs for various voices; church and piano music, to opus 76. Original and graceful compositions, but have not the lasting qualities of the great masters' works.	German.
1815 12 April. Oxford.	**1873** 28 January. Leipzig.	**PIERSON, Henry Hugo.** Pupil of Attwood and Corfe in England, and Rink and Reissiger in Germany. He did not hold any musical post. Was esteemed most in Germany, where he lived from 1845, and became acquainted with Mendelssohn, Spohr and Hauptmann. 2 Oratorios, " Jerusalem " and " Hezekiah " ; operas, performed in Germany; songs, including " Ye Mariners of England," and overtures.	English.
1815 15 May. Pesth.	**1888** 14 January. Paris.	**HELLER, Stephen.** Pupil of Halm at Vienna. Concert pianist and teacher in Paris, from '38. Visited London in '50 and '62. Pianoforte pieces and studies of light elegant style up to opus 157; also sonatas, and pieces with Ernst, the violinist.	Hungarian.
1815 19 June. Dublin.	**1899** 18 December	**GLOVER, John William.** Director of the music in the Catholic Pro-Cathedral, Dublin, in '48, succeeding Corri. Founded the Choral Institute of Dublin, in '51. 3 Operas (2 Italian), cantata, concertos, songs, church music, and an ode to Thomas Moore.	Irish.
1815 28 June. Halle.	**1892** 24 October. Halle.	**FRANZ, Robert.** Pupil of Schneider at Dessau. One of the greatest song writers. Organist at the Ulrichskirche and conductor of the Singakademie at Halle. 257 German lieder, 6 chorals, Psalms and other church-music, and part-songs ; also arrangements, and literary works.	German.
1815 Bologna.	**1882** 2 February. London.	**CAMPANA, Fabio.** Pupil at the Liceo, Bologna. Settled in London about 1850 as a teacher of singing. 5 Operas, produced in Italy, and 2 others in London; also Italian songs.	Italian.
1815 15 September Christiania.	**1868** 11 August. Grefsen.	**KJERULF, Halfdan.** Studied for a year with Richter at Leipsic. Gave material assistance to Grieg. 100 Songs, lyrics, Northern ballads, quartets and choruses for men's voices, and pianoforte pieces. Songs on poems by Björnson, Moore, Hugo and Lord Houghton.	Norwegian.
1815 19 September Malta.	**1883** 16 October. London.	**SCHIRA, Francesco.** Pupil of Basili at Milan Conservatorio. Professor of harmony and counterpoint at Lisbon Conservatorio in '35. Conductor at the Princess's in 1842, Drury Lane in '44, and again in '52, and at Covent Garden in '48. Italian operas ; a cantata for the Birmingham Festival ; songs, duets and trios ; an operetta, etc.	Maltese.

Born	Died	Name	Nationality
1815 20 September Schmarsou, n'r Demmin	**1882** 29 August. Paris.	**VOSS, Charles.** Studied in Berlin. Settled in Paris as pianist and teacher. Ephemeral pianoforte music ; also a concerto, etc.	German.
1815* 25 October. Genoa.	**1894** 19 February. Genoa.	**SIVORI, Ernesto Camillo.** The only pupil of Paganini ; also studied with G. Costa, Dellepiane, and later with Serra for composition. Travelled as solo-violinist throughout Europe and America, gaining much honour and admiration. First visited London in 1843. 2 Violin concertos, duets for violin and piano, duets for violin and bass, romances ; fantasias and other solos. *Various dates given.	Italian.
1816 17 February. Reichebach.	**1887** 30 April. Danzig.	**MARKULL, Friedrich Wilhelm.** Pupil of Schneider at Dessau. Conductor at Danzig, and organist of the Marienkirche ; also pianist and critic. 3 Operas, 2 Oratorios, symphonies, organ and vocal music.	German.
1816 20 February. Rome.	**1873** 3 July. London.	**PONIATOWSKI, Joseph Michael Xavier Francis John, Prince of Monte Rotondo.** Studied under Ceccherini at Florence. Followed Napoleon III to England, and produced an opera at Covent Garden in 1872. Tenor singer. 12 Operas, ballads, Mass, etc.	Italian.
1816 19 March. The Hague.	**1891** 17 January. The Hague.	**VERHULST, Johannes Josephus Herman.** Learnt the violin and theory at the Royal School of Music at the Hague, where afterwards he became Director of the Court Music. Conductor at Leipzig and Rotterdam. Friend of Schumann. Symphonies, overtures, quartets, church music, songs and part-songs—not much known outside of Holland.	Dutch.
1816 27 March. Canterbury.	**1893** 9 December. Windlesham. Surrey.	**ELVEY, Sir George Job (Mus.D.).** Brother of Stephen (1805). Pupil of Potter and Dr. Crotch at the Royal Academy. Organist of St. George's Chapel, Windsor, '35-'82, and conductor of the Choral Society of Windsor and Eton. Oratorios, odes, anthems, Festival March, and church music.	English.
1816 13 April. Sheffield.	**1875** 1 February. London.	**BENNETT, Sir William Sterndale.** Pupil of Lucas and Dr. Crotch, of W. H. Holmes for pianoforte, and later of Potter. In early life was influenced by Mendelssohn at Leipzig. Conductor of the Philharmonic in 1856. Principal of the Royal Academy in 1866, succeeding Lucas. Musical Professor at Cambridge University in 1856, *vice* Walmisley. Oratorio, cantata, symphonies, overtures, pianoforte concertos, sonatas and pieces ; chamber music, anthems, songs. part-songs and church music, about 60 works. " The Woman of Samaria " was first produced at Birmingham in 1867.	English.
1816 3 June. Liège.	**1849** 14 July. Stavelot.	**PRUME, François Hubert.** Travelled as a virtuoso violinist. Pupil of Habeneck. Professor at Liège Conservatoire in 1833. Violin studies and solos.	Belgian.

11

Born	Died	Name	Nationality.
1816 3 September	**1886** 23 April. London.	**PITTMAN, Josiah.** Pupil of S. S. Wesley, Moscheles, and Wartensee. Organist in London, and was *Maestro al cembalo* at Her Majesty's and Covent Garden Theatres. Church services, and arrangements for pianoforte.	English.
1816 26 December Bristol.	**1860** 19 March. London.	**PHILLIPS, William Lovell.** Pupil of Potter, and class-fellow of Sterndale Bennett at the Royal Academy, where he became professor of composition. Organist at St. Katherine's Church, Regent's Park. Symphony; songs, and theatrical works.	English.
1817 18 January. Antwerp.	**1876** 29 October. Brussels.	**GREGOIR, Jacques Mathieu Joseph.** Brother of E. G. Jacques (1822). Pianist, pupil of Rummel. Made concert tours on the Continent. Cantata, opera, pianoforte concerto and other pieces, and collaborated in duets with Vieuxtemps and Léonard; over 100 works in all.	Belgian.
1817 22 February. Copenhagen	**1890** 21 December Copenhagen	**GADE, Niels Wilhelm.** Entered the Royal orchestra at Copenhagen as violinist. Succeeded Mendelssohn as conductor of the Gewandhaus concerts at Leipsic from '45 to '48, thence to Copenhagen where he became organist, Hof-capellmeister and professor of music. Visited Birmingham in '76, to conduct his cantatas "Zion" and "The Crusaders." Was intimate with Mendelssohn and Schumann. 8 Symphonies, 12 cantatas, overtures, violin concerto and sonatas; piano sonatas and pieces, songs, part-songs, chamber-music, etc., to opus 64.	Danish.
1817 24 March. Paris.	**1871** 26 May. Moulins.	**MAILLART, Louis (called Aimé).** Pupil of Halévy and Leborne for composition, and Guérin for violin. 6 Comic operas, the best being "Les Dragons de Villars;" also some cantatas.	French.
1817 2 April. Pistoia.	**1897** 10 March. Florence.	**MABELLINI, Teodulo.** Pupil of the Istituto Reale Musicale in Florence, where he became professor, after studying for a time with Mercadante at Novara. Conductor and court-chapel-master at Florence from 1848. 9 Operas, 2 Oratorios, several cantatas, and much church music.	Italian.
1817 3 April. Angoulême.	**1863** 14 May. Paris.	**PRUDENT, Émile.** Pupil of the Paris Conservatoire. Pianist and teacher. Was well-known in England. Pianoforte concerto, studies, fantasias and smaller pieces; a trio, and a concerto-symphony; amounting to about 70 in number.	French.
1817 31 May. Paris.	**1897** 6 November Paris.	**DELDEVEZ, Édouard Marie Ernest.** Violinist and leader. Pupil of the Paris Conservatoire under Habeneck, Halévy and Berton. Conductor of the Opéra in '73, and of the Conservatoire concerts in '72-'77. Symphonies, quartets, quintet, trios, ballets, overtures, cantata, Requiem, sacred choruses, and dramatic works; also literary works.	French.

Born	Died	Name	Nationality
1817 Murcia.	1880 26 March. Madrid.	**SORIANO-FUERTES, Mariano.** Conductor at theatres of Seville, Cadiz and Barcelona. Teacher in the Conservatoire at Madrid. Several operettas (Zarzuelas); but he is best known by his literary works.	Spanish.
1817 2 October. Lidköping.	1901 22 August. Leckö.	**WENNERBERG, Gunnar.** Poet, and legislator of Sweden. Self-taught in music. Became a member of the Swedish Academy in 1867. Oratorio; Stabat Mater; Psalms of David, used extensively throughout Sweden; and " Songs of Freedom."	Swedish.
1817 27 October. Cracow.	1899 7 December. Nowogrod.	**KONTSKI, Antoine de.** Brother of Apollinaire (1825). Pianist. Pupil of Field. Settled in London in 1867. Made a professional world-tour in 1896-98. Many salon pieces for piano, and an opera.	Polish.
1817 12 November. Arnsberg.	1882 29 October. Gratz.	**NOTTEBOHM, Martin Gustav.** Pianist, pupil of L. Berger, Dehn and Sechter. Friend of Mendelssohn and Schumann. Teacher, and writer on musical subjects, particularly on Beethoven's life and work. Piano quartet, trios, solos, and variations.	German.
1817 12 November. Verona.	1893 16 October. Verona. (drowned himself.)	**PEDROTTI, Carlo.** Pupil of Foroni. Conductor of Italian-opera in Amsterdam from '40 to '45. Director of the Nuovo and Filarmonico theatres, Verona, in '45, and migrated to Turin in '68, undertaking similar posts. 14 Operas and light operas, the best being " Tutti in Maschera."	Italian.
1817 13 November. Paris.	1869 31 December. Paris.	**LEFÉBURE-WÉLY, Louis James Alfred.** Pupil of Halévy, Berton, Adam, and Séjan for organ. Remarkable for his extempore organ-playing. Held posts at churches in Paris, including St. Sulpice. Legion of Honour in 1850. Symphonies; chamber-music; a comic-opera; Masses; organ and harmonium works (the latter being his best).	French.
1817 13 November. Carmarthen.	1885 1 May. London.	**RICHARDS, Henry Brinley.** Pupil of the Royal Academy, winning the King's scholarship in 1835. Pianist in London, and lecturer on Welsh music. Overture; pianoforte pieces; sacred, and part-songs; songs, including " God Bless the Prince of Wales " (published in 1862).	Welsh.
1817 24 November. Wutzbach.	1905 26 December Dresden.	**SPINDLER, Fritz.** Pupil of F. Schneider at Dessau. Pianist. 2 Symphonies; trios; a pianoforte concerto; sonatinas; studies, and a great number of drawing-room pieces—330 in all.	German.
1818 6 February. London.	1891 6 August. Bois le Combes, n'r Paris.	**LITOLFF, Henry Charles.** Pupil of Moscheles. Toured as a pianist, and established the publishing firm bearing his name. 115 Published works, including several operas, overtures, symphony-concertos, a violin concerto, an oratorio, chamber and pianoforte music.	English.

Born	Died	Name	Nationality.
1818 11 March. Brescia.	**1897** 10 February. Milan.	**BAZZINI, Antonio.** Pupil of Camisoni at Milan. Travelled as a violinist, and was organist at St. Philip's Church, Brescia, in 1825. Professor of Milan Conservatorio in '73 and director of the same in 1882. Symphonic overtures, opera, sacred cantatas, string quartets and a quintet, violin concerto, and difficult solos.	Italian.
1818 12 March. Perpignan.	**1854** 15 June. St. Cloud.	**BOUSQUET, Georges.** Violinist ; pupil of the Paris Conservatoire. Critic. For a short time was conductor of the Italian Theatre, Paris. Operas, Masses, etc.	French.
1818 20 May. Bordeaux.	**1906** 30 September Paris.	**RAVINA, Jean Henri.** Pianist virtuoso and teacher. Pupil at the Conservatoire, and later, a joint professor there. Legion of Honour in 1861. Salon piano pieces, and some arrangements.	French.
1818 10 June. Mühlheim on Ruhr.	**1896** 23 June. Brussels.	**KUFFERATH, Hubert Ferdinand.** Pupil of David for violin, and Mendelssohn and Hauptmann for composition. Pianist to the King, Leopold I, and professor of counterpoint at the Brussels Conservatoire from 1872. A symphony ; string quartet and trio ; piano concerto and many pieces, songs, etc.	German.
1818 17 June. Paris.	**1893** 18 October. Saint-Cloud.	**GOUNOD, Charles François.** Pupil of Halévy, Paër and Lesueur at the Paris Conservatoire, and studied in Rome. Conductor of the Orphéon, Paris, in 1852. Member of the Institut de France in 1866, and was made Grand Officer of the Legion of Honour in 1880. Lived for some years in England and established that which became the Royal Choral Society. Several operas (including " Faust " and " Romeo and Juliet ") ; oratorios and sacred cantatas, including " The Redemption " (first performed in Birmingham, 1882); motets ; songs ; many church works, pianoforte music, etc.	French.
1818 30 June. Westminster.	**1901** 4 February. London.	**HOPKINS, Edward John (Mus.D.).** Brother of John (1822). Pupil of T. F. Walmisley. Organist of the Temple Church for over 50 years. He was a fine accompanist. Anthems, many church services, chants, Psalms, duets and trios, also a treatise on the organ.	English.
1818 Bagnères.	**1907** 12 February. Tunis.	**DANCLA, Jean Baptiste Charles.** Violinist and teacher ; pupil of Baillot at the Conservatoire, where he ultimately became professor in 1857. Teacher of Rivarde. Studies, fantasias, variations, etc., for violin.	French.
1818 15 July. Mannheim.	**1872** 3 June. Salzburg.	**ESSER, Heinrich.** Musical director at the Court Theatre, Mannheim, conductor at Mayence, and succeeded O. Nicolai as chapel-master at the Imperial Opera, Vienna, in 1847. 3 Operas ; symphonies ; suites ; lieder ; vocal duets and choruses ; string quartet, etc. ; about 100 works.	German.

Born	Died	Name	Nationality.
1818 24 July. Namur.	1897 8 July. Villers-sur- Mer.	**GODEFROID, Dieudonné Joseph Guillaume Félix.** Younger brother of J. J. Pupil of the Paris Conservatoire. Harpist. Oratorio ; 2 operas ; harp and pianoforte music.	Belgian.
1818 12 September Krotoschin.	1882 1 March. Berlin.	**KULLAK, Theodor.** Pupil of Czerny. Hofpianist to the King of Prussia in 1846. Founded a musical institution in Berlin. At first studied law and medicine. Pianoforte trio, and duets for pianoforte and violin; pianoforte concerto, studies and many solos; about 130 in number.	German.
1818 26 October. Bologna.	1891 3 July. Bologna.	**GOLINELLI, Stefano.** Pupil of Donelli for piano and Vaccaj for composition. Professor at the Liceo of Bologna, 1840-70. Toured as a pianist, visiting England in '51 and playing with Sivori and Patti. 200 Pianoforte works, including sonatas, preludes, toccatas, variations, and smaller pieces.	Italian.
1818 26 November. Bourges.	1884 30 September Vaast-la- Hougue.	**LACOMBE, Louis Brouillon.** Pupil of Czerny, Sechter and Seyfried. Toured as pianist. Lived in Paris from 1839. Operas, dramatic symphonies, chamber-music, melodrama, pieces and studies for pianoforte.	French.
1819 12 January. Heidelberg.	1882 27 October. Spezia.	**GUTMANN, Adolph.** Pupil and friend of Chopin. Pianoforte studies and ephemeral pieces.	German.
1819 11 February. Boston, U.S.A.	1890 30 June. Newport, Rhode Island.	**TUCKERMAN, Samuel Parkman (Mus.D.).** Pupil of Zeuner, and later studied in England. Organist and director of the choir at St. Paul's Church, Boston. Returned to England in 1856. Organist of Trinity Church, New York, in 1864. Church services, cantata, anthems, and part-songs.	American.
1819 26 February. London.	1895 25 March. London.	**STIRLING, Elizabeth.** Pupil of Wilson and E. Holmes for pianoforte and organ, and of Hamilton and G. A. Macfarren for harmony. Organist at All Saints', Poplar, and at St. Andrew's, Undershaft. Pedal fugues and other pieces for organ ; songs, duets and part-songs.	English.
1819 4 March. Munich.	1895 8 November London.	**OBERTHÜR, Charles.** Harpist : pupil of G. V. Röder. Came to England in 1844 and was befriended by Moscheles. 2 Operas ; cantatas ; a grand Mass ; concertino and a quartet for harps ; trio for harp, violin and 'cello, etc.	German.
1819 7 April. Bellaire.	1890 6 May. Paris.	**LEONARD, Hubert.** Pupil of Habeneck. Succeeded De Bériot as first professor of the violin at Brussels Conservatoire in 1847 to '67. Gave the first performance in Berlin of Mendelssohn's violin concerto. Violin concertos, studies, fantasias, elegies and salon pieces.	Belgian.
1819 8 April. Hamburg.	1875 31 December Vienna.	**EVERS, Carl.** Pupil of Carl Krebs. Pianist and teacher. Chapel- master at Grätz in 1841 to '72. Pianoforte sonatas, fugues, chansons, fantasias and part-songs.	German.

Born	Died	Name	Nationality
1819 18 April. Bordeaux.	**1898** 24 January.	**COMETTANT, Jean Pierre Oscar.** Pianist, critic and writer. Pupil of Elwart and Carafa. Pianoforte pieces, duets with violin, songs and choruses ; also books of musical literature.	French.
1819 21 June. Offenbach-on-Main.	**1880** 5 October. Paris.	**OFFENBACH, originally LEVY, Jacques.** Studied for a year at the Conservatoire, Paris. Worked chiefly in Paris, where he was conductor at the Theâtre Français. Visited London in 1844 as 'cellist, and in 1857 as conductor. Went to America in 1875. 90 Comic operas, operettas and pantomimes, the most popular being " The Tales of Hoffmann " ; also some early 'cello pieces.	German.
1819 27 June. Berlin.	**1905** 4 June. Berlin.	**LOESCHHORN, Albert.** Pupil of Ludwig Berger, and at the Royal Institute for Church music in Berlin, where he afterwards became professor of the pianoforte. Received the title of Royal Professor in 1868. Pianoforte studies, sonatas, quartets, etc.	German.
1819 2 July. Goffontaine	**1898** 21 April. Leipzig.	**GOUVY, Louis Theodore.** Pupil of Elwart, and studied in Italy. He previously studied law. A member of the Berlin Academy, and received the Legion of Honour in 1896. 7 Symphonies, a sinfonietta, symphonic-paraphrase, overtures, octets, sextets, quintets, quartets, trios, sonatas, piano works, songs, cantatas, choruses, and dramatic works ; 170 various works.	German. (French parents).
1819 26 August. Rosenau, Coburg.	**1861** 14 December London.	**ALBERT, Prince Consort of Queen Victoria.** The greatest promoter of music in this country. Improved the band at Buckingham Palace and Windsor, where many great works of Mendelssohn, Bach and Wagner were first performed in England. Anthems, church services, choruses with solo voice, 5 Collections of lieder and romances, canzonets, etc.	German.
1819 13 September Leipzig.	**1896** 20 May. Frankfort.	**SCHUMANN, Madame Clara Josephine.** Wife of Robert Schumann, daughter and pupil of F. Wieck. One of the world's greatest pianists. Toured the capitals, playing with Mendelssohn and Liszt, visiting London several times. Principal pianoforte teacher in the Conservatoire at Frankfort in '78. Piano concerto, fugues, romances, waltzes, etc. ; trio, songs, and lieder ; to opus 23.	German.
1819 6 October. Lambeth.	**1904** 17 June. Canterbury.	**LONGHURST, William Henry (Mus.D.).** Brother of J. A. (1809). Organist and master of the choristers at Canterbury Cathedral in 1873, succeeding Jones. Anthems, services, songs, and an oratorio.	English.
1819 8 October. London.	**1905** 3 October. London.	**MOUNSEY, Elizabeth.** Sister of Ann (1811). Organist of St. Peter's, Cornhill, from 1834 to '82. Mendelssohn, when visiting this country, frequently played on the organ of this church. Organ, piano and guitar works.	English.

Born	Died	Name	Nationality
1819 13 December Frome,	**1900** 3 January. Radley, Oxford.	**MONK, Edwin George (Mus.D.).** Pupil of H. Field for piano, G. Field for organ (at Bath), H. Philips for solo singing, and Macfarren for composition. Organist in Ireland in 1844, and of York Cathedral in 1859-83, succeeding Dr. Camidge. Astronomer, F.R.A.S. Anthems, church and secular works.	English.
1819 22 December Eilenburg.	**1885** 31 March. Wiesbaden.	**ABT, Franz.** Student of the Thomasschule, Leipsic. Chapel-master at Bernburg and Zürich in '41, and of the Hof-theater at Brunswick in '82. Over 400 works, chiefly lieder and songs for 1, 2, 3 and 4 voices; male and female choruses, and pianoforte music.	German.
1820 5 January. Paris.	**1884** 3 April. Paris.	**PRUMIER, Ange Conrad.** Harpist. Son of Antoine (1794). Pieces for harp.	French.
1820 23 January Petrograd.	**1871** 20 January. Petrograd.	**SEROV, Alexander Nicholaevich.** Critic, and writer on Russian music; later, contrived to combine in his operas the dramatic influence of Wagner with the National tendencies of his predecessor, Glinka. His wife, V. S. Bergman, also wrote operas. Operas, including "Judith" and "Rogneda"; a "Stabat Mater," "Ave Maria," orchestral works, incidental music, etc.	Russian.
1820 10 February. Altona.	**1901** 17 June. Altona.	**GURLITT, Cornelius.** Pupil of Reinecke. Organist and Director at the principal church at Altona. A great number of pianoforte pieces (chiefly educational); also an opera and 2 operettas.	German.
1820 13 February. Bartfeld.	**1882** 20 November. Wiesbaden.	**KÉLER BÉLA. Proper name, Albert von Kéler.** Pupil of Schlesinger and Sechter in Vienna. Took charge of Gung'l's band at Berlin, then of Lanner's in Vienna, and was chapel-master of the Kur orchestra at Wiesbaden. Overtures, dance and violin music of the brilliant type, up to op. 130.	Hungarian.
1820 20 February. Verviers.	**1881** 6 June. Algiers.	**VIEUXTEMPS, Henri.** Violinist: pupil of De Bériot, and studied counterpoint with Sechter, and composition with Reicha. Travelled much as a soloist. Played first in London in 1834, when he met Paganini. Visited America in 1844. Professor at Brussels Conservatoire in 1871. Solo-violinist to the Emperor at Petrograd from 1846 to '52. Violin concertos in E, F minor, A, D minor, A minor, and G.; Fantasie Caprice, Ballade et Polonaise, variations, etc.	Belgian.
1820 18 April. Spalato.	**1895** 21 May. Vienna.	**SUPPÉ, Franz von.** Pupil of Cigala, Ferrari and Seyfried. Conductor at theatres in Pressburg, Baden and Vienna. 2 Grand operas, 165 farces, comedies and vaudevilles; also a Mass and a Requiem. The overtures "Poet and Peasant" and "Morning, Noon and Night" are his best-known pieces.	Austrian.

Born	Died	Name	Nationality
1820 5 May. Minsk.	1872 4 June. Warsaw.	**MONIUSZKO, Stanislaus.** Pupil of Aug. Freyer and Rungenhagen. Teacher and organist of St. John's,Wilna, until 1858, when he became chapel-master of the opera in Warsaw, and later, professor of the Conservatorium there. Operas, ballets, overtures, Masses, cantatas, church music, songs, etc.	**Lithuanian.** (1st mention).
1820 22 May. Carlsruhe.	1849 22 February. Brunswick.	**FESCA, Alexander Ernst.** Son of Friedrich (1789). Pupil of Rungenhagen, W. Bach and Taubert. Pianoforte trios and other chamber-music, also 4 operas, the best of which is " Der Troubadour."	German.
1820 Munich.	1885 24 May.	**BÄRMANN, Karl.** Son of Heinrich, who was a friend of Weber. Toured as a virtuoso clarinettist, and was in the Court band at Munich. Clarinet studies, a " school," etc.	German.
1820 ?	1881 February. Paris.	**TALEXY, Adrien.** Conducted a series of French operas at St. James's Theatre, London. 6 Operettas, piano studies, a method, and many salon pieces.	French.
1820 30 August. Sheffield, Mass, U.S.A.	1895 6 August. Barley's Island.	**ROOT, George Frederick (Mus.D.).** Pupil of Webb at Boston. Became a music publisher at Chicago in '59-71. Cantatas and national songs, including " Tramp, tramp, tramp," " The Battle Cry," etc.	American.
1820 5 September. Brunswick.	1886 16 February. Königsberg.	**KÖHLER, Chr. Louis Heinrich.** Pupil of Bocklet for pianoforte, and Sechter for composition. Conductor at Marienburg and Elbing, then settled at Königsberg in 1847. 3 Operas, a ballet, many pianoforte fantasias, and educational works ; the studies opus 112 and 128 being the best.	German.
1820 5 September Frankenthal.	1901 1 May. Wiesbaden.	**VIERLING, Georg.** Pupil of Rinck and Marx. Organist at the Ober-kirche, Frankfurt-on-the-Oder, in '47. Royal Music-director at Berlin in '59, and professor of the Berlin Academy in 1882. Overtures, a symphony, choruses with orchestra, solo and part-songs.	German.
1820 December. Potsdam.	1879 14 October. Berlin.	**ECKERT, Carl Anton Florian.** Violinist, pianist and conductor. Pupil of Ries, Rungenhagen and Mendelssohn. Chapel-master at Stuttgart in 1861, vice Kücken, and became head-director at the Berlin Opera in '69, succeeding Dorn. 3 Operas, oratorios, much church music, a symphony, trio, songs, and a 'cello concerto.	German.
1820 27 December Albendorf.	1885 17 June.	**REIMANN, Ignaz.** Student of the Breslau Seminary. Principal teacher and choir-master at Rengersdorf in Silesia. A great amount of church music ; Masses, oratorios, Requiems, Te Deums, Litanies, and Offertories ; besides 9 overtures, wedding cantatas, etc.	German.

Born	Died	Name	Nationality
1821 21 January. London.		**MACIRONE, Clara Angela.** Pupil of Potter and Holmes for piano, Negri for singing, and Lucas for composition. Professor of the piano at the Royal Academy. Anthems, Te Deum, Benedictus, solo and part-songs, pianoforte pieces, etc.	English.
1821 1 March. Lysberg.	**1873** 25 February. Geneva.	**LYSBERG, Charles Samuel (pseudonym, Bovy-Lysberg).** Pupil of Chopin and Belaire. Professor of Geneva Conservatoire. 130 Pianoforte pieces, and one opera.	Swiss.
1821 18 March. London.	**1892** 13 July. London.	**STEPHENS, Charles Edward.** Pupil of Potter for piano, Hamilton for composition, and Blagrove for violin. Organist at several London churches. Symphonies, concert overtures, anthems, services, songs, ballads, string quartets, trios and piano music.	English.
1821 27 June. Berlin.	**1873** 26 May. Berlin.	**CONRADI, August.** Pupil of Rungenhagen. Organist and conductor at Berlin, Dusseldorf and Cologne; Chapel-master at Stettin in '49. 5 Symphonies, overtures, string quartets, dance-music, lieder, and an opera.	German
1821 7 October. Puderbach.	**1885** 14 September Berlin.	**KIEL, Friedrich.** Pupil of Kummer and Dehn. Teacher of counter-point, fugue and composition in the Hochschule für Musik, Berlin. Oratorio, Requiem, fugues, canons, and pieces for 'cello and piano: over 80 works in all.	German
1821 16 October. Lemberg.	**1883** 27 July. Baden, n'r Vienna.	**DOPPLER, Albert Franz.** Toured as a flautist. Professor of the flute in the Conservatorium at Vienna, and conductor of the ballet at the Court Opera. Several operas and ballets; overtures and concertos for flute.	Austria
1821 9 November. Guebwiller, Alsace.	**1910** 20 May. Paris.	**WEKERLIN, Jean Baptiste Théodore.** Pupil of Elwart for harmony, Ponchard for singing, and Halévy for composition. Became head librarian at the Conservatoire, Paris, in 1876. 6 Operas, 2 antique dramas, 2 ode-symphonies, many male and female choruses, motets, a Mass, a symphony, suite, 300 vocal airs, etc.	French
1822 8 January. Bergamo.	**1901** 18 July. n'r Bergamo.	**PIATTI, Alfredo Carlo.** The greatest violoncellist of his day. Pupil of his grand-uncle for 'cello, and Molique for composition. Came first to England in 1844 and afterwards spent much of his life in London. Teacher of Hausmann, Becker, Whitehouse, etc. 'Cello concertos, romances, fantasias, sonatas, songs with 'cello obbligato, violin romances, and many arrangements.	Italian
1822 13 January. Paris.	**1885** 23 January.	**CLEMENT, Felix.** Organist and director at various churches. Writer on musical history and archæology. Choruses; church music; a method for organ and a method of Plain-chant; editions of Roman Church music, etc.	French

Born	Died	Name	Nationality
1822 16 January. Hardway, n'r Gosport.	**1895** 27 June. Glasgow.	**LAMBETH, Henry Albert.** Pupil of T. Adams. City organist at Glasgow, and conductor of the Choral Union. Pianoforte pieces, songs, and Psalms.	English.
1822 1 March. Boom, n'r Antwerp.	**1853** 9 June. Brussels.	**AERTS, Egidius.** Flautist: pupil of Lahon, and studied composition under Fétis. Toured from 1837 to '40. Professor of the flute at Brussels Conservatoire in '47, and first flute at the Theatre. Symphonies, overtures, concertos, and other flute music.	Belgian.
1822 7 March. Lorient.	**1884** 5 July. Paris.	**MASSÉ, Felix Marie, known as Victor.** Pupil of Halévy at Paris. Chorus-master at the Académie in 1860, succeeded Leborne as professor of composition at the Conservatoire in '66, and succeeded Auber at the Institut in '72. Many operas, cantatas, songs, and some sacred works.	French.
1822 22 May. Bushey, Hertfordshire	**1890** 13 March. London.	**WYLDE, Henry (Mus.D.).** Pupil of Moscheles, and Potter at the Royal Academy where he afterwards became a professor of harmony. Founded the London Academy of Music in 1871. Cantatas, one on Milton's " Paradise Lost "; pianoforte concerto, sonatas, fantasias; English songs from Goethe and Schiller, vocal duets, etc.	English.
1822 27 May. Lachen.	**1882** 24 June. Frankfort.	**RAFF, Joseph Joachim.** Pupil of Liszt. Director of the Hoch Conservatorium at Frankfort from 1877. Met Mendelssohn at Cologne in 1846. 11 Symphonies; concertos for pianoforte, violin, and 'cello; sonatas, suites, string quartets, all kinds of pianoforte music, songs, 1 opera and 2 cantatas; to the opus No. of 216. Though his best works are unique, poor circumstances necessitated his writing "commercial" music.	Swiss.
1822 18 June. London.	**1896** 4 February. Oswestry.	**LESLIE, Henry David.** Pupil of C. Lucas. 'Cellist, and conductor of several musical societies. Operas, oratorio, cantatas, symphonies, chamber-music, overtures, anthems, solo and part-songs, and pianoforte music.	English.
1822 Männerstadt.	**1903** 31 January. London.	**LUTZ, Wilhelm Meyer.** Organist at St. Chad's, Birmingham, St. Ann's, Leeds, and of St. George's Cathedral, London. *Chef d'orchestre* at the Surrey Theatre, 1851-55, and of the Gaiety from '69. Operas, operettas, cantata, chamber-music, Grand Masses and other Roman Church music.	German.
1820 or 22 Pressburg.	**1877** 9 December. Vienna.	**HAUSER, Miska.** Violinist. Pupil of Böhm and Mayseder. Travelled much as a virtuoso, visiting London in 1850. Violin works.	Hungarian.

Born	Died	Name	Nationality.
1822 16 July. Crescentino.	1903 1 May. Brighton.	**ARDITI, Luigi.** Pupil of the Milan Conservatorio. Started his career as violinist. Conductor at Her Majesty's Theatre in 1858, Covent Garden, 1874-77, the Olympic in '92, also visited New York, Boston, Vienna and Petrograd. 2 Operas, overtures, a Commemoration Ode ;. The vocal waltz " Il Bacio " became popular.	Italian.
1822 15 August. Dessau.	1892 2 May. Leipzig.	**RUST, Wilhelm.** Pupil of his uncle W.F. (1787) and of F. Schneider. Professor of composition at the Stern Conservatorium, Berlin; organist at the Thomaskirche, Leipzig, and succeeded E. F. E. Richter at the Thomasschule in 1880. Vocal and pianoforte works, to opus 33.	German.
1822 6 September. Schmölz.	1909 2 February. Munich.	**HERZOG, Johann Georg.** Organist at Munich in 1842, Cantor in '49, and professor of the Conservatorium in '50. Director of the Singakademie and teacher in the university at Erlangen in '54. Organ school, fantasias, etc.	German.
1822 13 October. Erfurt.	1896 13 February. Bremen.	**REINTHALER, Karl Martin.** Pupil of Ritter and Marx. Studied theology. Organist at the Cathedral, and conductor of the Singakademie at Bremen in '58 ; a member of the Berlin Academy in '82, and was entitled Royal Professor in '88. Opera, symphonies, oratorio, Psalms and part-songs.	German.
1822 7 November. Turnhout.	1890 28 June. Antwerp.	**GREGOIR, Edourd Georges Jacques.** Brother of J. M. Joseph (1817). Pianist, musical journalist and critic. Oratorios, symphonic-oratorio, historical-symphony, comic operas, overtures, dramas, part-songs, many piano and organ works.	Belgian.
1822 10 December Liège.	1890 8 November. Paris.	# FRANCK, César. Important through the quality, originality, and the poetic mysticism of his works. His life was uneventful and placid, and lived for his Art alone. Studied first at Liège Conservatoire, then at Paris under Leborne, Zimmerman, Berton and Benoist. Took charge of the organ class at the Paris Conservatoire in 1872. Organist at Ste. Clotilde, Paris, from 1858. Symphonies, symphonic-poems, oratorios (including "Les Béatitudes"), cantatas, motets, solo and part-songs, chamber music, organ works, pianoforte music, and 2 operas.	Belgian. Naturalised French in 1870.
1822 16 December London.	1876 28 February. New York.	**HORSLEY, Charles Edward.** Son of William (1774). Pupil of Hauptmann and Mendelssohn. Organist at St. John's, Notting Hill, and at Christ Church, Melbourne, Australia, in '62. Oratorios, anthems, odes, pianoforte trio and pieces, songs, and music for Milton's " Comus."	English.

Born	Died	Name	Nationality
1822 24 December Crema (Lombardy).	**1889** 7 July. Parma.	**BOTTESINI, Giovanni.** Virtuoso bass-player, and conductor. Pupil of Rossi for bass, and Vaccaj and Basili for composition. First appearance in London, 1849. Conductor of the Italian Opera in Paris in 1855-57, at Palermo in 1861-63, also at Cairo, and London in '71. Operas, oratorio, many fantasias, duets and other pieces for the double-bass.	Italian.
1823 3 January. Zoerle- Parwys.	**1881** 30 January. Malines.	**LEMMENS, Nicholas Jacques.** Pupil of Fétis, and of Hesse for organ. Professor of the organ at Brussels Conservatoire in 1849. Resided much in England. Founded a College for Catholic organists at Malines in '79. Organ-school, sonatas, Offertories, etc.	Belgian.
1823 27 January. Lille.	**1892** 22 April. Paris.	**LALO, Edouard Victor Antoine.** Studied the violin at Lille Conservatoire, and later played the viola. Received the Legion of Honour in 1880. Symphonies, suites and rhapsodies for orchestra ; concertos and sonatas for violin, 'cello and piano ; piano trio, string quartets, songs, an opera, and a grand ballet.	French.
1823 7 February. Danzig.	**1895** 15 June. Baden, n'r Vienna.	**GENEE, Franz Friedrich Richard.** Pupil of Stahlknecht at Berlin. Chapel-master of theatres at Revel, Riga, Cologne, Düsseldorf, Amsterdam, Prague, etc., between 1848 and '67. Wrote many librettos for himself and other composers 14 Operettas and many part-songs.	German.
1823 10 March. Hull.	**1876** 22 January. St. Leonards.	**DYKES, Rev. John Bacchus (Mus.D.).** Father of John (1863). Pupil of Walmisley. Vicar of St. Oswald, Durham. Many church services, anthems, and hymn tunes, including " Nearer, my God, to Thee," " The day is past and over," etc.	English.
1823 Petrograd.	**1872** September.	**GALITZIN, Prince George.** Son of Prince Nicolas Borissovich. At Moscow, in 1842, founded a choir of 70 boys, whom he fed, clothed and educated, and also maintained an orchestra. An able conductor. Orchestral, chamber and vocal music.	Russian.
1823 3 August. Madrid.	**1894** 19 February. Madrid.	**BARBIERI, Francisco Asenjo.** Studied at the Madrid Conservatoire. Conductor, musicologist and teacher. Secretary of the Association for promoting Spanish opera. 75 Spanish operettas—called Zarzuelas.	Spanish.
1823 13 October. Esslingen.	**1894** 5 June. Stuttgart.	**FAISST, Immanuel Gottlob Friedrich (D.Phils.).** Studied without a teacher on Mendelssohn's advice. Founded an organ school at Stuttgart in 1847, and was appointed organist at the Shiftskirche in '65. Church and choral music, including male quartets, organ pieces, fugues, etc.	German.
1823 21 October. Puente de la Reina.	**1864** 11 February. Madrid.	**ARRIETA Y CORERA, Emilio.** Studied in Italy under Perelli and Mandanicci, and at the Milan Conservatorio. Professor of composition in 1857, and director in 1858, of the Royal Conservatory, Madrid. Operas.	Spanish.

Born	Died	Name	Nationality
1823 1 December. Marseilles.	1909 15 January. Lavaudon.	**REYER, Ernest.** Pupil of his aunt, Mme. Louise Farrenc. A follower of Berlioz's style. Succeeded David at the Institut in 1876. Musical writer and journalist. Officer of the Legion of Honour, 1886. Grand operas (including "Salammbô"), comic operas, cantatas, ballets, "Melodies" for voice and piano, songs, and sacred music.	French.
1823 10 December Chemnitz.	1903 19 September Hamburg.	**KIRCHNER, Theodor.** Pupil of C. F. Becker at Leipzig; disciple of Schumann. Organist at Winterthur in '43; conductor and teacher at Zürich in '62; director at Würzburg in '73; Leipsic in '83, and at Dresden Conservatorium in '83. About 100 piano pieces, lieder, violin and 'cello pieces, string quartet, and a serenade for piano trio.	German.
1823 10 December Prague.	1912 8 October. Kensington, London.	**KUHE, Wilhelm.** Pupil of Tomaschek. Lived in London from 1845. Professor at the Royal Academy, 1886 to 1904. Pianoforte pieces, fantasias, songs without words, etc.	Bohemian.
1823 25 December London ?	1886 17 December Nice.	**CHIPP, Edmund Thomas (Mus.D.).** Studied the violin, and was in the Queen's private band, 1843-45. Organist in London, Belfast, Edinburgh, and at Ely Cathedral in '66. Oratorio, a Sacred Idyl, many organ works, much church music, and songs.	English.
1824 25 January. London.	1880 22 January. London.	**COWARD, James.** Choir-boy at Westminster Abbey. Organist at several London churches, and the Grand Lodge of Freemasons. Conductor of the Western Madrigal Society, the Abbey, and City Glee Clubs, etc. Madrigals, anthems, glees, pianoforte and organ pieces.	English.
1824 28 January. The Hague.	1899 9 January. Amsterdam.	**COENEN, Johannes Meinardus.** Educated at the Hague Conservatorium. Bassoon-player in the Royal orchestra. Conductor at the Dutch theatre of Van Lier, Amsterdam, '51. Director of the music at the Palais voor Volksvlyt in 1865. Symphonies, overtures, ballet music, an opera, cantatas; concertos for clarinet and for flute; sonata for bassoon, clarinet and piano; chamber-music, etc.	Dutch.
1824 22 February. Berlin.	1881 9 October. Berlin.	**WÜERST, Richard Ferdinand.** Pupil of David for violin, and Mendelssohn for composition. Teacher of composition in Kullak's Conservatorium, and professor and member of the Academy of Arts, Berlin. 7 Symphonies, overtures, quartets, etc.	German.
1824 2 March. Leitomischl.	1884 12 May. Prague.	**SMETANA, Friedrich.** Pupil of Proksch and Liszt. The first Bohemian National composer. Director of the Philharmonic Society at Gothenburg in 1856, and conductor of the National Theatre at Prague from '66 to '74, when he resigned through deafness. Several Bohemian operas, 4 symphonic-poems, string quartets, pianoforte trio, part-songs, and a festival march.	Bohemian.

Born	Died	Name	Nationality.
1824 27 April. Norwich.	**1853** 28 October. London.	**BEXFIELD, William Richard (Mus.D.).** Mostly self-taught. Organist at Boston, Lincs., and later at St. Helen's, London. Lecturer on music. Oratorio ("Israel Restored"), anthems, and organ fugues.	English.
1824 13 June. Düsseldorf.	**1893** 18 January. Boston, U.S.	**EICHBERG, Julius.** Pupil of J. Rietz, and of the Brussels Conservatoire. Professor at Geneva in 1846. Director of the orchestra at the Boston Museum in '59, and established the Boston Conservatory of Music in '67. Operettas, string quartets, choruses, songs, pianoforte music, violin solos and studies.	German.
1824 23 June. Altona.	**1910** 10 March. Leipzig.	**REINECKE, Carl Heinrich Carsten.** Court-pianist at Copenhagen; Professor of piano and counterpoint at Cologne Conservatorium. Director at Breslau University; Conductor of the Gewandhaus concerts at Leipzig, and professor of composition at the Conservatorium (1860); and later, director of musical studies until 1902. Piano concertos, sonatas, etc.; chamber-music, concertos for violin and 'cello; symphonies, Masses, oratorios, cantatas, overtures, and an opera; also literature.	German.
1824 11 July. Liège.	**1898** 14 September Ghent.	**SAMUEL, Adolphe Abraham.** Father of Eugène (1863). Studied at Liège and Brussels. Professor of harmony at Brussels Conservatoire, 1860. Director of Ghent Conservatoire in 1871. Several operas, 7 symphonies, cantatas, choral works, songs, etc.	Belgian.
1824 1 August. Deal.	**1857** 20 January.	**FITZWILLIAM, Edward Francis.** Musical director at Haymarket Theatre in '53. Operetta, comic opera and other stage music, Te Deum, and songs.	English.
1824 19 August. Hanover.	**1898** 29 December Frankfort.	**GOLTERMANN, Georg Eduard.** Pupil of Prell and Menter for 'cello, and Lachner for composition. Toured as a concert 'cellist. Music director at Würzburg, and chapel-master at the Stadt Theatre, Frankfort, in 1874. Symphonies, 'cello concerto, and other pieces.	German.
1824 4 September Ansfelden.	**1896** 11 October. Vienna.	**BRUCKNER, Anton.** Pupil of Sechter and Kitzler. Organist of Linz Cathedral in 1855, and succeeded Sechter as organist of the Hofkapelle and professor of the Conservatorium Vienna, in 1867. Lecturer at the University in '75. Gave 6 organ recitals in the Albert Hall in 1871. 8 Symphonies, 3 Grand Masses, a Te Deum, motets, Psalms, choruses, songs, string quartet, etc.	Austrian.
1824 6 September Lille.	**1888** 15 April. Corbeil, n'r Paris.	**SEMET, Théophile.** Pupil of Halévy. Drummer at the Opéra for many years. Operas, vaudevilles, cantata, orchestral music, songs, and part-songs.	French.
1824 24 December Mayence.	**1874** 26 October. Mayence.	**CORNELIUS, Peter.** Pupil of Dehn at Berlin. Professor of harmony and rhetoric at Munich Conservatorium. Worked with Liszt and Wagner in promoting new musical ideals. Grand opera, comic opera, Lieder-cyclus, songs, duets, and choruses with solo voice.	German.

Born	Died	Name	Nationality
1825 13 January. Königsberg.	1884 4 January. Wiesbaden.	**EHLERT, Ludwig.** Pianist, critic and litterateur. Pupil of Mendelssohn at Leipsic. Directed the Cherubini Society at Florence. At Berlin in '69, Meiningen, and finally at Wiesbaden. Overtures, symphonies, Requiem, a sonata romantique, lieder, etc.	German.
1825 5 February. Frankfort-am-Main.	1883 7 March. London.	**GOLLMICK, Adolf.** Pupil of his father, Carl, for piano and H. Wolf for violin. Settled in London in 1844. Founded the Réunion des Beaux-Arts in 1847, the Westbourne Operatic Society in '64, and the Kilburn Musical Association in '79. Operas, operatic cantatas, symphony, piano quartet, pieces, and songs.	German.
1825 7 February. Banstead, Surrey.	1877 7 August.	**GABRIEL, Mary Ann Virginia.** Pupil of Pixis and Döhler for piano and Molique for composition. Cantatas "Dreamland" and "Evangeline," operettas and songs.	English.
1825 17 March. Prague.	1883 3 June. Paris.	**WEHLI, Karl.** Pianist : pupil of Moscheles and Kullak. Played in Europe, America, Australia, India, etc. Pianoforte sonatas, ballades, impromptus, nocturnes waltzes, etc.	Bohemian.
1825 30 June. Arras.	1892 3 November Paris.	**HERVÉ, real name, Florimond Ronger.** Pupil of the School of St. Roch. Organist of various churches in Paris. Conductor, librettist, singer, etc., of his own theatre. Conductor of the promenade concerts in London in '74, and later at the Empire Theatre. Operas, comic operas, operettas, ballets, songs, and a symphony with solo voices.	French.
1825 August. Bath.	1904 30 August. London.	**LODER, Kate Fanny.** Pupil of H. Field and Mrs. Anderson for piano, and Lucas for composition. Professor of harmony at the Royal Academy. Opera, overture, 2 string quartets, a violin sonata, 2 piano sonatas, studies and pieces.	English.
1825 12 August. London.	1889 6 April. Hereford.	**OUSELEY, the Rev. Sir Frederick Arthur Gore, Bart.** Succeeded Sir Henry Bishop as Professor of Music at Oxford. Was ordained priest, and appointed Precentor of Hereford Cathedral in 1855. Vicar of St. Michael's, Tenbury, in '56, and warden of the College, where his library of music and valuable manuscripts still remains. Operas, oratorios (including "Hagar"); cantatas, over 70 anthems, 11 church services; organ preludes, fugues and sonatas; 2 string quartets, solo and part-songs.	English.
1825 23 October. Warsaw.	1879 29 June. Warsaw.	**KONTSKI, Apollinari de.** Brother of Antoine (1817). Toured as a concert violinist. Solo-violinist to the Emperor of Russia in '53, and Director of Warsaw Conservatoire in '61. Violin works, fantasias, etc.	Polish.

Born	Died	Name	Nationality
1825 25 October. Vienna.	**1899** 3 June. Vienna.	**STRAUSS, Johann (Junior).** Studied composition under Dreschsler, and played the violin. Incorporated his father's two bands, and toured Europe. Director of the summer concerts at Petrograd, and conductor at the Court balls. 400 Waltzes, the most popular being "Blue Danube," many operettas, ballets, and orchestral pieces.	Austrian.
1825 14 November. Frankenstein.	**1903** 1 December Berlin.	**REISSMANN, August.** Writer of much musical literature, including the "General History of Music." Lecturer of musical history at the Berlin Conservatorium. Operas, dramatic scenas, ballet, oratorio; concerto, suite and sonatas for violin, and piano pieces.	German.
1825 16 December Dublin.	**1894** 24 March. Dublin.	**STEWART, Sir Robert Prescott, Knight (Mus.D.).** Organist of Christ Church Cathedral, and of Trinity College, Dublin, in 1844. Vicar-choral of St. Patrick's in '52. Professor in the University in '61, and at the Royal Irish Academy in '72. Cantatas, odes, glees, a fantasia on Irish Airs, etc.	Irish.
1826 16 February. Brunswick.	**1878** 21 May. Leipzig.	**HOLSTEIN, Franz von.** Studied under Griepenkerl, and also at Leipzig. Served in the Schleswig-Holstein campaign. Operas (some comic), concert overtures, a scena for soprano and orchestra, many songs, and instrumental works.	German.
1826 1 March. Bridgend, Glam.	**1913** 19 March.	**THOMAS, John.** "Pencerdd Gwalia," i.e. chief of the Welsh Minstrels. Studied under Chatterton (harp), Read (piano), Lucas and Potter (composition). Toured much on the Continent. Harpist to Queen Victoria, and professor of the Royal Academy and the Royal College. Harp concertos, symphony, overtures, quartets, 2 operas, cantatas, etc.	Welsh.
1826 7 April. Hamburg.	**1880** 9 April. Stockholm.	**BERENS, Hermann.** Pupil of Reissiger. Conductor of the Court Orchestra, and professor of the Academy at Stockholm. Operas, operettas, chamber and piano music.	German.
1826 11 April. Chelsea.	**1912** 29 April.	**LAHEE, Henry.** Pupil of Sterndale Bennett, Goss and Potter. Organist at Holy Trinity Church, Brompton, 1847-74. Cantatas, anthems, madrigals, glees, songs, and instrumental pieces.	English.
1826 1 June. Glogau.	**1883** 2 July. Leipzig.	**ZOPFF, Hermann.** Pupil of A. B. Marx and Kullak. Conductor, critic, editor and professor of singing. Teacher in the Berlin Conservatorium till 1864, thence to Leipzig. Operas, oratorios, cantatas, symphonic-poem, songs, piano pieces, and many didactic works.	German.
1826 3 June. London.	**1905** 7 June. London.	**STEGGALL, Charles (Mus.D.).** Father of Reginald (1867). Pupil of Sterndale Bennett. Organist at various London churches, and professor at the Royal Academy, 1851 to 1903. Was one of the founders of the Royal College of Organists. Anthems and church music.	English.

Born	Died	Name	Nationality
1826 Lemberg.	**1900** 10 March. Stuttgart.	**DOPPLER, Karl.** Brother of A. F. (1821). Toured as a flautist. Conductor at the National Theatre, Pesth, and was Hofkapellmeister in Stuttgart, 1865-98. Hungarian operas, ballets, and flute music.	Austrian.
1826 4 July. Pittsburg, Pennsylvania	**1864** 13 January. New York.	**FOSTER, Stephen Collins.** Studied at the Academy at Athens, Pennsylvania, and at Jefferson College, near Pittsburg. 175 Songs, including " Swanee Riber," " Massa's in de cold ground," " Old Black Joe," etc., and a waltz for 4 flutes.	American. (Irish descent.)
1826 13 August. Carlisle.	**1897** 10 May. Liverpool.	**BEST, William Thomas.** Pupil of John Norman. Organist at several churches in Liverpool and London, including St. Martin-in-the-Fields. Opened the organ in Albert Hall in 1871. Went to Australia in 1890. Church services, anthems, hymns ; fugues, sonatas, etc. for organ ; 2 overtures, an orchestral march, and piano pieces.	English.
1826 28 August. London.	**1905** 2 September London.	**MACFARREN, Walter Cecil.** Brother of Sir George (1813). Pupil of Holmes (piano) and Potter (composition). Professor of the piano at the Royal Academy, 1846-1903, and conductor of its concerts, 1873-1880. A director of the Philharmonic Society. 7 Overtures, a symphony, piano concerto and sonatas, etc. ; church services, chants and hymns ; madrigals and part-songs, and edited many classical works.	English.
1826 22 October. Casal-maggiore.	**1882** 4 February. Milan.	**QUARENGHI, Guglielmo.** Studied at the Milan Conservatorio, where he became professor of the violoncello in 1851. Chapel-master at Milan Cathedral in 1879. An opera, church music, 'cello method, and a treatise on bow instruments.	Italian.
1826 21 December Vienna.	**1905** 9 May. Germany.	**PAUER, Ernst.** Pupil of Dirzka and Mozart's son for piano, and Sechter and F. Lachner for composition. Toured as solo-pianist. Pianist to the Imperial Austrian Court in '66. Succeeded C. Potter at the Royal Academy. Examiner at Cambridge University in '79. Chamber-virtuoso to the Grand Duke of Hesse in 1893. Operas, pianoforte pieces, and many arrangements and editions of classical works.	Austrian.
1826 26 December Rotterdam.	**1904** February. Leyden.	**COENEN, Franz.** Brother of William (1837). Pupil of Vieuxtemps and Molique. Toured as a violinist, and afterwards became director of the Conservatorium, Amsterdam, until 1895. Cantatas, Psalm, symphony, and quartets.	Dutch.

Born	Died	Name	Nationality.
1826 31 December Shrewsbury.	**1904** 20 October. Worthing.	**HILES, Henry (Mus.D.).** Brother of John (1810). Conductor of several societies in Lancashire and Yorkshire, and organist of various churches. Lecturer on harmony and composition at Owens College in '76, at the Victoria University in '79, and became Professor at the Manchester College in '93. Oratorio, cantatas, anthems, glees, odes, operettas, overture ; fugues, sonatas, concert overture, etc. for organ ; piano pieces, songs, and theoretical works.	English.
1827 2 February. Hanover.	**1902** 15 October. Dresden.	**SCHMITT, Georg Aloys.** Son of Aloys (1788). Pupil of Vollweiler. Court chapel-master at Schwerin in '56. Visited London in 1860. Operas, operettas, orchestral works, and completed Mozart's C minor Mass.	German.
1827 9 February. Ensival, n'r Liège.	**1890** 17 December Brussels.	**DUPONT, Auguste.** Studied at Liège Conservatoire. Travelled as pianist. Professor of the Brussels Conservatoire in 1850. Piano concerto, concertstück, solo pieces, and songs.	Belgian.
1827 5 March. Paris.	**1905** 22 May. Saint-Germain.	**JONAS, Émile.** Rival of Offenbach in opera-bouffe. Professor of Solfège at the Paris Conservatoire (1847-66), of Harmony for military bands (1859-70), and director of music at the Portuguese Synagogue. Many operas and operettas (produced in Paris and London), and a collection of Hebrew tunes.	French. Jewish.
1827 6 March. Pernau.	**1903** 7 December. Münster.	**GRIMM, Julius Otto.** Pupil of the Leipzig Conservatorium (piano and composition). Conductor at Münster, and director of the Musical Academy there in 1878. Pianoforte pieces, songs, orchestral works, including a symphony, " Suite in canon form," and an ode for chorus and orchestra.	German.
1827 Simbirsh.	**1894** 8 July.	**KASHPEROV, Vladimir Nikitich.** Pupil of Fotta and Henselt in Petrograd, and Dehn in Berlin. Professor of singing at the Moscow Conservatoire, 1866-72. Several operas, produced at Milan, Florence, Venice, Petrograd and Moscow.	Russian.
1827 Falmouth.	**1885** 26 November. London.	**PHILP, Elizabeth.** Pupil of Garcia for singing and Hiller for composition. Singer and teacher. Songs and ballads, on words by Arnold and Longfellow.	English.
1827 22 August. Amsterdam.	**1909** 8 February. London.	**SILAS, Edouard.** Pupil of Lacombe and Kalkbrenner for piano, Benoist for organ, and Halévy for composition. Came to London in 1850 as a teacher and organist of the Catholic Chapel at Kingston-on-Thames. Teacher of harmony at the Guildhall School of Music and the London Academy. Symphonies, overtures, an opera ; piano concerto, pieces, duets, etc. ; oratorio, cantata, and a Mass.	Dutch.

Born	Died	Name	Nationality
1827 22 August. Vienna.	**1870** 22 July. Vienna.	**STRAUSS, Joseph.** The 2nd son of Johann (1804) and brother of Johann (1825). Conducted a band in a similar manner to his brother. 283 Works, which attained popularity.	Austrian.
1827 23 August. London.	**1875** 30 December. London.	**WALEY, Simon Waley.** Pupil of Moscheles, Bennett and Osborne for piano; Horsley and Molique for composition. Was a member of the committee of the London Stock Exchange. Piano concerto, pieces and trios; songs, and a choral setting of the 117th and 118th Psalms, contained in the "Musical Services of the West London Synagogue."	English. Jewish.
1827 8 September. Berlin.	**1888** 23 June. Dresden.	**NAUMANN, Emil.** Grandson of J. G. (1741). Pupil of Mendelssohn and Hauptmann. Court-director of sacred music at Dresden in '56. Succeeded Rust as organist of St. Thomas's, Leipzig, in 1880. Operas, oratorio, and much musical literature.	German.
1827 17 September Hooksiel.	**1896** 12 July. Bielefeld.	**MEINARDUS, Ludwig Siegfried.** Pupil of Riccius and A. B. Marx. Conductor of the Singakademie at Glogau in '53; teacher at the Dresden Conservatorium in '65; critic and composer at Hamburg in '74; organist at Bielefeld in '87. Oratorios, operas, symphonies, ballads for chorus, and much chamber music.	German.
1827 12 November. Oberoder-witz.	**1885** 30 October. Dresden.	**MERKEL, Gustav.** Pupil of Schneider for organ, also had instruction from Reissiger and Schumann. At Dresden was organist of the Waisenkirche in 1858, of the Kreuz-kirche in '60, Court-organist in '64, director of the Singakademie from '67 to '73, and professor at the Conservatorium in '61. Organ sonatas, fugues, etc.; pianoforte, violin music, songs, and motets—180 works in all.	German.
1827 26 November. Oppeln.	**1872** 23 March. Berlin.	**ULRICH, Hugo.** Pupil of Dehn. Was an orphan when twelve. Lived in Italy and was for a short time teacher at the Berlin Conservatorium. 3 Symphonies, 2 overtures, opera, quartet, piano trio, 'cello sonata, and various piano works.	German.
1828 8 February. Godiasco.	**1896** 30 April. Bergamo.	**CAGNONI, Antonio.** Pupil of the Milan Conservatorio. Chapel-master at Vigevano in 1856-63, of Novara Cathedral in '78, and director of the Istituto Musicale there. Chapel-master at Santa Maria Maggiore in Bergamo from 1886. 17 Operas, and sacred music.	Italian.
1828 8 March. London.	**1881** 16 April. Wandsworth Hospital.	**MARTIN, George William.** Chorister at St. Paul's under W. Hawes. Organist of Christ Church, Battersea, in 1849, and music-master at St. John's College in 1845-53. Glees, madrigals and part-songs.	English.
1828 3 June. Nîmes.	**1892** 13 May. Paris.	**POISE, Jean Alexandre Ferdinand.** Pupil of A. Adam at the Paris Conservatoire. Several light and comic operas; and an oratorio.	French.

Born	Died	Name	Nationality
1828 Orleans.	1915 26 August. Paris.	RILLÉ, François Anatole Laurent de. Pupil of Comoghio and Elwart. Part-songs, light operettas, small choral works, and church music.	French.
1828 31 July. Oudenarde.	1908 24 December. Brussels.	GEVAËRT, François Auguste. Pupil of Sommère and Mengal at the Conservatoire at Ghent, where he became organist at the Jesuits Church. "Chef de chant" at the Académie de Musique, Paris, in 1867, and succeeded Fétis as director of the Brussels Conservatoire in 1871. Operas, cantatas, Requiem, Psalm, choruses, ballads, orchestral fantasia ; and many historic and didactic works.	Belgian.
1828 5 August. Parma.	1886 30 March. Parma.	ROSSI, Giovanni Gaetano. Pupil of the Milan Conservatorio. Leader of the orchestra in the theatre at Parma; organist of the Court chapel (1852-73), and director of the Conservatorio (1864-73). Conductor at the Teatro Carlo Felice, Genoa (1873-79). 5 Operas, 3 Masses, oratorio, Requiem, and a symphony.	Italian.
1828 26 August. Copenhagen.	1892 22 February. Copenhagen.	SIBONI, Erik Anton Waldemar. Son of Giuseppe, the Italian singer. Pupil of Vogel, Hartmann, Moscheles, Hauptmann and Sechter. Teacher of our late Queen Alexandra, and her sister, the Empress of Russia. Organist and professor at the Royal Academy of Music of Sorö in Seeland (1864-83). 2 Danish operas, cantatas, quartets, trios, piano concertos and sonatas, symphonies, overtures and church music.	Danish.
1828 3 October. Berlin.	1897 23 February. Belin.	BARGIEL, Woldemar. Studied under Dehn and at the Leipzig Conservatorium. Professor at Cologne in 1859, chapel-master at Rotterdam in '65, and became professor at the Königliche Hochschule at Berlin in '74. Overtures, symphony, Psalms for chorus and orchestra, string quartets, piano trios, sonatas, suites, etc.	German.
1828 19 October. Inzago.	1856 3 May. Florence.	FUMAGALLI, Adolfo. Brother of Luca (1837). Pupil of Angeloni at the Milan Conservatorio. Travelled as a solo-pianist. Fantasias, capriccios, and some pieces with orchestra.	Italian.
1829 4 February. Beaune.	1903 18 December Hyères.	IVRY, Marquis Richard d'. Amateur. Operas, and a lyric comedy.	French.
1829 8 May. New Orleans.	1869 18 December Rio de Janeiro.	GOTTSCHALK, Louis Moreau. Pupil of Charles Hallé, Maleden, and Stamaty in France. Toured much as a pianist. 2 Operas, symphony, and many piano pieces.	American.
1929 9 May. Sinalunga.	1888 10 March. Florence.	PINSUTI, Ciro. Pupil of Potter in England, and Rossini in Italy. Professor of singing at R. Academy in 1856. Teacher of Grisi, Patti, etc. More than 230 songs, 35 duets, 14 trios, 45 part-songs, and operas.	Italian.

Born	Died	Name	Nationality
1829 4 June. Groningen.	1869 20 June. London.	**ASCHER, Joseph.** Pupil of Moscheles. Court pianist to the Empress Eugénie in Paris. Over 100 salon pieces for piano, mazurkas, galops, études, nocturnes, etc.	Dutch.
1829 5 August. Lübeck.	1886 1 May. Reval.	**STIEHL, Heinrich.** Pupil of Moscheles, Gade and Hauptmann. Organist in St. Petersburg in '53 ; afterwards at Vienna, London, Belfast (where he founded the Cecilia Society), Hastings; and was organist, professor and conductor at Reval, Russia, in 1880. 2 Operas, orchestral pieces, quartets, trios and sonatas : to opus 172.	German.
1829 21 August. Hamburg.	1907 24 February. London. Buried at Malvern.	**GOLDSCHMIDT, Otto.** Husband of Jenny Lind. Pupil of J. Schmitt, Grund and Mendelssohn. Came to England in '48, and went to America as conductor in '51. Vice-Principal of the Royal Academy in '63, and was a member of the Royal Swedish Academy, etc. Oratorio, choruses, piano concerto, studies, trio, songs and part-songs.	German.
1829 28 August. Golk n'r Meissen.	1908 December. Berlin.	**DIETRICH, Albert Hermann.** Pupil of Rietz, Hauptmann and Moscheles at Leipzig, and later with Schumann at Düsseldorf. Hofkapellmeister at Oldenburg in '61, and retired to Berlin in 1890. Operas, symphonies, overture; concertos for horn, violin and 'cello ; piano sonatas, etc.	German.
1829 4 October. Hamburg.	1908 17 May. Chelsea.	**BLUMENTHAL, Jacob.** Pupil of Grund, Bocklet, and Sechter in Vienna, and of Herz at the Paris Conservatoire. Came to London in '48, where he became pianist to Queen Victoria ; also a fashionable teacher. Many piano pieces, and numerous songs.	German.
1830 8 January. Dresden.	1894 12 February. Cairo.	**BÜLOW, Hans Guido von.** The foremost pianist of the School of Chopin and Liszt. Conductor of the Royal opera at Munich in '67, and director of that Conservatorium in '67. Appeared first in England in 1873. Chapel-master of the Hoftheater at Hanover in '78. Piano-teacher at Frankfort and Berlin ; conducted and played in most European capitals. Orchestral, and pianoforte works.	German.
1830 13 January Vicenza.	1887 25 June. Milan.	**FILIPPI, Filippo.** Studied Law at Padua. Writer and critic. Promoted Wagner's music in Italy. Chamber-music, pianoforte pieces, and songs.	Italian.
1830 1 February. Darmstadt.	1913 10 November. Great Bookham.	**SCHLOESSER, Carl Wilhelm Adolph.** Son of Louis (1800). Came to England from Frankfort in '54. Professor at the Royal Academy until 1903. Pianoforte music, and songs.	German.
1830 11 February. Berlin.	1913 3 November Munich.	**BRONSART, Hans von.** Pupil of Dehn for composition, and Kullak and Liszt for piano. Succeeded Bülow at Berlin in '65. General-Intendant at Weimar in '87. Piano concerto, polonaise, etc. ; a cantata for double choir and orchestra, and an opera.	German.

Born	Died	Name	Nationality
1830. 13 April. Copenhagen.	**1904** 15 January. Weimar.	**LASSEN, Eduard.** Pupil of Brussels Conservatoire, and later of Liszt, whom he succeeded as Court music-director, and conductor of the opera at Weimar in 1861. Operas, symphonies, cantatas, Te Deum, a set of works for voice and orchestra, and many songs.	Danish.
1830 18 May. Kerzthely.	**1915** 2 January. Vienna.	**GOLDMARK, Carl.** Pupil of Jensa and Böhm for violin, and Preyer for harmony. Was engaged in the theatre band at Raab, and settled in Vienna as piano teacher in 1850. 5 Operas; symphonies and symphonic-poem; overtures; violin concertos, suites and sonatas; choruses, part-songs, Psalms; quartets, quintets and trios, etc.	Hungarian. (Jewish.)
1830 22 June. Lancut.	**1915** 14 November. Dresden.	**LESCHETIZKY, Theodor.** Pianist: chief teacher of Paderewski. Was for a time professor at the Petrograd Conservatorium, and settled in Vienna in 1878. Appeared first in London in '64. Opera, and piano pieces.	Polish. (Austrian.
1830 22 July. Ealing.	**1903** 26 October. Eastbourne.	**OAKELEY, Sir Herbert Stanley (Mus.D.).** Pupil of Dr. Elvey, J. Schneider at Dresden, and Breidenstein at Leipzig. Composer of music to Her Majesty in Scotland in 1881. Professor of Edinburgh University 1865-91. Cantatas, motets with orchestral accompaniment; songs, anthems, services; piano, organ and orchestral music.	English.
1830 31 August. Ostritz.	**1908** 13 September Dresden.	**KRETSCHMER, Edmund.** Pupil of Otto for composition, and Schneider for organ. Organist at the Catholic church, and of the Court at Dresden. Operas, Masses, and choruses with orchestra.	German.
1830 25 September Hanover.	**1916** 27 July. Stolpe.	**KLINDWORTH, Karl.** Pupil of Liszt. Came to London in 1854 as pianist and conductor. In 1882 returned to Germany, where he conducted the Berlin Philharmonic concerts. Professor at the Moscow Conservatorium in '68. Established a school in Berlin. Pianoforte works and arrangements.	German.
1830 16 November. Wechwoty-netz.	**1894** 20 November. Peterhof.	**RUBINSTEIN, Anton Gregor.** The most eminent pianist after Liszt. Visited England first in 1842; toured extensively. Chamber-virtuoso to the Grand Duchess Helen of Russia in '48. Founder and principal of the Petrograd Conservatorium, 1862-67. Operas, sacred operas, cantatas, symphonies, overtures, piano concertos, sonatas, violin sonatas, trios, quartets, quintets, songs, and every form of piano work; to Op. 119, also some without opus numbers.	Russian.

Born	Died	Name	Nationality
1831 1 January. London.	1894 24 March. London.	**WESTBROOK, William Joseph (Mus.D.).** Pupil of R. Temple. Organist of St. Bartholomew's, Sydenham, from 1851. Conductor of the South Norwood Musical Society for 13 years. Examiner in music to the College of Preceptors. Oratoriette, madrigals, canons, songs, part-songs and many organ pieces; also many arrangements and text translations.	English.
1831 21 February. Vienna.	1903 16 May. Dresden.	**RAPPOLDI, Eduard.** Pupil of Thalberg (piano), Jansa, Böhm, Hellmesberger (violin), Sechter and Hiller (composition). Teacher at the Hochschule, Berlin, with Joachim, and a member of that master's quartet. Royal Professor in 1876, and soon afterwards became concert-master at Dresden, and teacher in that Conservatorium. Symphonies, quartets, sonatas and songs.	Austrian.
1831 26 February. Bolognola.	1901 18 January. Rome.	**MARCHETTI, Filippo.** Pupil of Conti. President of the Reale Academy of St. Cecilio, Rome, in 1881, and Director of the Liceo Musicale in 1885. Operas (the best being " Ruy Blas "), romances and ballads.	Italian.
1831 10 June. Prague.	1898 22 January. Prague.	**REMY, W. A. (Dr. Jur.).** Proper name, Wilhelm Mayer. Pupil of C. F. Pietsch; teacher of Busoni, Heuberger, Kienzel, etc. Conductor and teacher in Vienna. Symphonies, symphonic-poem, concert-opera, overtures, choruses and other vocal and orchestral works.	Bohemian.
1831 13 June. London.	1897 20 November. Streatham, London.	**BANISTER, Henry Charles.** Pupil of C. Potter at the Royal Academy, where he became professor of harmony in 1853. Professor at the Guildhall School of Music in 1880, and taught at the Royal Normal College for the Blind. Symphonies, overtures, songs, piano pieces, and many didactic works.	English.
1831 28 June, Kitsee, n'r Pressburg.	1907 15 August. Berlin.	**JOACHIM, Joseph (Dr.).** The greatest solo-violinist and quartet leader of his time. Pupil of Hauser, Hellmesberger and Böhm for violin, and Mendelssohn for composition. Visited London first in 1844. Leader of the Grand Duke's band at Weimar in '49. Principal of the Hochschule at Berlin from its foundation in '68. 3 Violin concertos and other solos with orchestra; overtures and songs.	Hungarian.
1831 9 August. Dettingen.	1911 5 September. Esslingen.	**FINK, Christian.** Pupil of Dr. Kocher at Stuttgart, and Schneider at Dresden for organ. Principal of the seminary at Esslingen, and organist of the principal church there. Organ works, choruses, Psalms, and songs.	German.
1831 22 August. Sidbury, Devon.	1915 10 June. Dulwich.	**CUMMINGS, William Hayman (Mus.D.).** Organist and concert tenor-singer. Professor of singing at the Royal Academy, 1879-96. Succeeded Barnby as principal of the Guildhall School of Music in 1896, and was conductor of the Sacred Harmonic Society. Cantata, glees, songs, anthem, and a morning service.	English.

Born	Died	Name	Nationality.
1831 3 September. Breslau.	**1902** 1 February. Leipzig.	**JADASSOHN, Salomon (D.Phil.).** Pupil of Hesse, Lüstner and Brosig, and later of Liszt and Hauptmann. Teacher of harmony, counterpoint and composition at the Leipzig Conservatorium, and was appointed Royal Professor in 1893. Symphonies, overtures, serenades, piano concertos, quartets, quintets, sextets, Psalms and other choral works, over 100 in all. Also didactic works.	German.
1831 September. Southampton	**1879** 31 October.	**ROBINSON, Mrs. Fanny.** Wife of Joseph. Pupil of Bennett and Thalberg. Helped with her husband in reviving the Irish Academy. Numerous piano pieces and a cantata, " God is love."	English.
1831 14 October. Totis.		**SINGER, Edmund.** Pupil of Böhm for violin and Preyer for composition. Toured as a solo-violinist. Leader and solo-violinist at the German Theatre at Pest in 1846 ; leader of the Court band at Weimar under Liszt ; professor of the violin at the Stuttgart Conservatorium, and leader of the Court band in 1861. Violin concert pieces, fantasias, studies, etc.	Hungarian.
1831 25 December Vienna.	**1877** 28 October. Vienna.	**HERBECK, Johann.** Mostly self-taught. Professor at the Conservatorium, Vienna, in '58 ; Court chapel-master in '66 and director of the Court opera in '71. Symphony, symphonic-variations, and other orchestral ; string quartets, Masses, songs, part-songs, and choruses.	Austrian.
1832 19 January. Prague.	**1875** 17 March. Bozen.	**LAUB, Ferdinand.** Violinist : pupil of Milner at Prague. Visited England first in '51. Succeeded Joachim at Weimar in '53, and was followed by Singer. Professor of the violin at the Moscow Conservatorium in '66. Violin solos, etc.	Bohemian.
1832 28 January. Münster.	**1902** 7 September. Braunsels- on-Lahn.	**WÜLLNER, Franz.** Pupil of Carl Arnold, Schindler and F. Kessler. Professor of piano at the Munich Conservatorium in '56, and was Court chapel-master to the King in '64. Succeeded Bülow at the King's new School of Music and at the Court theatre in '69. " Royal professor " in '75. Succeeded Hiller as director of Cologne Conservatorium in '84. Cantata, motets, Masses, Stabat Mater, Lieder for mixed chorus, Psalms, pianoforte and chamber music.	German.
1832 13 April. Trieste.	**1911** 18 December. London.	**RANDEGGER, Alberto.** Pupil of Lafont for piano and Ricci for composition. Musical director of theatres at Fiume, Zara, Brescia, and Venice. Came to England in '54 and became professor of singing at the Royal Academy and at the Royal College. Conducted at several London theatres, the Queen's Hall Choral Society, and the Norwich Festival 1881-1905. Operas (tragic and comic), cantatas, Psalms, anthems choruses, songs, etc.	Hungarian.

Born	Died	Name	Nationality
1832 3 June. Paris.	1918 October. Paris.	**LECOCQ, Alexandre Charles.** Pupil of Halévy at the Paris Conservatoire. Followed in the style of Offenbach. Many comic operas, operettas, songs, etc.	French.
1832 17 July. Stockholm.	1876 10 February.	**SÖDERMAN, August Johan.** Studied under Richter and Hauptmann at Leipsic. Chorus-master at the Royal Opera, Stockholm, in 1860. A member of the Swedish Academy of Music. Operettas, cantatas, overtures; Mass for solos, chorus and orchestra; "Sacred songs for organ"; vocal trios, quartets; part-songs, ballads, songs, etc.	Swedish.
1832 23 July. Buda-Pesth.	1900 14 November. London.	**POLLITZER, Adolphe.** Pupil of Böhm and Alard for violin, and Preyer for composition. Leader of the Opera in London in '51, and of the New Philharmonic, etc. Professor of the violin at the London Academy in '61, and became principal in 1890, succeeding Wylde. Caprices and solos for violin.	Hungarian.
1832 21 September Kochowitz.	1915 1 April. Stuttgart.	**ABERT, Johann Joseph.** Pupil of the Prague Conservatorium. Succeeded Eckert as chapel-master at Stuttgart from 1867 to '88. 4 Operas, symphonies, symphonic-poem, and smaller pieces.	Bohemian.
1832 21 September Hamburg.	1892 9 June. Berlin.	**LANGHANS, Friedrich Wilhelm (Dr.).** Pupil of David and Alard for violin, and Richter for composition. Violinist, professor of musical history, and writer. Symphony, violin sonata, and quartet.	German.
1832 22 October. Posen.	1885 15 February. New York.	**DAMROSCH, Leopold (Mus.D.).** Pupil of Ries, S. W. Dehn and Böhmer. Leader of the Court orchestra at Weimar under Liszt, in '57. Conductor of the orchestra at Breslau 1862-71. Then lived at New York as violinist and conductor of the Oratorio Society, Symphony Society, Opera, etc. Concertos and solos for violin, overtures, songs, choruses and church music.	German.
1832 28 November. Dürkheim.	1887 7 March. Manchester.	**HECHT, Eduard.** Pupil of Rosenhain, Hauff and Messer. Settled in Manchester in '54, where he conducted the St. Cecilia Choral Society in 1860, the Stretford Choral Society in '79, was lecturer at Owens College in '75. Symphony, cantata, choruses, string quartets, songs, part-songs, marches for military band, etc.	German.
1833 7 May. Hamburg.	1897 3 April. Vienna.	**BRAHMS, Johannes.** Pupil of Marxsen and was influenced by Schumann. Associated with the violinists Remenyi and Joachim. Director of the Court concerts and of the Choral Society at Cologne, 1854-58. Conductor of the Singakademie in Vienna and of the Gesellschaft der Musikfreunde for a short time. His life was uneventful and peaceful. Buried near Beethoven and Schubert. Symphonies, concertos (piano, violin and violin and 'cello), sonatas, quintets, quartets, trios, overture, cantatas, motets, choruses, Requiem, Psalms, many piano works, and about 200 songs—to the opus number of 122.	German.

JOHANNES BRAHMS.

Born	Died	Name	Nationality
1833 24 May. Narva.	**1896** 12 April. Munich.	**RITTER, Alexander.** Violin pupil of Schubert of Dresden. Conductor at the Town Theatre of Stettin in '56. Was one who fought for the cause of Wagner's music. Operas, string quartet, and symphonic-poems.	Russian. (German parents.)
1833 September Birmingham.	**1858** 24 August. Birmingham.	**BACHE, Francis Edward.** Brother of Walter (1842). Studied under Sterndale Bennett in London, then Hauptmann and Plaidy at Leipzig, and Schneider at Dresden. Overtures, 2 operas, piano concerto, trio, many solos ; songs, romance for 'cello, etc.	English.
1833 4 October. London.	**1893** 31 August. Remonchamps.	**CUSINS, Sir William George.** Pupil at Brussels Conservatoire under Fétis in '44, and at the Royal Academy in '47 under Lucas, Bennett, Potter and Sainton. Played the violin and piano in public, and was organist to the Queen's Private Chapel : Professor at the Royal Academy. Conductor of the Philharmonic Society, '67 to '83, and was appointed Master of the Music to the Queen in 1870. Oratorio " Gideon," overtures, piano concerto, marches, songs, etc.	English.
1834 0 January. Paris.	**1896** July. St. Germain-en-Laye.	**SALOME, Théodore César.** Pupil of the Conservatoire. Organist, professor of solfège at the Conservatoire ; and chapel-master at the Lycée Saint-Louis. Various organ pieces, and several orchestral works.	French.
1834 1 February. Lemberg.	**1895** 13 October. Warsaw.	**ZARZYCKI, Alexander.** Director of the Conservatorium of Warsaw. Violin pieces, a piano concerto, etc.	Austrian, Polish.
1834 15 March. Tralee.	**1919** 13 March.	**O'LEARY, Arthur.** Studied at Leipsic under Moscheles, Plaidy, Hauptmann, Richter and Rietz, and under Potter and Bennett at the Royal Academy, London, where he became professor, 1856-1903. His wife also wrote songs. Orchestral pieces, songs, and dance music.	Irish.
1834 9 May. Cranbourne.	**1916** 26 December	**THORNE, Edward H.** Pupil of Elvey. Organist at Henley, Chichester Cathedral, several London churches, and lastly at St. Anne's, Soho, from '91. Church services, Psalms, a festival march, funeral march, toccata and fugue, overture, organ voluntaries, piano pieces, songs and part-songs.	English.
1834 8 June. Winchester.	**1897** 8 April. Cambridge.	**GARRETT, Dr. George Mursell.** Pupil of S. Elvey and S. S. Wesley. Organist of Madras Cathedral in '54 ; St. John's College, Cambridge, in '57 ; and succeeded J. L. Hopkins as organist to the University in '73. Church services, cantata, songs, part-songs, and organ pieces.	English.
1834 10 June. London.		**BERGER, Francesco.** Studied under Ricci and Lichl at Trieste, and later under Hauptmann, Plaidy and Moscheles at Leipzig. Piano professor at the Royal Academy, London, and the Guildhall School of Music. Overture and incidental music, 100 piano pieces, and 100 songs.	English. (Italian parents.)

Born	Died	Name	Nationality
1834 13 June. Quedlinburg.	1899 10 January. Berlin.	**BECKER, Albert Ernst Anton.** Pupil of Bönicke and Dehn. Teacher of composition in Scharwenka's Conservatorium, Berlin, in 1881, and director of the Domchor in '91. Opera, oratorio, motets, Mass, songs, symphony, pieces for violin and orchestra, chamber music, and organ works. Best in sacred music.	German.
1834 22 June. Strasburg.	1891 22 July. Antwerp.	**RITTER, Frédéric Louis (Dr.).** Pupil of Hauser, Schletterer and Georges Kastner, his cousin. Spent several years in America, conducting orchestras and choral societies in New York. Choruses, songs, Psalms, symphonies, overtures, piano concerto, and organ works.	French.
1834 8 July. Cheltenham.	1885 29 July. London.	**THOMAS, Robert Harold.** Pupil of Sterndale Bennett, Potter (theory), and Blagrove (violin). Professor of the piano at the Royal Academy and the Guildhall School of Music. Overtures, piano pieces, and songs.	English.
1834 17 August. Harlebeke.	1901 8 March. Antwerp.	**BENOIT, Pierre Léopold Léonard.** The chief promoter of the Flemish musical movement, and director of the Flemish School of Music at Antwerp in 1867. Pupil of Fétis. Flemish operas, dramas, oratorios, cantatas, choral symphony, choruses with orchestra, and songs.	Belgian.
1834 1 September Cremona.	1886 16 January. Milan.	**PONCHIELLI, Amilcare.** Pupil of the Milan Conservatorio. Chapel-master at Bergamo in 1881, and in the same year his opera "Promessi Sposi" was performed in Birmingham. Operas, ballets and cantatas.	Italian.
1834 31 October. Petrograd.	1887 16 February. Petrograd.	**BORODIN, Alexander Porphyrievich.** Disciple of Balakirev. A great "poet" in national music. Professor of medicine, and author of many important treatises on chemistry. 2 Symphonies, 2 string quartets, symphonic sketch and a scherzo for orchestra; songs, piano suite and pieces, an opera "Prince Igor," and an unfinished opera ballet.	Russian.
1834 25 November. Brussels.	1902 31 October. Brussels.	**COLYNS, Jean-Baptiste.** Student, then professor of the violin at the Brussels Conservatoire, and in 1888 at Antwerp. Toured as a solo-violinist, visiting England in '73. Operas and violin works.	Belgian.
1835 18 January. Vilna.	1918 1 March. Petrograd.	**CUI, César Antonovich.** Disciple of Balakirev. Studied in early life under Moniuszko. Lieut.-General of Engineers. President of the Imperial Russian Musical Society. Writer on music. 8 Operas, including "William Ratcliff" and "The Saracen"; suites and pieces for orchestra; suites and pieces for violin; string quartet, choruses, piano works, and many songs.	Russian.
1835 26 January. Moscow.		**BESEKIRSKIJ, Wasil Wasiliewich.** Pupil of Léonard for violin, and Dameke for composition, at Brussels. Toured extensively as solo-violinist, appearing first at the Philharmonic, London in 1868. Violin concerto, solos, etc.	Russian.

Born	Died	Name	Nationality.
1835 4 February. Vienna.	**1916** 28 December Vienna.	**STRAUSS, Eduard.** Third and youngest son of Johann (sen'r). Pupil of Preyer for composition. Took his brother Johann's place at Petrograd and made repeated tours with his orchestra. 200 Dance pieces.	Austrian.
1835 1 March. Oundle.	**1909** 5 December. Hackney.	**PROUT, Ebenezer (Mus.D.).** Pupil of C. Salaman. Organist at various chapels in London. Conductor of the Hackney Choral Association, 1876-90. Professor of harmony and composition at the National Training School, the Royal Academy in '79, and the Guildhall School of Music in '84. Symphonies, string quartets, quintets, cantatas, Psalms, ode, services, organ concertos, overtures and orchestral suite. Best known for his theoretical works.	English.
1835 30 March. Mainz.	**1916** 26 December Munich.	**SCHOLZ, Bernhard E.** Pupil of E. Pauer and S. W. Dehn. Teacher in the Royal School at Munich in 1856 ; chapel-master of the Court Theatre, Hanover, in '59 to '65 ; succeeded Raff in 1883, as director of Dr. Hoch's Conservatorium at Frankfort. 8 Operas, symphony, piano concerto, overtures, string quartets ; pieces for solo, chorus and orchestra; songs, etc.	German.
1835 4 May. Nottingham.	**1907** 25 October. London.	**TURPIN, Edmund Hart (Mus.D.).** Organist at St. George's, Bloomsbury, in 1869, and St. Bride's, Fleet Street, 1886. Conducted the London orchestra at the Cardiff Eisteddfod in 1883. Editor of some musical journals. Oratorios, cantatas, Masses, Stabat Mater, anthems, services, a symphony-overture, chamber-music, piano pieces, and songs.	English.
1835 21 May. Moscow.	**1881** 23 March. Paris.	**RUBINSTEIN, Nicholas.** Brother of Anton Gregor (1830). Pupil of Kullak and Dehn. Founded the Russian Musical Society in 1859 and the Conservatorium at Moscow in 1864. Teacher of Taneiev, Siloti and Sauer. Several pianoforte works, etc.	Russian.
1835 Murcia.	**1906** 26 February.	**CABALLERO, Manuel Fernárdez.** Pupil of Albeniz and Eslava at the Madrid Conservatoire. Became totally blind. Over 200 stage works in 1, 2, 3 and 4 acts, also church music, and songs.	Spanish.
1835 Rathmines, Dublin.	**1907** 20 August.	**TORRANCE, Rev. George William, M.A. (Mus.D.)** Organist at Dublin. Lived in Australia from 1869 to '97. Oratorios, opera, madrigals, hymns, and much sacred music.	Irish.
1835 Danzig.	**1918** Helsingfors.	**FALTIN, Richard.** Studied at Danzig, Dresden and Leipzig. Settled in Finland in early life, and became the chief promoter of Finnish music. Organist of St. Nicholas Church, Helsingfors, and musical director at the University, succeeding Frederick Pacius. Important choral works, and arrangements of Finnish folksongs.	German.

Born	Died	Name	Nationali
1835 10 July. Lublin.	**1880** 2 April. Moscow.	**WIENIAWSKI, Henri.** Pupil of Massart at Paris. Toured as a solo-violinist, sometimes with Rubinstein. Solo-violinist to the Emperor of Russia, 1860. Professor of the violin at Brussels Conservatoire for a few years, succeeding Vieuxtemps. 2 Violin concertos (in F sharp and D.), difficult solos and studies, up to Opus 22.	Polish.
1835 10 August. Komorn.	**1893** 30 April. Pesth.	**BELICZAY, Julius von.** Pupil of Hoffmann and F. Krenn in Vienna. Professor of theory in the National Music Academy at Pesth. 2 Symphonies, 3 string quartets, trio; Serenade and an Andante for strings; "Ave Maria" for solo, chorus and orchestra; a Mass, piano music, and songs.	Hungaria
1835 18 September Nœstved.	**1915** 27 July. Copenhagen.	**KRYGELL, Johan Adam.** Entered Copenhagen Conservatory at the age of 32. Organist of St. Matthew's Church from 1880. Oratorio, Mass, Requiem; organ concerto, fugues and other pieces; also songs.	Danish.
1835 7 October. Coburg.	**1913** 26 February. Dresden.	**DRAESEKE, Felix August Bernhard.** Pupil of the Leipzig Conservatorium. Disciple of Liszt. Teacher in the new Conservatorium at Munich in '68, and held a similar post at Dresden in '76, succeeding Wüllner. Wrote the libretto to his first opera. Operas, symphonies, overtures; concertos for violin, 'cello and piano; quartets, quintet, Requiem, Adventlied; piano sonatas and pieces; 'cello solos, and vocal works.	German
1835 9 October. Paris.	**1922** 16 December Algiers.	**SAINT-SAËNS, Charles Camille.** Pupil of Stamaty, Benoist and Halévy. Organist of St. Merri in '53 and of the Madeleine, '58 to '77. Travelled much throughout Europe as a pianist. Knight of the Legion of Honour in '67 and an officer of the same in '84. Succeeded Reber as a member of the Institut in 1881. Operas including "Samson and Delilah"; ballets, symphonies, symphonic-poems, concertos (violin, 'cello and piano), orchestral suites, chamber music, sonatas for various instruments, choruses, church music, and many piano works, to opus 105.	French.
1835 2 November Marseilles.	**1901** 13 January. Paris.	**COHEN, Jules Émile David.** Pupil of the Paris Conservatoire. Inspector of music under Napoleon III; professor at the Conservatoire for 35 years, and chorus-master at the Opéra for 20 years, at Paris. Many operas, choruses, symphonies, Masses, choral works, and piano pieces.	French.
1835 12 December Versailles.	**1908** 14 February. Paris.	**PFEIFFER, Georges Jean.** Pupil of Damcke and Maleden. Was partner in the piano firm of Pleyel, Wolff & Cie. Symphonies, overtures, chamber-music, operettas, pianoforte pieces and studies, symphonic-poem, sonatas, concertos, and an oratorio.	French.

Born	Died	Name	Nationality
1836 21 February St. Germain du Val.	**1891** 16 January. Paris.	**DELIBES, Clément Philibert Léo.** Pupil of Le Couppey, Benoist, Bazin and A. Adam. Organist of St. Pierre de Chaillot and St. Jean St. François in 1862-71. Accompanist at the Théâtre Lyrique in '53. Professor of advanced composition at the Conservatoire in 1881, succeeding Reber. Member of the Institut in '84, *vice* Massé. Many operas, comic operas, operettas, ballets, scenas, choruses, cantata, Mass, etc. ; the comedy " Coppé- lia " being his best-known piece.	French.
1836 21 February. Copenhagen.	**1898** 18 July. Copenhagen	**HARTMANN, Emil.** Brother of J. P. Pupil of Gade, whom he succeeded as director of the Musical Society at Copenhagen. Operas, symphonies, overture, choral cantata, concertos for violin and 'cello ; serenade for piano, clarinet and 'cello ; and many songs.	Danish.
1836 18 April. Potes.	**1903** 28 September Santander.	**MONASTERIO, Jesus de.** Pupil of De Bériot at Brussels. Toured as a concert violinist. Violin professor at the Conservatoire, Madrid. Violin and church works.	Spanish.
1836 15 August. Norwich.	**1908** 10 February. Durham.	**ARMES, Philip (Mus.D.).** Pupil of J. L. Hopkins. Organist of Chichester Cathedral in 1861, and of Durham in 1832, *vice* Henshaw. Professor of music at Durham University in 1897. Oratorios " Hezekiah," " St. John," and " St. Barnabas " ; services, anthems, hymns, a 5-part madrigal, and organ music.	English.
1836 16 August. Nottingham.	**1901** 17 July. Oxford.	**FARMER, John.** Pupil of the Leipzig Conservatorium. Teacher of music at Zurich; music-master at Harrow, 1862-85; organist in Balliol College, Oxon, from '85, where he was succeeded by Walker. Oratorio, Requiem, a fairy opera, " Nursery Rhymes," Quadrilles for chorus and orchestra, songs, etc.	English.
1836 31 December Nijny- Novgorod.	**1910** 16 May. Petrograd.	**BALAKIREV, Mily Alexeivich.** *Founder of the New Russian School*, having under his guidance C. Cui, Moussorgsky, Rimsky-Korsakov. and Borodin. Helped to establish the Free School of Music in Petrograd in 1862. Director of the Imperial Chapel and conductor of the Imperial Russian Musical Society in '69. Overtures, symphonic-poems, symphony, songs, folk-songs and national songs ; piano pieces and arrangements.	Russian.
1837 12 January. Königsberg.	**1879** 26 January. Baden- Baden.	**JENSEN, Adolph.** Pupil of Ehlert and F. Marpurg. Chapel-master at Posen for a short time, and teacher of the piano at Tausig's school at Dresden. Many songs, piano pieces, overture, chorus with solo and orchestra, and an opera ; about 70 works,	German.

Born	Died	Name	Nationality.
1837 2 February. Munich.	1911 16 November.	**ZENGER, Max.** Self-taught. Conductor at the Royal Opera House, Munich (1869), Court conductor at Carlsruhe (1872), and of the Oratorio Society ('78-'85). Operas, oratorio, 100 songs, part-songs, string quartets, sonata for horn, works for various instrumental combinations, choruses, symphonies, and an overture.	German.
1837 12 March. Boulogne.	1911 29 March. Paris.	**GUILMANT, Félix Alexandre.** Pupil of Lemmens. Organist at Boulogne, and of the Trinité, Paris, from 1871. Played in England on several occasions. 2 Symphonies, 7 sonatas and many concertos for organ ; chorus with solo and orchestra ; Masses, motets, organ and harmonium pieces.	French.
1837 25 April. Dublin.	1894 18 August. London.	**LEVEY, William Charles.** Son and pupil of R. M. (1811). Studied later under Auber, Thalberg and Prudent in Paris. Conductor at Drury Lane (1868-74), then at Covent Garden, Adelphi, Princess's, Avenue and Grecian Theatres. 2 Operettas, dramas, incidental music, a cantata, pianoforte pieces, and songs.	Irish.
1837 30 April. Norwich.	1913 13 September Birmingham.	**GAUL, Alfred Robert (Mus.B.).** Pupil of Dr. Buck. Organist successively at Fakenham, St. John's, Ladywood, Birmingham, and St. Augustine's, Edgbaston. Teacher at the Midland Institute, and conductor of the Walsall Philharmonic Society in 1887. Oratorio " Hezekiah," sacred cantatas (" The Holy City " best-known), Psalms, hymns, chants, part-songs, and piano pieces.	English.
1837 29 May. Inzago.	1908 June. Milan.	**FUMAGALLI, Luca.** Brother of Adolfo (1828). Pianist ; played in Paris in 1860. Piano pieces, and an opera given in 1875 at Florence.	Italian.
1837 23 June. New Orleans.	1892 6 May. Paris.	**GUIRAUD, Ernest.** Saw his first opera performed at the age of 15. Professor of harmony and accompaniment at the Paris Conservatoire in 1876, succeeding Baptiste ; and professor of advanced composition there in 1880, replacing Massé. Decorated with the Legion of Honour in '78. Several operas, orchestral suites, and a caprice for violin and orchestra.	American. (French parents.)
1837 6 July. Grodkowice.	1921 23 January. Cracow.	**ZELENSKI, Wladyslaw.** Director of Cracow Conservatory, 1883-1921. Operas ; symphonies, overtures and other orchestral works ; piano concerto, violin and piano sonatas, quartets, trio, and 80 songs.	Polish.
1837 11 July. Carcassonne.		**LACOMBE, Paul.** Pupil of Bizet. A corresponding member of the Institut in 1901, succeeding Benoît. Symphonies, symphonic overture, suites and pieces for piano and for orchestra, violin sonatas, trios, Mass, Requiem, and many songs.	French.
1837 28 July.	1913 20 March.	**BARNEKOW, Christian.** President of the Music Society at Copenhagen. Cantatas, chamber music, sacred and secular songs.	Danish.

Born	Died	Name	Nationality.
1837 24 August. Rosney.	**1924** June. Paris.	**DUBOIS, François Clément Théodore.** Pupil of A. Thomas at the Conservatoire. Chapel-master of Ste. Clotilde in '66, and of the Madeleine, succeeding Saint-Saëns as organist there in 1877. Succeeded Elwart as professor of harmony at the Conservatoire in '71, and became the head in 1896. Took Gounod's place at the Académie in '94. Operas and other dramatic works, symphonies, suites, etc. for orchestra ; ode, choruses, piano pieces, songs, church and chamber music.	French.
1837 16 October. London.	**1898** 29 April. London.	**BARNETT, John Francis.** Pupil of the Royal Academy, London, and the Conservatorium, Leipzig. Performed on the piano in England and Germany. Oratorios, cantatas, symphonies, overtures; suites and sketches for orchestra ; concerto and sonata for flute ; concerto, sonatas and pieces for piano ; quintets, quartets and trios.	English.
1837 9 November. London.	**1876** 4 March. Paris.	**HOLMES, Alfred.** Brother of Henry (1839). Self-taught. Visited all parts of Europe playing violin-duets with his brother. Symphonies (one, "Joan of Arc", with solos and chorus) ; overtures, and an opera.	English.
1837 7 November Rotterdam.	**1918** 19 March.	**COENEN, Willem.** Brother of Franz (1826). Settled in London in '62, and played the piano in public. Oratorio " Lazarus," piano music, and songs.	Dutch.
1837 9 December. Strasburg.	**1912** 12 February. Paris.	**WALDTEUFEL, Emil.** Pupil of the Paris Conservatoire under Marmontel and Laurent. Pianist to the Empress Eugénie. Many hundreds of waltzes.	French.
1837 28 December Salem, Mass.	**1909** 3 April. Boston, Mass.	**LANG, Benjamin Johnson (M.A.).** Studied with F. G. Hill of Boston, and later in Germany. Conductor, organist, pianist, and teacher in Boston. Oratorio " David," symphonies, overtures, chamber-music, piano pieces, songs, and church music.	American.
1838 6 January. Cologne.	**1920** 2 October. Berlin-Friedenau.	**BRUCH, Max.** Pupil of Breidenstein, Hiller, Reinecke and Breuning. Musical director at Coblenz in '65 ; chapel-master to the Prince of Schwarzburg-Sondershausen in '67-70 ; director of the Stern Singing Society, Berlin, in '78 ; director of the Liverpool Philharmonic Society, 1880-83 ; director of the Orchesterverein at Breslau, 1883-90 ; director in the branch of composition at the Hochschule, Berlin, in '92. Symphonies, violin concertos, quartets, solos with orchestra, sonatas, choruses, oratorio, operetta, piano music, and songs ; to Opus 79.	German.

Born	Died	Name	Nationality
1838 17 March. Goldingen.	**1889** 15 February. Moscow.	**DAVIDOV, Charles.** Studied the 'cello under Schmidt at Moscow and Schuberth at Petrograd, and composition under Hauptmann at Leipzig. Leading 'cellist in the orchestra, and professor at the Conservatorium, Leipzig. First 'cello at the Petrograd opera, and became director of the Conservatoire in 1876. Visited London first in 1862. 4 'Cello concertos, orchestral suite and symphonic sketch, sextet, quintet, quartets, songs, many 'cello pieces and studies.	Russian.
1838 3 April. Vesoul.	**1906** December. Vézelise.	**BOISDEFFRE, René de.** Lived in Paris from 1842, and was known as a composer in 1864. Symphony, cantatas, piano sonatas, trios, quartets, quintets, and a sextet.	French.
1838 11 April. London.	**1923** 20 June. Vittel, Vosges.	**ROECKEL, Joseph Leopold.** Son of Professor Roeckel. Pupil of Eisenhofer at Würzburg and Götze at Weimar. His wife wrote piano pieces under the name of Jules de Sivrai. Settled in England. Cantatas, scena for baritone and orchestra, many songs, and some instrumental compositions.	English.
1838 16 April. Prague.	**1897** 20 September Prague.	**BENDL, Karel or Karl.** Conducted at Brussels, Amsterdam and Paris. In 1865 was appointed conductor of the Choral Society Hlahol at Prague, until '79, when he became conductor of the Baron Dervies's private band in Milan, Lugano and Nice. Operas, operettas, choruses, a Mass and smaller choral works ; string quartet, violin sonata, songs and ballads.	Bohemian.
1838 8 June. Leeds.	**1897** 15 May. At sea.	**NAYLOR, John (Mus.D.).** Organist at All Saints', Scarborough (1873), organist and choir-master at York Minster (1883-97). Conductor of the York Musical Society for many years. Cantatas, anthems, and services.	English.
1838 16 June. Oxford.	**1901** Pittsburg, U.S.A.	**ARCHER, Frederick.** Organist at Oxford ; Brooklyn, U.S., in '81, and later at New York. Conductor at Glasgow, Boston ('87), and of the Pittsburg orchestra (1895-98). Cantata, piano pieces, songs, and didactic works.	English.
1838 Moscow.	**1881** 24 January. Moscow.	**ASANTSCHEWSKY, Michel Von.** Pupil of Hauptmann and Richter at Leipzig. Director of the Petrograd Conservatorium, 1870-76. Collected a library of books on musical subjects. Piano pieces and a trio ; sonata for 'cello and piano, etc.	Russian.
1838 Lisbon.	**1903**	**d'ARNEIRO, Count.** Pupil of V. Schira (composition and singing) and Soares (piano). Operas, symphony-cantata, and piano pieces.	Portuguese
1838 29 July, Tarbes.	**1906** 19 February. Tarbes.	**LASSERRE, Jules.** Pupil of the Paris Conservatoire. Travelled as solo 'cellist. Came to England in '69 and played principal 'cello under Sir Michael Costa. Violin and 'cello solos, and a " method."	French.

Born	Died	Name	Nationality
1838 3 August. Paris.	**1889** 24 November. Great Marlow.	**CLAY, Frederic.** Pupil of Molique and Hauptmann. A famous whist-player. Many light operas, incidental music, 2 cantatas, and many songs.	French.
1838 12 August. York.	**1896** 28 January. London.	**BARNBY, Sir Joseph.** Pupil of the Royal Academy. Organist at several London churches, including St. Anne's, Soho, from 1871 to '86. Conductor of the London Musical Society, '78-86, succeeded by Mackenzie. Precentor of Eton in '75, and became principal of the Guildhall School of Music in '92. Many anthems, services, part-songs, solos, trios, etc., 246 hymn tunes, and an oratorio.	English.
1838 25 October. Paris.	**1875** 3 June. Bougival, n'r Paris.	**BIZET, Georges. Proper name Alexandre César Léopold.** Pupil of the Paris Conservatoire under Marmontel (piano), Benoist (organ), Zimmermann (harmony), and Halévy (composition). Became the latter's son-in-law in '69. Operas, his best being " Carmen " ; operettas, orchestral suites, overtures, and songs.	French.
1838 13 December Chartres.	**1873** 5 March. Paris.	**CASTILLON, Alexis de.** Pupil of Victor Massé and César Franck. Joined with Duparc and Saint-Saëns in the foundation of the Société Nationale de Musique. Quintets, quartets, trios, sonata for violin and piano, piano concerto ; march, symphonic-sketch, overture, etc., for orchestra; choruses, many songs, and piano pieces.	French.
1838 17 December Rotterdam.	**1897** 11 March. London.	**TOURS, Berthold.** Studied at Brussels and Leipzig. Resided in London from 1861, teaching and playing the violin in various orchestras. Became editor for Novello and Co, in 1878. Anthems, services, hymns, songs, piano and violin pieces, and a tutor for violin.	Dutch.
1839 9 January. Portland, Maine.	**1906** 25 April.	**PAINE, John Knowles (Mus.D.).** Pupil of the Hochschule, Berlin. The first professor of Harvard University from '75 to 1905., and was College organist from 1862 to '82. Operas ; dramatic ; symphonies, symphonic-poems, oratorios, cantatas, and a Mass.	American.
1839 10 March. Hartford, Connecticut.	**1909** 6 October. Brooklyn, New York.	**BUCK, Dudley.** Studied at Leipzig under Hauptmann, Richter and Reitz, and the piano under Plaidy and Moscheles. Organist at Hartford, Chicago, Boston and New York, where he also conducted the Apollo Club. 2 Oratorios, cantatas, many choruses for men's voices, anthems, services, songs, organ pieces, grand-opera, comic-opera, symphony, etc.	American.
1839 16 March. Karevo.	**1881** 16 March. Petrograd.	**MOUSSORGSKY, Modeste Petrovich.** Follower of Dargomijsky. Excelled as a vocal writer rather than instrumental. Revealed in his works a true picture of nature and humanity, and may be termed a " musical nihilist." National operas and dramas, songs, choruses with orchestra, sketches for piano, and orchestral pieces.	Russian.

Born	Died	Name	Nationality
1839 17 March. Vaduz.	**1901** 25 November. Munich.	**RHEINBERGER, Joseph Gabriel.** Studied at the Munich Conservatorium, where he afterwards became professor of piano, composition and organ. Organist of the Court Church, Munich, and conductor of the Choral Society. He was entitled Royal Professor. Organ concertos, sonatas, fugues, etc. ; ditto for piano ; symphonies, overtures, chamber music, and all kinds of choral and church works, to the opus number of 197.	Austrian.
1839 12 April. Paris.	**1903** 26 October. Paris.	**JONCIÈRES, Victorin de.** Pupil of Elwart and Leborne. Received the Cross of the Legion of Honour in 1877. Grand-operas and other dramatic, choruses, symphony, orchestral suite and other pieces, overture, and a violin concerto.	French.
1839 19 May. London ?	**1884** 4 December London ?	**SMITH, Alice Mary.** (Mrs. Meadows White). Pupil of Sterndale Bennett and G. A. Macfarren. 2 Symphonies, overtures, concerto for clarinet, piano quintets and trios, string quartets, 5 cantatas, songs, duets, etc.	English.
1839 11 July. Compinas.	**1896** 16 September Pará.	**GOMEZ, Antonio Carlos.** Pupil of the Milan Conservatorio. Director at the Conservatorium at Pará in 1895. Operas and other dramatic works, produced in Italy ; also cantatas.	Brazilian. (Portuguese parents.)
1839 17 July. Worms.	**1916** 11 September Berlin.	**GERNSHEIM, Friedrich.** Pupil of Pauer, Rozenheim, Hauff and of the Leipzig Conservatorium. Teacher and pianist in Paris, Saarbruck, Cologne, and conductor at Rotterdam in '74. Teacher at the Stern Conservatorium, 1890-97, and director of the Sternscher Gesangverein till 1904. 4 Symphonies, concertos for violin and piano, overture ; piano and string quartets and quintets ; violin sonatas, and many choral works.	German.
1839 14 August. Königgrätz.	**1915** 28 October. Petrograd.	**NAPRAVNIK, Edward Franzevich.** Studied at the Organ School, Prague, where he became teacher. Organist of the Imperial Theatres, Petrograd, and succeeded Liadov in 1869 as chief chapel-master. Conducted the concerts of the Russian Musical Society from 1869 to '81. 4 Operas, 4 symphonies, symphonic-poem, overture, suites, piano concerto, various chamber-music, choruses, songs, and piano works, to opus 70.	Bohemian. (Russian school.)
1839 7 November. London.	**1905** 9 December San Francisco	**HOLMES, Henry.** Brother of Alfred (1837). Violin soloist and quartet player ; professor at the Royal College until 1894. After quitting his brother at Paris, removed to Copenhagen and Stockholm about 1865. 4 Symphonies, 2 cantatas, overture, 2 string quintets, a violin concerto, solos, and many songs.	English.

Born	Died	Name	Nationality
1840 13 January. Bruges.	**1908** 19 June. Paris.	**WAEFELGHEM, Louis Van.** Pupil of Brussels Conservatoire under Meerts for violin and Fétis for composition. Solo violinist at the Opera in Buda-Pesth. Examiner for viola at the Paris Conservatoire, also played the viola in London, in various quartets. From 1895 devoted himself entirely to the viole d'amour, and became the finest player of the 19th century on that ancient instrument. Solos and pieces for the viole d'amour, and restored the old music for the instrument.	Belgian.
1840 18 January. Berlin.	**1916** 31 December. Berlin.	**RUDORFF, Ernest.** Pupil of Clara Schumann (piano), Ries (violin), Hauptmann and Reinecke (composition). Professor at Cologne Conservatorium in 1865, and founded the Bach Society there in '67. Professor at the Hochschule, Berlin, under Joachim in '69, and succeeded Max Bruch as conductor of the Stern Singing-Society in 1880. Symphonies, symphonic-variations, overtures and ballade for orchestra, choruses, part-songs, songs, and piano works.	German.
1840 2 February. Nantes.	**1910** 4 July. Vernouillet.	**BOURGAULT-DUCOUDRAY, Louis Albert.** Pupil of Ambroise Thomas at the Conservatoire, where he lectured on musical history from 1878. Grand opera, comic opera, cantata, a Stabat Mater, orchestral suite, and other works depicting Grecian scenes.	French.
1840 13 February. Berlin.	**1906** 13 September London.	**JACOBI, Georges.** Pupil of De Bériot and Massart for violin, Réber, Gevaërt and Chéri for composition. First violinist at the Grand Opéra, Paris, and conductor of the Bouffes Parisiens in 1869. For many years conductor of the Alhambra Theatre, and became professor at the Royal College in '96. 103 Grand ballets and divertissements, comedy-operas, 2 concertos and many pieces for violin, concertino for viola, and many songs.	German.
1840 22 February. Rotterdam.	**1911** 7 July. Stuttgart.	**LANGE, Samuel de.** Son of Samuel (1811); brother of Daniel (1841). Pupil of Verhulst and A. Winterberger for organ. Organist and teacher at Lemberg, Rotterdam, Basle, Cologne, and Stuttgart, there becoming director of the Conservatorium in 1900. 8 Organ sonatas, 3 symphonies, oratorio, " Moses "; piano concerto, 3 quartets, trio, quintet, sonatas for violin and for 'cello, and many part-songs for male voices.	Dutch.
1840 25 February. Romsey, Hants.	**1898** 12 February. London.	**WESTLAKE, Frederick.** Pupil of the Royal Academy, where he became pianoforte professor in 1863. Mass and other church works; a duet for 'cello and piano, songs, part-songs, and piano solos.	English.

Born	Died	Name	Nationality.
1840 26 February. Ratibor.		**HOLLÄNDER, Alexis.** Pupil of Schnabel, Hesse, Böhmer and the Berlin Royal Academy. Pianist and teacher of singing. Instructor at Kullak's Academy in 1861, and conducted the Cecilia Society in 1870. Suite for violin and piano ; piano quintet and solos ; choruses, songs, and studies.	German.
1840. 8 March. Verona.	**1891** 23 July. Monza.	**FACCIO, Franco.** The greatest Italian conductor of his time. Pupil of Ronchetti at the Milan Conservatorio, where he became professor of harmony in 1868, succeeding Croff. Conductor at the Teatro Carcano and at La Scala. Visited England in 1889, conducting the performance of " Otello " at the Lyceum Theatre. Operas, cantata, symphony, overture, songs, etc.	Italian.
1840 28 March. Berlin.	**1889** 13 July. London.	**ZOELLER, Carli.** Pupil of the Berlin Conservatorium under Ries (violin), Gärich (harmony), and Grell (counterpoint). Settled in London in 1873, becoming bandmaster of the 7th (Queen's Own) Hussars, and later of the 2nd Life Guards. Played on, and wrote about the viole d'amour. 4 Overtures, and other orchestral pieces ; violin concerto, comic operetta, lyric drama, quintet, quartet, songs, and church music.	German.
1840 25 April. Kamsko-Votinsk.	**1893** 25 October. Petrograd.	# TCHAIKOVSKY, Peter Ilitch. The best-known Russian composer. Pupil of Zaremba and Anton Rubinstein at the Russian Musical Society at Petrograd. Professor of harmony at Moscow Conservatorium from 1866 to '78 ; afterwards devoting his life solely to composing and conducting. Visited London for the first time in 1888. 8 Operas, the best being " Eugen Oniegen " and " The Queen of Spades " ; 6 symphonies, symphonic-poems, 4 suites, marches ; 3 concertos for piano and 1 for violin ; 3 string quartets, choruses, piano trio and many solos, and 107 songs ; to the opus No. of 79, and 18 works without opus numbers.	Russian.
1840 11 May. Rome.	**1911** July. Rome.	**CAPOCCI, Filippo.** Son of Gaetano (1811). Organist at the Lateran, Rome (1873), and succeeded his father as chapel-master in 1898. A great number of organ works, including 5 sonatas, published by Augener, Laudy, Cocks, Kistner and Leduc.	Italian.
1840 6 June. London.	**1901** 31 March. Verona.	**STAINER, Sir John (Mus.D.).** Pupil of Bayley (harmony), Dr. Steggall (counterpoint), and G. Cooper (organ). Organist of Tenbury College in '56 ; Magdalen College, Oxford ; Oxford University ; and of St. Paul's Cathedral, London, from 1872 to 1888, succeeding Goss. Principal of the National Training School in 1881, succeeding Sullivan. Decorated with the Legion of Honour in 1880. Oratorios, cantatas, anthems, church services and other sacred pieces, " The Crucifixion " being his most popular work.	English.

Born	Died	Name	Nationality.
1840 24 June. Aix-la-Chapelle.	**1884** 17 May. Petrograd.	**BRASSIN, Louis.** Pupil of Moscheles at the Leipzig Conservatorium. First pianoforte teacher at the Stern Conservatorium, Berlin, 1866 ; professor at Brussels Conservatoire (1869-78), and held a similar post at Petrograd in 1884. 2 German operettas, and many pianoforte pieces.	Belgian.
1840 2 August. Petrograd.	**1913** 17 June. Munich.	**STARCK, Ingeborg. (Frau von Bronsart).** Pupil of Henselt and Liszt. Toured as a solo-pianist. Operas ; " Kaiser Wilhelm March," played in Berlin to celebrate the return of the troops in 1870 ; a piano concerto and other pieces, songs, and string music.	Russian. (Swedish parents.)
1840 September Christiania.	**1911** 14 June. Copenhagen.	**SVENDSEN, Johan Severin.** The greatest conductor and the 3rd greatest composer of Norway. Pupil of the Leipzig Conservatorium under Hauptmann, David, Richter, and Reinecke. Conductor of the Christiania Musical Association, and teacher of composition (1872-77). Court conductor at Copenhagen in 1883. Visited London in 1878 and 1888. 2 Symphonies, 4 Norwegian Rhapsodies, 2 overtures; concerto for violin and 1 for 'cello; marches, cantata; string quartets, quintet and octet ; songs, etc.	Norwegian.
1840 4 October. Rouen.	**1910** 16 August. Paris.	**LENEPVEU, Charles Ferdinand.** Pupil of Savard and A. Thomas. Professor of composition at the Paris Conservatoire in 1894, and a member of the Institut in 1896. Decorated with the Legion of Honour, 1887. Operas (one produced at Covent Garden in 1882), a lyric-drama, ode, Requiem, choruses, songs, and piano pieces.	French.
1840 3 November London.	**1883** 5 July. London.	**CLARK, Rev. Frederick Scotson.** Studied in London, Leipsic and Stuttgart. Organist in various London churches, and at Exeter College, Oxford. In 1865 founded a " College of Music " for the organ and church music. Over 500 organ and pianoforte pieces, and a method for harmonium.	English.
1840 December. Charleston.	**1896** 24 June. London.	**POZNANSKI, Barrett Isaac.** Pupil of Vieuxtemps (violin) and Bagge (composition). Director of the Illinois Conservatoire ; travelled as a violinist ; came to London in 1879. Pieces for violin, and an instruction book.	American.
1840 December. Königsberg.	**1876** 3 December.	**GOETZ, Hermann.** Pupil of L. Köhler, and the Stern Conservatorium in Berlin, under Bülow (piano) and Ulrich (composition) Organist at Winterthur and Zürich. 2 Operas ; symphony ; cantata ; Psalm 87 for solo, choir and orch' ; concertos for piano and for violin ; quintet, quartet and trio for strings and piano ; songs ; piano sonata, and pieces.	German.
1841 8 January. Ambert.	**1894** 13 September Paris.	**CHABRIER, Alexis Emmanuel.** Mostly self-taught. Operas, operettas, scena for mezzo-soprano and female chorus, a rhapsody and Spanish airs for piano, and other pieces.	French.

Born	Died	Name	Nationalit
1841 28 January. Baldenheim.	**1890** 28 May. Strasburg.	**NESSLER, Victor E.** Conductor of various male choral societies at Leipsic ; of the Stadt Theater in 1870, and the Carolatheater in '79. Many German operas, and part-songs.	German. (Alsatian.
1841 10 February. Huddersfield.	**1924** 27 March. Windsor.	**PARRATT, Sir Walter.** Pupil of his father and G. Cooper. Organist of Magdalen College and St. Giles' Church, Oxford, in 1872, succeeding Stainer. Choir-master of Jesus and Trinity chapels, and conductor of the Musical Society and glee clubs. Appointed to St. George's Chapel, Windsor, in '82, and conductor of the Windsor Madrigal Society. Professor of the organ at the Royal College in 1883 to 1909. Master of the Queen's Musick and private organist to Her Majesty in 1893. Anthems, songs, dramatic; and organ pieces.	English.
1841 19 February. Tortosa.	**1922** 19 August. Barcelona.	**PEDRELL, Felipe.** Self-taught. The acknowledged head of modern Spanish music. Professor of musical history and æsthetics at the Royal Conservatorium of Madrid. Several operas (produced in Spain and Italy), musical dramas, and valuable editions of ancient church music.	Spanish.
1841 5 April. Paris.	**1886** 6 April. Paris.	**RITTER, Theodore.** (properly Bennet). Pupil of Liszt. 2 Operas (" Marianne " produced at Paris, and " La dea risorta " at Florence in 1865), and drawing room pieces for piano.	French.
1841 14 May. Parma.	**1919** 21 February. Turin.	**BOLZONI, Giovanni.** Violinist and conductor. Director of the Liceo at Turin in 1889. Operas, symphony, suites and overtures ; sextet for reeds and horn, and a string quartet.	Italian.
1841 21 May. Merthyr Tydvil.	**1903** 17 February. Penarth.	**PARRY, Joseph (Mus.D.).** Father of J. H. P. (1864). Studied under Sterndale Bennett, Garcia and Steggall at the Royal Academy. Professor at Aberystwyth University, and lecturer at Cardiff. Oratorios, cantata and other choral works, operas, overtures, string quartet, etc.	Welsh.
1841 11 July. Rotterdam.	**1918** 31 January. California.	**LANGE, Daniel de.** Son of Samuel (1811). Pupil of Ganz and Servais for 'cello, and Verhulst for composition. Director of the Amsterdam Conservatorium in 1895. Conductor of several choral societies. Performed old Netherlandish music with a party which came to London in 1885. 2 Symphonies, cantata, overture, opera, Mass, Requiem, Psalms, and a 'cello concerto.	Dutch.

Born	Died	Name	Nationality
1841 8 September. Mühlhausen. n'r Kralup.	1904 1 May Prague.	**DVOŘÁK, Antonin.** Pupil of A. Liehmann, Hanche and Pitzsch for organ. Played the violin and viola in the National Theatre, Prague, and became organist of St. Adalbert's Church in 1873. Conducted his works in England in 1884, '86, '91 and '96. Director of the National Conservatory, New York, from '92 to '95. Principal of the Prague Conservatorium in 1901. Introduced two new forms into the sonata, i.e. the " Dumka " and " Furiant." 9 Operas, symphonies, poems, variations and other orchestral works ; oratorios, cantatas including " The Spectre's Bride " ; overtures, concertos for piano, violin and 'cello, string quartets, trios, etc. ; piano works and songs, amounting to 120 works.	Bohemian.
1841 4 September Orenburg.	1907 15 February. Nice.	**BLARAMBERG, Paul Ivanovich.** Pupil of Balakirev. National operas, symphony, symphonic-poem, a Scherzo for orchestra; Fantasia for solo, female chorus and orchestra; sketch for male chorus, folk-songs arranged for chorus, and songs.	Russian.
1841 5 September Leeds.	1920 9 February. Oxford.	**ROBERTS, John Varley (Mus.D.).** Organist and choirmaster at Halifax in 1868 ; succeeded W. Parratt as organist at Magdalen College, Oxford, in 1882 ; founded the University Glee and Madrigal Society in 1884 ; and from 1885 to '93 was organist of St. Giles', Oxford. Cantatas and Psalms for voices and orchestra, 50 anthems, 6 church services, songs, and organ pieces.	English.
1841 11 October. Basle.	1927	**HEGAR, Friedrich.** Studied at Leipzig under David (violin), Hauptmann, Rietz and Plaidy. Conductor of the Symphony and Oratorio concerts at Zurich ; and founded the Conservatoire there in 1875. Succeeded Joachim as director of the Royal Academy of Music, Berlin, in 1907. Oratorio, many choruses, ballad, etc. ; overture, a 'cello and a violin concerto, string quartets, and songs.	Swiss.
1841 November. Warsaw.	1871 17 July. Leipzig.	**TAUSIG, Carl.** Pupil of Liszt, and the most remarkable virtuoso-pianist of his time. Toured the German and Russian towns as pianist, and opened a School of piano-playing at Berlin. Piano concerto, studies and pieces, many arrangements for piano, and fingered editions of standard works.	Polish.
1842 3 January. Berlin.	1902 16 July. Berlin.	**HOFMANN, Heinrich Karl Johann.** Pupil of Kullak (piano), Dehn and Wüerst (composition). Devoted his life to composition from 1873. Operas, cantatas, orchestral suites, serenades, etc., choruses, octets, quartets, trios, 'cello concerto, songs, duets, and piano pieces—about 100 works.	German.

Born	Died	Name	Nationalit
1842 22 January. Paris.	1924 10 May. Paris.	**MARÉCHAL, Charles Henri.** Pupil of the Conservatoire under Benoist (organ), Chauvet (counterpoint), and V. Massé (composition). Chorus-master at the Théâtre Lyrique in 1867, and inspector of musical education in '96. Several operas, sacred drama, cantatas; orchestral, vocal and instrumental works.	French.
1842 24 February. Padua.	1918 10 June. Milan.	**BOITO, Arrigo.** Pupil of the Milan Conservatorio under Mazzucato. A worthy poet. Librettist of his operas " Mefistofele," " Nerone " and " Orestiade," also of other composers' operas, including Verdi's " Otello " and " Falstaff." Inspector-general of technical instruction in the Conservatori of Italy in 1892. Operas besides the above mentioned, and an early cantata.	Italian.
1842 11 April. Lyons.	1901 16 August. Paris.	**AUDRAN, Edmond.** Pupil of the École Niedermeyer, Paris. Organist of the church of St. Joseph, Marseilles, in 1861. Many comic operas (produced in France and England) Funeral march, Mass, motets, and songs.	French.
1842 12 May. St. Etienne.	1912 13 August. Paris.	**MASSENET, Jules Frédéric Émile.** Pupil of the Paris Conservatoire, where he succeeded Bazin as professor of advanced composition in 1878. Decorated with the Legion of Honour in '76, and became a member of the Académie des Beaux-Arts in '78. Many operas, lyric dramas, lyric comedies, several orchestral suites, oratorios, choruses, melodies for one and two voices, piano music for 2 and 4 hands, and a piano concerto.	French.
1842 13 May. London.	1900 22 November London.	**SULLIVAN, Sir Arthur Seymour.** The most famous writer of comic operas. Choir-boy at the Chapel Royal; studied at the Royal Academy and at the Leipsic Conservatorium. Organist of St. Michael's, Chester Square, and director at St. Peter's, Cranley Gardens. Conducted the Promenade concerts in '78 and '79, and the Leeds Festival from '83 to '98, succeeding Costa. Buried at St. Paul's Cathedral. Many comic operas, music to Shakespeare's plays, oratorios, cantatas, 13 anthems, 56 hymns, songs, overtures, marches, symphony, concerto, piano pieces, a duet for 'cello and piano, etc.	English
1842 14 May. Szepes-Váral-lya.	1894 27 October. Vienna.	**CZIBULKA, Alphons.** A military bandmaster. Much dance-music, and 6 operettas.	Hungari
1842 29 May. Vienna.	1899 31 December Baden, n'r Vienna.	**MILLÖCKER, Karl.** Pupil of the Conservatorium der Musikfreunde, Vienna. Chapel-master at Graz in 1864; conductor and composer to the Theater-an-der-Wien, Vienna. Numerous operettas, farces, etc. (popular throughout Austria and Germany), and piano pieces.	Austria

Born	Died	Name	Nationality.
1842 London.		**NIXON, Henry Cotter** (Mus.B.). Son of H. G. (1796). Pupil of Deval, H. Smart, Dr. Steggall and G. A. Macfarren. Organist at Hull, Woolwich, Blackheath, Spanish Place, & St. Leonard's. Symphonic-poem, piano trio, sonatas for violin and 'cello, overture, concertstück for piano and orchestra, madrigals, part-songs, and songs.	English.
1842 6 July. Ongar.	1895 15 July. London.	**PRENTICE, Thomas Ridley.** Pupil of the Royal Academy under W. and G. A. Macfarren for piano and composition respectively. Organist of Christ Church, Lee Park, 1872. Professor of the piano at the Guildhall School in 1880, and at the Blackheath Conservatoire in 1881. Cantata, anthems, part-songs, pianoforte pieces, and instruction books.	English.
1842 11 August. Adorf.	1924 7 December.	**BECKER, Reinhold.** Violinist. Director of the Men's Choral Society at Dresden, 1884-94. 2 Operas, symphonic-poem, symphony, violin sonatas, string quartets, songs, choruses, and 2 violin concertos : to about Op. 150.	German.
1842 31 August. Paris.	1907 6 March. Paris.	**DUVERNOY, Victor Alphonse.** Pupil of the Conservatoire, where he afterwards became master of the piano class. 2 Operas, symphonic pieces, overture, chorus with soli and orchestra, chamber music, and many piano pieces, some with orchestral accompaniment.	French.
1842 14 September Holliston, n'r Boston.	1923 14 October. Cambridge, Mass.	**WHITING, George Elbridge.** Studied the organ under Morgan at New York, Best in England, and theory with Haupt and Radecke at Berlin. Organist and conductor at Hartford (Conn.) Boston, Albany, and at Holy Cross Cathedral. Principal and organ instructor in the New England Conservatory. Organ studies and concert pieces, cantatas, choruses, marches, symphony, suite for orchestra, suite for 'cello and piano, church music, part-songs, piano concerto and pieces.	American.
1842 15 December London.	1907 11 November. Putney.	**GADSBY, Henry.** Organist at St. Peter's, Brockley ; succeeded Hullah as professor of harmony at Queen's College, London, in '84, and was one of the original professors at the Guildhall School of Music. Cantatas, choruses, anthems, services, songs, part-songs, symphonies, organ concerto, string quartet, overtures, and music to plays.	English.
1842 26 December Ghent.	1917 7 April. Mons.	**EEDEN, Jean Baptiste van den.** Pupil of the Conservatoriums of Ghent and Brussels. Succeeded Huberti as director of Mons Conservatoire in 1878. Opera, several oratorios, cantatas, symphonic-poem ; suites, a scherzo, and a march for orchestra ; songs and part-songs.	Belgian.

Born	Died	Name	Nationality.
1843 14 February Paris.	1919 21 December. Paris.	**DIÉMER, Louis.** Pupil of Marmontel, Bazin and A. Thomas at the Conservatoire, succeeding the former at the same institution in 1888 as professor of the piano. Concertos and concertstücken for piano and orchestra, chamber music, songs, and piano solos.	French.
1843 27 March. Cambridge.	1916 23 June. London.	**MACLEAN, Charles Donald.** Studied under Hiller at Cologne. Organist at Exeter College, Oxford. Symphonic-poems, oratorio, cantata, piano concerto, trio, etc.	English.
1843 8 April. Copenhagen.	1923 13 July. Frederiksburg.	**HAMERIK, Asger.** Pupil of Gade and Haberbier at Copenhagen, Bülow at Berlin (piano); and Berlioz, whose only pupil he claims to be. Resided in America from '72 to '98. 6 Symphonies, 4 operas, 2 choral trilogies, Requiem, orchestral suites, and many smaller works.	Danish.
1843 28 May. Rome.	1914 15 December. Rome.	**SGAMBATI, Giovanni.** Pupil of Barberi and Natalucci. Court pianist and director to Emmanuel III; and founded, together with Penelli, the Liceo Musicale in Rome. Conducted in London in 1882 and '91. Piano concerto, suites, nocturnes, fugues, études, etc.; symphony, string and piano quartets and quintets, Requiem, motet, organ works and many songs; about 50 works in all.	Italian.
1843 29 May. Paris.	1917 10 February Paris.	**PESSARD, Émile Louis Fortuné.** Student, and later professor of harmony at the Paris Conservatoire. Operas, orchestral, chamber music, and songs.	French.
1843 10 June. Graz.	1900 9 October. Wiesbaden.	**HERZOGENBERG, Heinrich von.** Studied at Vienna and Graz. Conductor of the Bach Society in Leipzig, and professor at the Hochschule, Berlin. Cantatas, choruses, Masses, Psalms, Requiem, symphonies, quartets, trios, sonatas for violin and 'cello, organ fantasias, songs, duets, piano pieces and duets: about 100 works.	Styrian.
1843 15 June. Bergen.	1907 4 September. Bergen.	**GRIEG, Edvard Hagerup.** The greatest Norwegian composer. Pupil of the Leipsic Conservatorium, and later of Gade. Established and conducted the Philharmonic Society at Christiania from 1867 to '80. Visited London in 1888, '89, '94 and '96. Piano concerto, sonata, ballade, etc.; overture and suite ("Peer Gynt") for orchestra; string quartet; sonatas for violin and for 'cello; many songs, song cycles, choruses, and works for string orchestra; about 70 works in all.	Norwegian.

Born	Died	Name	Nationality
1843 19 June. Paris.	**1917** 8 September. Paris.	**LEFEBVRE, Charles Édouard.** Pupil of the Conservatoire, where he succeeded Benjamin Godard as professor of the instrumental ensemble class in 1895. Cantatas, motets, Psalm and other church music, operas, comic opera, lyric poem, choruses, symphony, overtures, serenades, orchestral scenes, sonatas, trios, quartets, and a suite for wind instruments.	French.
1843 4 September. St. Mikulás.		**BELLA, Jan Levoslav.** Studied at Vienna. Catholic priest. Symphonic-poem, motets, Masses, hymns, songs and Slovak folk-songs.	Slovak.
1843 3 December. Brünn.	**1915** 19 March. Copenhagen	**NERUDA, Franz Xaver.** 'Cellist ; member of the Royal orchestra at Copenhagen, and succeeded Gade in '92 as director of the musical society there, whilst also conducting a society at Stockholm. Brother of Lady Hallé, the famous violinist, with whom he toured. Orchestral and chamber music ; 'cello concerto, etc., to opus 74.	Moravian.
1843 25 December. Königsberg.	**1895** 26 November Cologne.	**JENSEN, Gustav.** Brother of Adolph (1837). Pupil of his father, Dehn, Laub and Joachim. Teacher of harmony and counterpoint at the Cologne Conservatorium in 1872. Concerted chamber music, and editions of old violin music.	German.
1844 20 January. Christiania.	**1910** 22 July. Venice.	**SELMER, Johan Peter.** Pupil of Chauvet and A. Thomas in Paris, and later of Richter, Jadassohn and O. Paul at Leipzig. Gave a concert of his own works in Christiania in 1879. Described as the Berlioz of Norway. 60 Orchestral works, the finest being " Prometheus" ; also male choruses, and songs.	Norwegian.
1844 26 January. Huddersfield	**1912** 14 March. Liverpool.	**PEACE, Albert Lister (Mus.D.).** Organist at Glasgow Cathedral, '79, and St. George's Hall, Liverpool, in '97, succeeding Best. Cantata ; anthems ; church services, and organ works.	English.
1844 19 February. Visby.		**ANDRÉE, Elfrida.** Studied at Stockholm, Copenhagen and Berlin. Organist at Gothenburg Cathedral in 1867. Opera, symphony, organ symphonies, cantata, Mass, piano quintet and trio, and songs.	Swedish.
1844 6 March. Tikhvin.	**1908** 8 June. Petrograd.	**RIMSKY-KORSAKOV, Nicholas Andreievich.** Pupil of Balakirev, whom he assisted at the Court Chapel. Retired from the Navy in 1873 ; professor of composition and instrumentation at the Petrograd Conservatorium in '71 ; inspector of naval bands till '84. Conducted the Russian Symphony concerts at Petrograd from '86 to 1900. 13 Operas, symphonies, suites, overtures, chamber music, piano concerto, choruses, and cantatas, sacred works, 80 songs, and 140 Russian folk-songs. He completed operas by Dargomijsky, Borodin, and Moussorgsky.	Russian.

Born	Died	Name	Nationality
1844 10 March. Pampeluna.	1908 21 September Biarritz.	**SARASATE, Pablo Martin Meliton, of Navascues.** Pupil of Alard (violin) and Reber (harmony) at the Paris Conservatoire. Toured much as a solo-violinist. He was renowned for his delicacy and purity of tone. Violin solos and duets in the form of Spanish dances, romances, and fantasies.	Spanish.
1844 23 March. Nancy.	1925 9 December. Paris.	**GIGOUT, Eugène.** Pupil at the Maîtrise of Nancy Cathedral, and later at Niedermeyer's school of religious music in Paris, where he became organ professor in 1902. Travelled as a virtuoso-organist, and was organist of St. Augustin in 1863. Many important organ works, piano sonata, and vocal and church music.	French.
1844 6 April. Bonn.		**LUDWIG, Joseph.** Pupil of Grünwald and Joachim for violin, and Hiller for composition. Came to London in 1870. Succeeded Jansa as professor at the London Academy of Music ; and became a noted quartet leader. 2 Symphonies, quartet, and pieces for violin and 'cello.	German. Naturalised English.
1844 8 May. Kiel.	1929 17 September	**GRÄDENER, Hermann Theodor Otto.** Son of C. G. P. (1812). Studied at the Vienna Conservatorium, where he became professor of harmony, etc., in 1882. Organist at Gumpendorf in '64 ; member of the Court orchestra at Vienna, and lector for harmony, etc., at the University. Caprice, Sinfonietta and overture for orchestra; octet, quintets, quartets, trios, violin concerto, sonata for 2 pianos, organ works, etc.	German.
1844 3 June. Montpellier.	1926 8 January. Paris.	**PALADILHE, Émile.** Pupil of Halévy at the Conservatoire. Legion of Honour, and a member of the Institut. Grand opera, comic operas, cantata, lyric-drama, 2 Masses, a symphony, and songs.	French.
1844 ? Paris.	1908 20 August. Cauterets.	**VARNEY, Louis.** Son of P. J. A. (1811). 35 Operettas, including "Les Forains," "Le Pompier de service," and " Les Demoiselles de Saint Cyr," produced in Paris, Berlin and Vienna.	French.
1844 14 July. Furtwangen.	1922 21 February. London.	**BERINGER, Oscar.** Studied at Leipzig under Moscheles, Richter and Plaidy, and at Berlin under Tausig and Ehlart. Professor at Tausig's school in Berlin ; founded a piano school in London, 1873-97, and became professor at the Royal Academy in 1885. Andante and Allegro for piano and orchestra, piano sonatinas and pieces, and songs.	German.
1844 9 September York.		**CRESER, William (Mus.D.).** Studied under G. A. Macfarren. Organist successively at York, Grinton, Scarborough, Leeds, and in 1891 became organist of the Chapel Royal, St. James, and composer to Her Majesty's Chapels Royal. Several oratorios, cantatas, Mass, Psalms, operetta, orchestral suite, chamber music, violin sonata, and organ pieces.	English.

Born	Died	Name	Nationality
1844 11 September Lambourne, Berks.	**1916** 23 February. London.	**MARTIN, Sir George Clement.** Pupil of Stainer, whom he succeeded as organist of St. Paul's Cathedral in 1888. Private organist to the Duke of Buccleuch at Dalkeith in '71 ; Master of the Choristers at St. Paul's in '74, and succeeded Cooper as deputy organist in '76. 7 Anthems, church services with orchestra, Te Deum, songs, etc.	English.
1844 16 October. Lillé.		**MATHIEU, Emile.** Pupil of Brussels Conservatoire. Director of the Academy at Louvain in '81, and succeeded Samuel as director of the Conservatoire Royal at Ghent in '91. Te Deum for soli, chorus and orchestra; poems for the same combination; Ballads from Goethe for voice and piano; operas, and comic operas.	Belgian.
1844 31 October. Darkehmen.	**1906** 9 June. Königsberg.	**BERNEKER, Konstanz.** Studied at the Academy for Church Music, Berlin. Cathedral organist, director of the Academy of Singing, lector at the University, and teacher in the Conservatorium at Königsberg. Oratorios and cantatas.	German.
1844 3 November. Döbör.	**1908** 4 April. Berlin.	**SUCHER, Joseph.** Husband of the prima donna Fräulein Rosa Hasselbeck. Conductor at the Comic Opera at Vienna, the City Theatre at Leipzig, Hamburg in '79, and the Hofoper at Berlin in 1888. Operas, cantatas, Masses, overtures, and a song-cycle.	Hungarian.
1844 1 December. London.	**1891** 28 December London.	**CELLIER, Alfred.** Organist of All Saints', Blackheath, in 1862 ; director of the Ulster Hall Concerts, Belfast, in '65 ; and conductor of the Belfast Philharmonic Society. Organist of St. Alban's, Holborn, in '68; conductor at the Prince's Theatre, Manchester, '71-75 ; the Opera Comique, London, '77-'79, and joint conductor with Sullivan of the Promenade concerts, '78-'79. Operas (grand and comic), operettas, suite for orchestra, a setting of Gray's " Elegy," songs and incidental music to plays, and piano pieces.	English.
1844 5 December Oldbury, Worc.	**1924** 18 March. Westminster.	**BRIDGE, Sir John Frederick.** Pupil of J. L. and John Hopkins and John Goss. Organist of Westminster Abbey from 1882, and Deputy from 1875, succeeding James Turle. Conductor of the Royal Choral Society in '96, succeeding Sir Joseph Barnby ; also of the Highbury Philharmonic Society and the Western Madrigal Society. Appointed First King Edward Professor of Music in the Universities of London in 1903. Oratorios, cantatas, choruses, motet, many anthems, church services, hymns, part-songs, overture and other orchestral music.	English.
1845 26 January. Drammen.	**1916** 11 May. Christiania.	**CAPPELEN, Christian.** Studied at Leipzig and Dresden. Succeeded Lindeman as organist of Our Saviour's Church, Christiania, from 1887. Organ works, cantatas, choruses, songs, and piano pieces—32 works.	Norwegian.

Born	Died	Name	Nationality
1845 22 February. Lyons.		**WIDOR, Charles Marie.** Studied in Belgium under Lemmens (organ) and Fétis (composition). Conducted in London in 1888 and 1909. Organist at St. Sulpice, Paris ; succeeded Franck as professor of the organ at the Conservatoire, and in '96 succeeded Dubois as professor of composition there. Operas, symphonies, choruses, Masses, motets, organ works, sonatas for violin and 'cello, piano concertos and pieces, suite for flute, chamber music, and songs ; nearly 100 works.	French.
1845 2 March. Oxford.		**GLADSTONE, Dr. Francis Edward.** Pupil of S. S. Wesley. Organist at the Cathedrals of Llandaff (1866), Chichester ('70), and Norwich ('77), and Christ Church, Lancaster Gate ('81–'86). Cantatas, Masses, anthems, services, songs, and an overture.	English.
1845 18 April. Graz.	**1925** October.	**GERICKE, Wilhelm.** Studied at the Vienna Conservatorium under Dessoff. Conductor at Vienna, and of the Symphony Orchestra at Boston, U.S.A. Operetta, Requiem, overture, chamber music, choruses, and songs.	Styrian.
1845 13 May. Parmiers.	**1924** 4 November Paris.	**FAURÉ, Gabriel Urbain.** Pupil of Niedermeyer, also of Dietsch and Saint-Saëns. Organist at St. Sulpice, St. Honoré, and at the Madeleine. Professor of composition at the Paris Conservatoire, and became Director in 1905, succeeding Dubois. Songs, lyrics, music to plays, operettas, symphony, orchestral suite, violin concerto and Romance, Elégy for 'cello, piano quintets, vocal duets, quartets, etc.	French.
1845 6 August. Marseilles.	**1902** 11 September Paris.	**BERNARD, Émile.** Pupil of Marmontel, Reber and Benoist at the Paris Conservatoire. Organist of Notre-Dame des Champs until 1895. Cantata, chorus, overture, concerto and suite for violin, 'cello sonata, concertstück and pieces for piano, quartet, trio, and songs.	French.
1845 14 November. Wiesbaden.	**1920** 29 October.	**PERABO, Ernst.** Pianist ; pupil of Moscheles, Richter and Reinecke. Worked in America. Piano pieces, studies and arrangements, and songs.	German.
1846 5 January. London.	**1893** 24 March. London.	**WINGHAM, Thomas.** Pupil of the Royal Academy under Sterndale Bennett and Harold Thomas, and became professor of the piano at the same institution in 1871. Organist at All Saints', Paddington, in '64, and musical director at the Brompton Oratory from 1882. Improved the music of the Roman Church. 4 Symphonies, 6 overtures, serenade, piano concerto, opera, 2 string quartets, septet, Masses, Te Deum, and motets.	English.

Born	Died	Name	Nationality.
1846 8 January.	**1903** March. Cap d'Ail.	**CAHEN, Albert.** Pupil of César Franck for composition, and Mme. Szarvady for piano. Operas, ballets, a Biblical drama, a poème-mythologique, and a set of songs.	French.
1846 10 February. Petrograd.	**1926** 29 July.	**ADAJEWSKI, Ella von.** Pupil of Henselt, and of the Petrograd Conservatory. Choruses for the Russian Church, operas, Greek sonata for clarinet and piano ; vocal, chamber and piano pieces.	Russian.
1846 24 February. Castellamare, di Stabia.	**1922** 27 January. London.	**DENZA, Luigi.** Studied at the Naples Conservatorio under Mercadante and Serrao. Professor of singing at the Royal Academy, London, in 1898. Opera and over 500 songs. His Neapolitan ditty "Funiculì Funiculà" was used by R. Strauss in his Italian suite, through the impression that it was a genuine folk-song.	Italian.
1846 14 March. Mülheim.	**1915** 26 October. Leutesdorf.	**BUNGERT, August.** Pupil of Kufferath, the Cologne Conservatorium, and Kiel. Music-director at Kreuznach. Followed Wagner's method of opera writing. A tetralogy of operas, a comic opera, orchestral works, a piano quartet, piano pieces, songs, etc.	German.
1846 7 April. Berlin.		**RIES, Franz.** Pupil of Massart and Vieuxtemps for violin, and Kiel for composition. Violin soloist, and viola player in the Vieuxtemps quartet. Came to London in 1870. Founded a publishing firm in Dresden in '74. 4 Suites and solos for violin and piano, string quintet and quartets, dramatic overture, piano pieces, and songs.	German.
1846 9 April. Ortona sul mare.	**1916** 2 December Rome.	**TOSTI, Francesco Paola.** Studied at Naples under Pinto (violin), Conti and Meradante (composition). Visited London first in 1875, and in 1880 became teacher of singing to the Royal Family of England. Numerous songs and 15 vocal duets (Italian, French and English) which have become very popular.	Italian.
1846 29 April. Hamburg.	**1918** 25 March. Brooklyn.	**SCHRADIECK, Henry.** Violinist ; pupil of Léonard and David. Professor in the Conservatoriums of Moscow, '64, Leipsic, '74, Hamburg, '89, New York, and Philadelphia. Concert-director at Hamburg in '68, and at Leipsic in '74. Violin studies, exercises, etc.	German.
1846 2 May. Warsaw.	**1909** 23 July. Wiesbaden.	**NOSKOWSKI, Zygmunt.** Pupil of Moniuszko in Warsaw, and Kiel in Berlin. Director of the Music Society, Warsaw, 1881, and professor at the State Conservatory in 1888. Symphonies, symphonic-poems, 3 operas, ballet, cantatas, 4 quartets, and about 100 songs and choral works.	Polish.

Born	Died	Name	Nationality
1846 8 May. Budapest.	1913 9 March. London.	**KORBAY, Francis Alexander.** Pupil of Moronyi and Volkmann. Tenor singer in the grand opera at the National Theatre, Budapest (1865-'68); toured Europe and America as solo pianist, and became professor of singing at the Royal Academy, London, 1894-1903. Orchestral piece "Nuptiale," Hungarian overture, and songs.	Hungarian.
1846 26 May. Paris.	1910 20 August. Noirmoutiers.	**COQUARD, Arthur.** Pupil of César Franck. Lecturer and critic. Several operas, dramatic scenes for voice and orchestra, symphonic works, a sacred trilogy, choruses, lyrics, etc.	French.
1846 18 June. Prague.	1913 7 August. Baden, n'r Vienna.	**POPPER, David.** The greatest 'cellist of his time. Pupil of Goltermann. Toured extensively, and became professor at the Royal Conservatoire, Budapest, in 1896. 'Cello concertos and many pieces, string quartet, etc.	Bohemian.
1846	1906	**WEGELIUS, Martin.** Studied in Vienna and Leipzig. Organiser of the Helsingfors Conservatory, instituted 1882, of which he was director until his death. Teacher of Sibelius, Kuula, Melartin, Järnefelt, and several other Finnish composers. Cantatas, choral work, songs, and educational works.	Finnish.
1846 24 August. Perpignan.	1925 6 July. Paris.	**TAUDOU, Antoine.** Pupil of the Paris Conservatoire, and of Reber. Professor of harmony and accompaniment at the Conservatoire in 1883, and was a good violinist. Cantatas, violin concerto, quartets, quintet, trios for various combinations, orchestral pieces, songs, and piano pieces.	French.
1846 4 November Nantes.	1904 3 November. Paris.	**SERPETTE, Henri Charles Antoine Gaston.** Pupil of A. Thomas at the Conservatoire. Began life as an advocate. Cantata, and many light operas.	French.
1846 7 November. Prossnitz.	1907 17 September Vienna.	**BRÜLL, Ignaz.** Pupil of Epstein, Rufinatscha and Dessoff. Toured as a concert-pianist, and came to London in 1878. Several operas, ballet, symphony, overture, concertos (2 for piano and 1 for violin), sonatas, trio, piano pieces, and songs—about 100 works.	Moravian
1846 22 December Gothenburg.		**HALLÉN, Johan Andréas.** Studied at Gothenburg, Leipzig, Munich and Dresden. Conductor of the Philharmonic Society and the Royal Opera, Stockholm; teacher of composition at the Conservatorium; and critic from 1909. Operas, symphonic-poems, suites, overtures, rhapsodies, oratorio, cantatas, quartet, piano pieces, and songs.	Swedish.
1846 31 December Posen.	1901 18 August. Charlottenburg.	**KLEINMICHEL, Richard.** Pupil of the Leipzig Conservatorium. Chapel-master at the Stadtheater at Leipzig and held similar posts at Danzig, Magdeburg and Berlin. Operas, symphonies, piano works and arrangements.	German.

Born	Died	Name	Nationality.
1847 7 February. Munich.	**1889** 17 August. Vienna.	**FRANK, Ernest.** Studied the piano under Fontaine, and composition under Franz Lachner. Chapel-master at Würzburg in '68, Vienna in '69, Mannheim in '72, Frankfort in '77, and of the Court Opera at Hanover in '99, succeeding Von Bülow. 3 Operas, songs and part-songs, also finished an opera by Goetz, and translated Stanford's "Veiled Prophet" and Mackenzie's " Colomba."	German.
1847 15 February. Frauenthal.	**1927** February.	**FUCHS, Robert.** Professor of theory at the Vienna Conservatorium from 1875. 5 Serenades for string orchestra, 2 operas, piano concerto, a Mass, and chamber music.	Styrian.
1847 16 February. Samter, n'r Posen.	**1917** 16 July. Bad Nauheim	**SCHARWENKA, Ludwig Philipp.** Brother of Xaver (1850), and husband of the well-known violinist. Pupil of Kullak, Wüerst and Dorn. Teacher of composition at his brother's conservatorium at Berlin in '81, and director of the same in '91. Symphonic-poem, 2 symphonies, a Festal Overture, Serenade, choral works, piano trio and many pieces for piano, studies for violin and 'cello, and songs—over 100 works.	German.
1847 10 April. Birmingham.	**1900** 11 June. Birmingham.	**HEAP, Charles Swinnerton.** Pupil of Dr. Monk at York ; Moscheles, Hauptmann, and Reinecke at Leipzig, and W. T. Best at Liverpool. Conductor of the Birmingham Philharmonic Union in 1870-86, and of the Festival Choral Society in '95, also of the Societies of Wolverhampton and Hanley. Cantatas, anthems, songs, overtures, trio, quintet, and organ pieces.	English.
1847 29 April. Copenhagen.	**1909** 7 May. Copenhagen.	**ANDERSEN, Karl Joachim.** The most eminent of a family of flute-players. A member of the Royal band at Copenhagen 1869-77. Went to Berlin in '81 and was one of the founders of the Philharmonic Orchestra in which he was flautist for ten years. Conductor of the Palace orchestra at Copenhagen from '93. Concertstücke for flute and orchestra, studies and pieces, to opus 62.	Danish.
1847 13 May. Förde, n'r Bergen.	**1925** 26 November.	**HAARKLOU, Johannes.** Studied at the Leipzig Conservatorium, and that of Berlin under Kiel and Haupt. Conductor of symphony concerts. 5 Operas, 3 symphonies, suite ; violin and a piano concerto, violin sonata, oratorio, cantatas, choruses, piano and organ pieces, and songs.	Norwegian.
1847 25 May. Antwerp.	**1922** 25 December Brussels.	**GOOVAERTS, Alphonse Jean Marie André.** Self-taught. Began the efforts for the reform of church music in 1874. Masses, Ave Maria and several other church pieces, Lieder and Scenas, Flemish songs, choral music, pieces for violin, and many literary works.	Belgian.
1847 24 June. Toulouse.	**1916** 16 May. Toulouse.	**SALVAYRE, Gervais Bernard.** Pupil at the Conservatoire under Benoist (organ), Thomas and Bazin (fugue). On returning from Rome to Paris became chorus-master at the Opéra	French.

Born	Died	Name	Nationality
1847
Derby.		Populaire. Decorated with the Legion of Honour in 1880.
Grand operas, ballets, drama, sacred symphony, symphonic-overture, Stabat Mater and Psalm, cxiii for soli, chorus and orchestra.
DAVENPORT, Francis William.
Pupil of G. Macfarren. Professor of the Royal Academy in 1879, and of the Guildhall School of Music in 1882.	English.
1847
5 July.
Cologne.	1925
14 November.
London.	Symphonies, overture, prelude and fugue for orchestra, 10 pieces for 'cello and piano, trio, songs, and part-songs.
ZIMMERMAN, Agnes.
Pupil of the Royal Academy, London, under Potter, Steggall, Pauer, and G. Macfarren. Known as a concert pianist.	German.
1847
1 August.
Florence.	1912
3 October.
London.	Sonatas for piano ; violin and piano ; and violin, 'cello and piano ; songs, duets, part-songs, piano solos, and fingered editions.
PAPINI, Guido.
Violin-soloist : pupil of Giorgetti. Prinicpal Violin Professor at the Dublin Royal Academy from '93 to '96 ; then lived in London.	Italian.
1847
22 August.
Edinburgh.	1935
28 April.
London.	2 Violin concertos, a " school," solos, trios, quartets, and songs.
MACKENZIE, Sir Alexander Campbell.
The greatest Scottish composer. Pupil of Uhlrich (violin), Stein (theory), in Germany, and Sainton and Lucas in London. Principal of the Royal Academy in 1888, Feb. 22nd, succeeding Sir George Macfarren. Conductor of the Philharmonic Society, 1892-99. Conductor of the Scottish Vocal Music Association in 1873, and was precentor at St. George's Church, Edinburgh.	Scottish.
1847
17 November.
West Bromwich.		Operas, comic operas, cantatas, choral odes, anthems, songs, overtures, concertos for piano and violin, suites, pieces, organ works, and oratorios.
ROGERS, Roland (Mus.D.).
Pupil of S. Grosvenor. Organist at West Bromwich in '58, Wolverhampton in '62, Tettenhall in '67, and Bangor Cathedral in 1871-'91.	English.
1847
30 November.
Cöthen.	1902
3 August.
Dessau.	Symphony, cantatas, anthems, services, Psalms, songs, part-songs, and organ solos.
KLUGHARDT, August Friedrich Martin.
Theatrical conductor for 20 years, then Court music-director at Weimar in '69, Neustrelitz in '73, and Dessau in '82.	German.
1847
1 December.
Holmestrand.	1907
6 June.
Christiania.	5 Operas, oratorio, Psalms for soli and chorus ; 5 symphonies, 5 overtures, 2 suites ; concertos for oboe, violin and 'cello ; and much chamber music.
BACKER-GRÖNDAHL, Agathe Ursula.
Pianist ; pupil of Kjerulf in Norway, Kullak in Berlin, and Bülow in Florence. Frequently visited England.
Many songs and pianoforte pieces.	Norwegian

Born	Died	Name	Nationality.
1847 16 December Paris.	**1903** 28 January. Paris.	**HOLMÈS, Augusta Mary Anne.** Pupil of César Franck. Wrote the librettos to her operas. Operas, symphonies, symphonic-poems, suites and odes ; choruses, Psalms, songs, etc.	French. Irish parents.
1848 21 January. Paris.		**DUPARC, Marie Eugène Henri Fouques.** Pupil of César Franck. Symphonic-poems, and songs with orchestral accompaniment.	French.
1848 5 February. Orvieto.	**1921** 2 February. Rome.	**MANCINELLI, Luigi.** 'Cellist in Florence and Rome, where, in 1874, he was raised to conductor. At Bologna in 1881 became Principal of the Liceo Musicale, conductor of the Teatro Comunale, and chapel-master of San Petronio. Visited London frequently from 1884 as conductor. Operas, oratorios, Intermezzi, dramas, Masses and sacred pieces.	Italian.
1848 27 February. Bournemouth	**1918** 7 October. Rustington.	**PARRY, Sir Charles Hubert Hastings, Bart.** The most important English composer between the times of Purcell and Elgar. Pupil of Sterndale Bennett, G. A. Macfarren and Pierson. Professor of Music at Oxford University in 1900, succeeding Stainer ; Director of the Royal College in 1894, succeeding Grove ; Examiner in the London University in '91. Oratorios, choruses, madrigals, songs, anthems, Te Deum, symphonies, overtures, suite, piano concerto, string quartets, trios, a nonet for wind, violin sonata and partita, and organ works.	English.
1848 9 March. Liège.		**MARSICK, Martin Pierre Joseph.** Pupil of Léonard, Massart and Joachim for violin, and Kufferath for composition. Solo-violinist and quartet leader. Professor of the violin at the Paris Conservatoire in '92, succeeding Massart. 3 Concertos, and pieces for violin, and songs.	Belgian.
1848 12 March. Augsberg.	**1907** 2 January. Kissingen.	**KISTLER, Cyrill.** Pupil of the Munich Conservatorium under Wüllner, Rheinberger and Fr. Lachner. Principal of a private music school at Bad Kissingen. He also published music. Opera, comic opera, choruses, songs, organ and orchestral pieces.	German.
1848 17 March. Tipton, Staffs.	**1922** 10 March. New York.	**NICHOLL, Horace Wadham.** Pupil of Samuel Prince. Organist at Dudley, '67, Stoke-on-Trent, '68, Pittsburg, U.S., and New York, '78. 4 Oratorios, 2 symphonies, symphonic-poems, symphonic-fantasias, orchestral suite and fugue ; 12 symphonic preludes and fugues for organ ; anthems, songs, piano pieces, and chamber-music.	English.
1848 5 May. Vienna.	**1906** 21 December Vienna.	**GOLDSCHMIDT, Adalbert von.** A follower of Wagner. Studied law until his 20th year. Known for the originality of his dramatic works, one of which was eulogised by Liszt. Operas or music-dramas, symphonic-poem, and about 100 songs.	Austrian.

Born	Died	Name	Nationality
1848 31 July. Paris.	**1903** 28 January. Paris.	**PLANQUETTE, Robert.** Pupil at the Paris Conservatoire. Several operettas and comic operas, for the French and English stage ; also songs and chansonnettes.	French.
1848 17 December Middletown, Conn.	**1903** 6 December. Chicago.	**GLEASON, Frederick Grant.** Studied under Buck in Hartford, at the Leipzig Conservatorium, in Berlin, and in London with Beringer. Organist at several churches in America. Romantic operas, cantatas, sacred choruses, part-songs, a symphonic-poem, chamber music, organ and piano pieces.	American.
1849 16 June. Croydon.		**SHAKESPEARE, William.** Pupil of Molique, and at the Academy under Bennett, at the Leipzig Conservatorium, and at Milan under Lamperti for singing. Professor of singing in 1878, and conductor of the concerts in 1880, at the Royal Academy. Piano concertos, sonatas, pieces with orchestra, trio, string quartets, overtures, and a symphony.	English.
1849 18 August. Paris.	**1895** 10 January. Cannes.	**GODARD, Benjamin Louis Paul.** Pupil of Hammer for violin, and of the Conservatoire under Reber for harmony. Played the viola in several chamber-music societies. Grand operas, comic operas, dramatic overtures and poems, symphonies, suites; 2 violin concertos, and a sonata ; string quartets, trios, songs, and piano music.	French.
1849 23 September Moscow.	**1927**	**IVANOV, Michael Mikhailovich.** Pupil of Tchaikovsky (harmony) and Dubuque (piano) at the Moscow Conservatoire. Writer and critic. 2 Operas, symphony, 3 orchestral suites, cantatas, a Requiem, songs, and piano pieces.	Russian.
1849 26 September Wismar.	**1926** January. Würzburg.	**RITTER, Hermann.** Inventor of the " Viola Alta," and toured as a player of the instrument, attracting the attention of eminent composers, including Wagner. Professor of musical history and esthetics, and of the viola at the Würzburg Royal School of Music. Received the title of Court Professor from Emperor Ludwig II of Bavaria. Compositions and arrangements for the Viola Alta.	German.
1849 29 September Milan.		**ZAVERTAL, Ladislaus.** Son of W. H. (1821). Conductor and composer to the theatre at Milan in '69. Conductor at Glasgow in '71, and master of the Band of the Royal Artillery in '81, succeeding Smythe. Initiated the Sunday Concerts in the Albert Hall. Operas, operetta, and symphonies.	Italian.
1849 16 October. Thornbury, Glos.	**1919** 16 October. Slough.	**LLOYD, Charles Harford.** Organist of Gloucester Cathedral in 1876, succeeding S. S. Wesley, and conducted the Three Choir Festivals in '77 and '80. Organist of Christ Church Cathedral, Oxford, in '82, succeeding Corfe, and conducted the Choral Society in succession to Parratt. Teacher of organ and composition at the Royal College, 1887-92, and succeeded Barnby at Eton College in '92. Cantatas, choruses, anthems, church services, madrigals, organ concerto, and a sonata.	English.

Born	Died	Name	Nationality
1849 16 October. Hamburg.	**1904** 4 August. Hamburg.	**KRUG, Arnold.** Son and pupil of Diedrich, studied also at the Leipzig Conservatorium. Conductor of his own Choral Society at Hamburg, and teacher at the Conservatorium. Symphony, symphonic-prologue, suite and other orchestral; violin concerto, string quartet, piano quartets, trio, choral works, etc.—about 100 works.	German.
1849 4 November. ßengenrieden.	**1919** 6 December. Mainz.	**STEINBACH, Emil.** Brother of Fritz (1855). Studied at the Leipzig Conservatorium. Conductor of the Town Band at Leipzig in 1877. Director at the Town Theatre at Mainz in 1898. Orchestral works, chamber-music, and songs.	German.
1849 6 November. Liverpool.		**COWARD, Sir Henry (Mus.D.).** Known as a great choral conductor. Initiated the Sheffield Festival in 1896, and made a world tour with his choir in 1911. Cantatas, anthems, songs, and didactic works on choir-training.	English.
1850 5 January. Petrograd.	**1915** 20 June. Petrograd.	**TANÉIEV, Alexander Sergeievich.** Pupil of Reichel at Dresden, Rimsky-Korsakov and Petrov at Petrograd, was influenced by Balakirev. Operas, symphonies, suites, quartets, pieces for violin and piano, choruses, part-songs, and a symphonic-poem.	Russian.
1850 6 January. Posen.	**1924** 8 December. Berlin.	**SCHARWENKA, Franz Xaver.** Brother of L. P. (1847); pupil of Kullak and Wüerst. Visited England first in 1879. Director of his own Conservatorium in Berlin from 1881 to '91, when he proceeded to New York in order to establish a branch of his institution, and there became famous as a concert pianist. 3 Piano concertos, 2 sonatas and many pieces of Polish character; trio, quartet, sonatas for 'cello, a symphony, and an opera—about 100 works.	German.
1850 18 February. Breslau.	**1934** 10 September Aviemore.	**HENSCHEL, Isidor Georg (Sir).** Pupil of Moscheles (piano), Reinecke and Richter (theory), Kiel (composition), Goetze and Schulze (singing) at the Leipsic and Berlin Conservatoriums successively. Appeared first in England as a bass singer in '77. Conducted the Boston Symphony Orchestra from '81 to '84. Established the London Symphony Concerts. Professor of singing at the Royal College in '86, succeeding Jenny Lind. Operas, operetta, 2 orchestral serenades, Te Deum, Requiem, quartets, ballad for violin, incidental music to "Hamlet," etc.	German. (Naturalised English, 1890.)
1850 25 February. Arras.		**GEORGES, Alexandre.** Studied at the school for religious music under Niedermeyer, and later became professor there. Comic operas, lyric opera and lyric drama, symphonic-poems, songs and chansons for voice and orchestra.	French.

Born	Died	Name	Nationality
1850 9 March. Lyons.	**1906** 29 July. Paris.	**LUIGINI, Alexandre Clément Léon Joseph.** Pupil of the Paris Conservatoire for violin. Leader of the orchestra in the Grand Théâtre at Lyons, becoming conductor in 1877, and was professor of the Conservatoire there. At Paris was conductor of the Opéra Comique from 1904. Ballets, symphonic music, cantatas, chamber music, and a comic opera.	French.
1850 14 March. Rengersdorf.	**1906** 24 May. Charlotten- burg.	**REIMANN, Heinrich.** Son of Ignas (1820). Critic and conductor ; teacher of theory and organ at the Scharwenka-Klindworth Conservatorium. Organist of the Philharmonic, and of the great church in the Augusta-Victoriaplatz in Berlin. Founded a Bach Society in 1898. Preludes, fugues, etc., for organ ; piano duets, choruses, songs, Lieder, and literature.	German.
1850 15 March. Vittoria.		**SERRANO, Emilio.** Court pianist to the Countess of Girgenti ; Director of the Royal Opera, and Professor of the Conservatoire of Madrid. Teacher of Del Campo, Gómez, etc. Grand operas, including " Irene de Otranto " and " Gonzalo de Cordoba " ; symphonic-poem, piano concerto, string quartet, etc.	Spanish.
1850 9 April. Taubenheim.	**1903** 4 September. Munich.	**ZUMPE, Hermann.** Court chapel-master at Munich in 1900. Conducted Wagner's operas in London in 1898. Operettas, operas, overture, and songs.	German.
1850 or 48 28 April. Aarhus, Jutland.	**1909** 10 November. Berlin.	**SCHYTTE, Ludwig Theodor.** Pupil of Rée, Neupert, Gebauer, Gade, Taubert, and Liszt. Teacher of the piano in Horák's Academy at Vienna. Was originally a chemist. Opera, comic opera, operetta, songs and many pieces for piano, and a concerto.	Danish.
1850 16 May. Norwich.	**1929** 19 November.	**MANN, Arthur Henry (Mus.D.).** Organist at Wolverhampton (1870), Tettenhall ('71), Beverley Minster ('75), and organist and director of the choir at King's College, Cambridge, in '76. Chorus-master of the Norwich Festival in 1902. Oratorio, anthems, Te Deum, church services, and hymn tunes.	English.
1850 17 May. Trapani.	**1922** 7 January. Florence.	**SCONTRINO, Antonio.** Pupil at the Palermo Conservatorio under Alfana and Platania for composition. Toured as a double-bass player. Professor of counterpoint at the Reale Instituto Musicale at Florence. 4 Operas, incidental music, overture, string quartets ; violin, 'cello and double-bass pieces ; sacred works, and 50 songs.	Sicilian.
1850 20 May. Helston, Cornwall.		**FANING, Eaton (Mus.D.).** Pupil of the Royal Academy, under Sterndale Bennett and Steggall, where he became professor of the piano in 1878. Professor at the Guildhall in '82, and at the Royal College, where he also conducted the Choral Class. Director of the Music at Harrow School in '85, while conducting several London societies. 2 Operettas, symphony, overture, string quartets, Mass, Magnificat, anthems, choruses, songs, duets and part-songs.	English.

Born	Died	Name	Nationality
1850 2 June. Liège.	1918 Brussels.	RAWAY, Érasme. Became an Abbé ; taught music and geography until 1880, then became choir-master at Liège Cathedral. One of the founders of modern Belgian music. Melodrama, 4 symphonic works, and songs.	Belgian.
1850 5 June. Grosswanz- leben.		BARTH, Richard. Violinist. Pupil of Beck and Joachim. Director of Music of the University of Marburg, and of the Conservatorium at Hamburg (1908). Violin sonatas, trio, quartet, and violin solos.	German.
1850 18 June. Graz.	1914 28 October. Vienna.	HEUBERGER, Richard Franz Joseph. Conductor and choirmaster at Vienna ; became a teacher in the Conservatorium in 1902, also a critic. 3 Operas, 2 ballets, 4 operettas, cantatas and orchestral works.	Styrian.
1850 27 June. Ostergarn.		HÄGG, Jakob. Studied at the Stockholm Conservatorium. Member of the Royal Academy, Stockholm. Overtures, suite, string quartet, trio, violin and 'cello sonatas, piano pieces, and songs.	Swedish.
1850 4 July. Hammerfest.		OLSEN, Ole. Pupil of Lendermann, and at Leipzig under Richter, Paul and Reinecke. Piano teacher and choirmaster at Christiania, and succeeded Svendsen as director of the Musical Society. Director of the Band of the 2nd Infantry Brigade. Critic and poet. Librettist of his 3 operas. 3 Operas, a fairy comedy, symphonic-poems, symphony, oratorio, cantatas, songs and piano pieces.	Norwegian.
1850 21 September Prague.	1922 10 March. Leipzig.	SITT, Hans. Teacher of the violin at the Leipzig Conservatorium in 1883, and conductor of the Bach Society and other Associations. Violin concertos, concertinos, solos, studies and duets, pieces for 'cello and piano, songs, overtures, male-choruses, etc.—about 120 works.	Bohemian.
1850 18 October. Mauritius.	1909 16 November.	THOMÉ, Francis Lucien Joseph. Pupil of Marmontel and Duprato at the Paris Conservatoire. Operas, ballets, incidental music to plays, songs, and piano pieces.	French. (school.)
1850 20 November. Ratton Park, Sussex.	1892 20 March. London.	THOMAS, Arthur Goring. Pupil of E. Durand in Paris, Sullivan and Prout at the Royal Academy, and of Max Bruch. Operas, comic operas, cantatas, orchestral suite, songs, duets, etc.	English.
1850 1 December. Copenhagen.	1926 25 February.	LANGE-MÜLLER, Peter Erasmus. Essentially self-taught. Operas, plays (of contemporary Danish poets), 2 symphonies, violin concerto, piano trio ; cantata, Psalms, and other choral works.	Danish.
1850 21 December Czáslau.	1900 10 October. Prague.	FIBICH, Zdenko. Pupil of the Leipsic Conservatorium under Moscheles, Richter and Jadassohn, also of V. Lachner at Mannheim. Teacher at Wilna and conductor at	Bohemian.

Born	Died	Name	Nationality.
		Prague. His fame is overshadowed by Dvořák and Smetana. 6 Operas, 6 melodramas, 3 scenic-melodramas, a melodramatic trilogy, 7 symphonic-poems, symphony overture, chamber-music for various combinations, many songs, and 352 piano pieces—700 works in all.	
1850 29 December Salamanca.	1923 2 December. Madrid.	BRETON, Tomás. Conductor of the Union Artístico-Musical. Visited London as conductor in 1891. Lectured and wrote in favour of Spanish National Opera. Operas, many operettas (Zarzuelas), symphonies, symphonic-poems, suites, violin concerto, oratorio, string quartets, trio, quintets, sextets, etc.	Spanish.
1851 9 January. Faenza.	1923 14 December Milan.	GALLIGNANI, Giuseppe. Studied at the Milan Conservatorio, where he became director in 1897. Several operas, vocal chamber music, and sacred works.	Italian.
1851 25 January. Antwerp.	1912 26 May. Antwerp.	BLOCKX, Jan. Pupil of the Antwerp school of music and of the Leipzig Conservatorium. Succeeded Benoit as director of the Antwerp Conservatoire in 1902. Operas, lyric-drama, comic opera, ballets, cantatas, oratorio, chamber-music, symphony, symphonic-poem, suite, church music, etc.	Belgian.
1851 29 January. Terni.	1922 17 November. Rome.	FALCHI, Stanislao. Director of the Liceo, Rome, 1902-15. Operas, overtures, Requiem, vocal and instrumental chamber-music.	Italian.
1851 9 February. Ohlau.		FIEBACH, Otto. Organist and musical director at the Königsberg University. 5 Operas and an oratorio, also didactic works.	Silesian.
1851 23 March. Villena.	1909 25 March.	CHAPÍ, Ruperto. Studied at the Royal Conservatory, Madrid. Played the piccolo and cornet. 168 Works for the stage; symphonies, symphonic-poems, oratorio, motets, string quartets, trio, pieces for violin and piano, and marches for military band. Important only as regards the evolution of Spanish music.	Spanish.
1851 27 March. Paris.	1931 3 December. Paris.	INDY, Paul Marie Théodore Vincent d'. Pupil of Diemer, Lavignac and César Franck. Director and teacher of composition at the Schola Cantorum, Paris. The leader of the "Franck" school. Symphonies, symphonic variations and ballad; overtures, operas, comic opera, incidental music, many songs (sacred and secular), trio, quartet, sonatas, pieces and ensemble music for various instruments.	French.
1851 17 May.		BENDIX, Victor Emanuel. Pupil of Copenhagen Conservatorium, and of Gade. Pianist, teacher and conductor of various societies in Copenhagen. 4 Symphonies, piano concerto, trio, songs and romances.	Danish.

Born	Died	Name	Nationality.
1851 23 June. Greenfield, Mass.		**EDDY, Hiram Clarence.** Pupil of D. Buck, and of Haupt and Loeschhorn at Berlin. Toured on the Continent and was organist at various churches. Director of the Hershey School of Musical Art and conductor of Philharmonic Vocal Society at Chicago. Preludes, fugues and canons for organ.	American.
1851 France.		**SIMON, Anton Yulievich.** Pupil at the Paris Conservatoire. Conductor of the Théâtre Bouffe, Moscow, in 1871. Superintendant of the Imperial Theatres and musical director of the Alexandrovsky Institute. Operas, ballets, symphonic-poems, overtures, concertos for piano and clarinet, piano trios, string quartet, ensemble pieces for wind, choruses, songs, many piano pieces, and violin and 'cello pieces.	French.
1851 November. Paris.	**1926** 4 November.	**WORMSER, André Alphonse Toussaint.** Pupil of the Paris Conservatoire under Bazin and Marmontel. Operas, pantomimes and other works.	French.
1851 November. London.	**1922** 18 December. London.	**FOSTER, Myles Birket.** Pupil of the Royal Academy under Sullivan and Prout (composition), Westlake (piano), Pettitt ('cello) and Horton (oboe). Organist at various London churches ; the Foundling Hospital (1880-92) ; Her Majesty's Theatre ; and was choirmaster at St. Alban's, Holborn. Symphony, overtures, quartet, trios, cantatas (sacred and secular), anthems including " Oh for a closer walk with God," part-songs, and church services.	English.
1852 4 January. London.	**1932** 23 August. Hampstead.	**CORDER, Frederick.** Pupil of the Royal Academy, and at Cologne under Hiller. Conductor at Brighton, and professor of composition at the Royal Academy from 1889. Operas, operettas, overtures, incidental music ; orchestral suites, scenes and pieces ; cantatas, choruses with orchestra, pieces for violin and piano.	English.
1852 7 January. Kingston, Jamaica.	**1935** 6 October. London.	**COWEN, Sir Frederic Hymen.** Pupil of Goss and Benedict, and studied for a short time at Leipzig. Conductor of the Philharmonic Society (1888-92), succeeding Sullivan, and again in 1900 succeeding Mackenzie ; also conducted the Hallé Orchestra, Manchester ('96 to '99), and the Societies of Liverpool and Bradford, and Scarborough Festival. Operas, operettas, oratorios, cantatas, anthems, part-songs, songs (nearly 300), symphonies, suites, overtures, marches, piano-concerto, chamber music, and solos.	English. (Came to **England** at the age of 4.)
1852 22 May. un-le-Roi.	**1920** 12 February. London.	**SAURET, Emile.** Violinist ; the last pupil of De Bériot. Toured as a violin soloist in America, England, and on the Continent. Violin Professor at the Stern Academy in Berlin (1880), at the Royal Academy, London (1890) succeeding Sainton, at Chicago (1903-6), and then taught privately at Geneva. Violin concertos, solos, and difficult studies.	French.

Born	Died	Name	Nationality
1852 23 June. Paris.	1914 3 January. Moscow.	**PUGNO, Stéphane Raoul.** Pupil of the Conservatoire. Organist of St. Eugène (1872-92), and chorus-master of the Ventadour Theatre '74. Professor of harmony at the Conservatoire ('92-96), and of the piano ('96-1901). Oratorios, many operas, piano sonatas, and songs.	French.
1852 28 June. Schönenwerd.	1921 25 December. Basle.	**HUBER, Hans (D.Phil.).** Studied at the Leipzig Conservatorium. Succeeded Bagge as director of the music school at Basle. 2 Operas; 7 symphonies and other orchestral pieces; concertos for violin and piano; quintets, quartets, trios, 'cello sonata, piano pieces and songs, oratorios, choruses, piano pieces, etc.	Swiss.
1852 Tarnopol.		**KAAN DE ALBÉST, Jindrich.** Pupil of the Organ School at Prague. Director of the Prague Conservatorium, 1907-18. Operas, ballets, orchestral works, 3 piano concertos, 3 violin sonatas, organ sonata, a melodrama and piano studies.	Polish.
1852 24 August. Turin.	1905	**JUNCK, Benendetto.** Pupil of Mazzucato at Milan. Songs, string quartet, and 4 violin sonatas.	Italian.
1852 30 September. Dublin.	1924 29 March. London.	**STANFORD**, Sir Charles Villiers. Pupil of O'Leary and Sir R. Stewart, also of Reinecke at Leipzig, and Kiel at Berlin. Organist of Trinity College, Cambridge, succeeding J. L. Hopkins, in 1873; conductor of the University Musical Society, and became Professor of Music in the University of Cambridge in '87, on the death of Macfarren. Professor of composition at the Royal College from its opening in '83. Conductor of the Leeds Festival in 1901. 7 Symphonies, overtures, quartets, trios, concertos for violin, piano and clarinet, sonatas, oratorios, anthems, church-music, choruses, songs, piano and organ works, 7 operas, 4 Irish Rhapsodies to-opus 177.	Irish.
1852 25 November. Paris.		**HILLEMACHER, Paul.** Worked in collaboration with his brother Lucien (1860), both studying at the Paris Conservatoire. Operas, comic operas, lyric dramas, a Légende symphonique, and songs.	French.
1853 1 January. Waldeck.		**KOESSLER, Hans.** Pupil of Rheinberger at Munich. Teacher at Dresden Conservatorium in 1877. Director of advanced school for composition at the Music Academy, Budapest, in 1920. 2 Symphonies, symphonic-variations, violin concerto and sonata, string quartets, quintets, Psalms, Mass, chamber-songs, and an opera.	German.
1853 3 January. Mewe.	1916 22 January. Frankfort-on-Main.	**KNORR, Iwan.** Pupil of the Leipzig Conservatorium under Moscheles, Richter and Reinecke. Principal teacher of composition at the Hoch Conservatorium in Frankfort-on-Main (1883), where he taught many notable men. Orchestral, chamber-music, pianoforte, songs, operas and didactic works.	German.

Born	Died	Name	Nationality
1853 2 February. Ightham, Kent.	**1919** January.	**SELBY, Bertram Luard-** Pupil of the Leipsic Conservatorium under Reinecke, and Jadassohn. Organist at Salisbury Cathedral ('81-83), and succeeded J. Hopkins at Rochester in 1900. Opera, cantatas, anthems, services, songs, organ pieces, quintets for piano and strings, violin sonata, piano pieces, etc.	English.
1853 5 March. Salem, Mass.		**FOOTE, Arthur William.** Studied only in America. Church organist and piano teacher at Boston. Symphonic-poem, overtures, suites, serenade, cantatas, songs, church and chamber-music, and didactic works.	American.
1853 12 March.	**1904** 6 December.	**BARTHOLDY, Conrad Johan.** Cantor at St. Matthew's, Copenhagen. Operas.	Danish.
1853 6 June. Stockholm.	**1918** 1 March. Stockholm.	**SJÖGREN, Emil.** Pupil of the Stockholm Conservatoire, and later at Berlin under Kiel (composition) and Haupt (organ). Organist at St. John's Church, Stockholm, from 1891. Piano sonatas and pieces, violin sonatas, organ pieces, and vocal solos.	Swedish.
1853 8 June. Amsterdam.		**HOLLANDER, Benno.** Pupil of Massart (violin) and Saint-Saëns (composition). Professor of the violin at the Guildhall School of Music in 1887. Leader of the London Symphony Orchestra, and in 1903 founded an orchestral society called the " B.H." 2 Violin concertos, fantasia, septet, quartets, trios, sonatas for violin and piano, symphony, and songs.	Dutch.
1853 11 June. Neuve- Maison.	**1904** 1 October. Paris.	**ROUSSEAU, Samuel Alexandre.** Pupil of César Franck at the Paris Conservatoire. Chapel-master at Sainte-Clotilde ; and chorus-master of the Concert Society of the Conservatoire. Operas, comic opera, Masses, motets and other church music, secular choral pieces, and pieces for violin, piano, organ and harmonium.	French.
1853 2 August. Posen.	**1919** 5 October. Dresden.	**NICODÉ, Jean Louis.** Pupil of Kullak (piano), Wüerst (harmony), and Kiel (composition). Professor of the Royal Conservatorium, Dresden, in 1878, and director of the Philharmonic Concerts in 1885. Symphonic-opera, poems, odes, variations, suites and other orchestral music ; sonatas, studies, and solos for piano ; 'cello sonata, songs, etc.	German.
1853 6 August. Rochester.	**1929** 29 March. London.	**BRIDGE, Dr. Joseph Cox.** Pupil of his brother, Sir Frederic, whom he assisted on the organ of Manchester Cathedral. Organist of Exeter College, Oxford, in '71, and of Chester Cathedral in '77 ; founded the Chester Musical Society, and conducted the Bradford Festival,'86-89. Director of the Trinity College, London. Oratorio, symphony, cantatas, operetta, anthems, Requiem Mass, songs, organ and piano music.	English.

Born	Died	Name	Nationali
1853 24 August.		**STCHERBATCHEV, Nicholas Vladimirovich.** Pianist ; studied in Rome, and afterwards became associated with the Russian School. Orchestral pieces, many various works for piano, and songs.	Russian.
1853 30 December Montluçon.		**MESSAGER, André Charles Prosper.** Pupil of Niedermeyer and Saint-Saëns. Conductor at the Paris Opéra-Comique, and " Artistic Director " at the Royal Opera, Covent Garden, in 1901. Many successful comic operas, operettas and ballets, also a symphony, cantata, etc.	French.
1854 24 February. Barnstaple.		**EDWARDS, Henry John (Mus.D.).** Pupil of his father, John (1808-94), afterwards of Bennett, Macfarren, Banister, and Cooper. Organist at Barnstaple Parish Church, and conductor of Exeter Oratorio Society in '96. Oratorios, cantatas, motets, Psalms, songs, part-songs, and a Triumphal march for orchestra.	English.
1854 3 March. Vienna.		**REINHOLD, Hugo.** Pupil of the Vienna Conservatorium under Bruckner, Dessoff and Epstein. Suite for piano and strings ; pieces for string orchestra ; quartet, piano music and songs—about 60 works in all.	Austria
1854 27 March. Sinay.	**1912** 28 October. Brussels.	**TINEL, Edgar.** Pupil at the Brussels Conservatoire under Brassin, Gevaert and Kufferath. Succeeded Lemmens as director of the Institute for church music at Malines, in 1882, and succeeded Kufferath as professor of counterpoint at the Brussels Conservatoire. Oratorios, choruses, Te Deum and other sacred works ; orchestral suite, music drama, and songs.	Belgian
1854 13 May. Leipzig.		**KLENGEL, Paul (D.Phil.).** Brother of Julius (1859). Violinist, pianist and conductor at Leipsic, Stuttgart and New York, returning to Leipsic in 1903. Songs, violin suites, viola pieces, etc.	German
1854 18 May. Amsterdam.	**1924** 9 December.	**ZWEERS, Bernard.** Studied under Jadassohn at Leipzig. Teacher of composition at Amsterdam Conservatory. Taught many of the modern Dutch composers. 3 Symphonies, choral works, and stage music.	Dutch.
1854 19 June. Lucca.	**1893** 7 August. Milan.	**CATALANI, Alfredo.** Studied at Modena and at the Naples Conservatorio under Donizetti and Crescentini. Director of the theatre at Messina and later at Correggio. Chapel-master at Modena, and keeper of the Este Library. 4 Operas, a Requiem, church music and archæological works.	Italian.
1854 Hukvaldy.		**JANÁČEK, Leoš.** Conductor of the Philharmonic Society at Brno 1881-88 ; now professor of the Master-School of composition there. Several operas ; symphonic-poem ; choruses (some with orchestra), song-cycle, etc.	Moravi

Born	Died	Name	Nationality
1854 4 July. Leipzig.		**ZOELLNER, Heinrich.** Studied at the Leipzig Conservatorium. Teacher at Cologne Conservatorium ; went to New York in 1890 ; teacher at Leipzig Conservatorium in 1902, and joined Stern's Conservatorium in 1907. Operas, cantata, oratorio, choruses, 4 symphonies, 5 string quartets, songs, etc.	German.
1854 23 August. Breslau.	1925 8 March. Paris.	**MOSZKOWSKI, Mortiz.** Pupil of the Stern Academy at Dresden, and of that of Kullak at Berlin. Concert pianist. Visited London for the first time in 1886 and for the last time in 1908. Operas, symphony, suites, concertos for piano and violin ; 'cello and violin pieces ; piano solos and duets ; and songs.	German.
1854 1 September. Siegburg.	1921 27 September Neustrelitz.	**HUMPERDINCK, Engelbert.** Pupil of Hiller, F. Lachner and Rheinberger. Professor at the Hoch Conservatorium, teacher of harmony in the Vocal School, and musical critic in Dresden. Head of the Meister-Schule for composition at Berlin in 1900. Operas, of which " Hänsel and Gretel " was most successful ; choral ballad, and smaller choral and orchestral works.	German.
1854 13 November. Lowell, Mass.	1931 4 April. Boston, U. S.	**CHADWICK, George Whitefield.** Pupil of Thayer at Boston, and of Reinecke, Jadassohn and Rheinberger at Munich. Director of the New England School of Music in 1897, and organist of the Second Universalist Church. Operas and operettas, 3 symphonies, 6 overtures, choruses, 5 string quartets, quintet, piano and organ pieces, and about 50 songs.	American.
1855 21 January. Paris.	1899 10 July. Limy.	**CHAUSSON, Ernest.** Pupil of César Franck. Secretary to the Société Nationale de Musique. Lyric dramas, 3 symphonic-poems, a symphony, vocal and instrumental pieces with orchestra ; trio, quartet ; " Concert " for piano, violin and string quartet ; organ, piano and violin solos.	French.
1855 26 January. Paris.	1922 10 March.	**HERVEY, Arthur.** Pupil of B. Tours and Marlois. Musical critic to " Vanity Fair " and the " Morning Post " in '92. Opera, operetta, dramatic overture, tone-poems, scena for baritone and orchestra, and songs.	French. (Irish. parents.)
1855 15 February. Leobschütz.	1915 6 December. Berlin.	**HOLLÄNDER, Gustav.** Pupil of David at Leipzig and Joachim at Berlin. Professor of the violin at Kullak's Academy in '75, at the Cologne Conservatorium in '81, and director of the Stern Conservatorium in Berlin in '94. Toured as a soloist and quartet leader. 4 Violin concertos ; sonata, suite, pieces, and works for strings.	German.
1855 13 March. Prague.	1903 19 September Schloss Alt- Erlaa.	**RÜCKAUF, Anton.** Pupil of Proksch, and later studied at Vienna. Accompanist to Gustav Walter. Songs, ballads, a violin sonata, pianoforte quintet, piano solos and duets, and an opera.	Bohemian.

Born	Died	Name	Nationality.
1855 9 April. Vienna.	**1907** 26 April. Vienna.	**HELLMESBERGER, Joseph (Junr.).** Son of namesake (1828). Solo-violinist at the Court Opera, Vienna, in '78 ; professor at the Conservatorium, and played second violin in his father's quartet, succeeding him as leader in '87. Chapelmaster of the Court Opera in 1900. 6 Operettas, and ballets.	Austrian.
1855 29 April. Petrograd.	**1914** 28 August. Novgorod.	**LIADOV, Anatol Constantinovich.** Pupil of Rimsky-Korsakov at the Petrograd Conservatoire, where he became professor of harmony and composition; and also held a similar post at the Imperial Court Chapel. Many piano works, songs, choruses, and orchestral pieces, numbering about 60 works in all.	Russian.
1855 10 May. Leipzig.		**RÖNTGEN, Julius.** Pupil of his father, Engelbert (1829-97), and later of Hauptmann, Richter, Plaidy and F. Lachner. Succeeded Verhulst as director of the Maatschappij tot Bevordering der Tonkunst in 1886, and was conductor of the Felix Meritis Society at Amsterdam. Piano concerto, sonatas, suites, ballade, etc. ; sonatas for violin and 'cello ; serenade for wind ; a Liederspiel, songs, symphonies, and 2 operas.	German.
1855 17 June. Grünsfeld.	**1916** 13 August. Munich.	**STEINBACH, Fritz.** Brother of Emil (1849). Pupil of the Leipzig Conservatorium. Conductor of the orchestra of the Grand Duke of Meiningen, with which he made a sensational performance in London in 1902. Succeeded Wüllner as Town Chapel-master and Director of the Conservatorium at Cologne in 1902. Septet, 'cello sonata, orchestral and vocal music.	German.
1855 23 June. Dieppe.		**WHITE, Maude Valérie.** Studied at the Royal Academy under Sir G. A. Macfarren and Davenport. Songs to words by Shelley and Herrick, of which " My soul is an enchanted boat " is the finest ; also a vocal quintet, an opera, and piano pieces.	French. (English parents.)
1855 Klatovy.		**KLIČKA, Josef.** Pupil of Skuhersky. Organist at Prague, and professor at the Conservatorium. Oratorios, Masses, opera, choruses, Psalms, organ sonata and concert fantasies, string quartets, quintets, trio, sextet, many pieces for harp, and Ballad of Bohemian music.	Bohemian.
1855 6 September Berlin.		**HUMMEL, Ferdinand.** Studied under Rudorff, Grabau, Kiel and Bargiel. Pianist. Piano concerto, male and female choruses, 4 'cello sonatas, violin sonata, horn sonata, overture, symphony piano suite and pieces, quintet, quartet, and stage works.	German.

Born	Died	Name	Nationality
1855 29 September Castellamare.		**ESPOSITO, Michele.** Studied at the Naples Conservatorio under Cesi (piano) and Serrao (composition). Professor of the piano at the Royal Irish Academy, Dublin, 1884, and conductor of the Dublin Orchestral Society. Cantata, operetta, symphony, overture, violin sonata, songs, and piano pieces—about 80 works.	Italian.
1855 5 October. Steubendorf-Leobschütz.	**1911** 8 October. Breslau.	**FILKE, Max.** Pupil of Brosig, and of the Leipzig Conservatorium. Choir-master of Breslau Cathedral in 1891, and teacher at the school for church music. Masses with orchestra, Te Deum, Requiem, Litany and much church music ; over 100 works.	German.
1855 12 October. Lébénji Szent Miklos.	**1922** 23 January. Leipzig.	**NIKISCH, Arthur.** One of the greatest orchestral conductors in history. Pupil of the Vienna Conservatorium. Conductor of the Leipzig Opera in '74 ; Boston, U.S. Symphony Orchestra in '87 ; the Gewandhaus, Leipzig (succeeding Reinecke) ; and the Berlin Philharmonic. Visited London several times. Symphony, cantata, string quartet, and violin sonata	Hungarian.
1855 24 November. Lublin.		**BIERNACKI, Michal Marjan.** Pupil of Roguski and Zelenski at Warsaw Conservatory. Professor and director of the Musical Society, Warsaw, from 1902 to '05. Symphonic works, cantatas, Masses, choral pieces, and songs ; also theoretical works.	Polish.
1855 23 December York.		**GRAY, Alan (Mus.D.).** Pupil of Dr. Monk. Musical director at Wellington College in '83 ; succeeded Stanford as organist of Trinity College, Cambridge, in '92, and conductor of the University Musical Society. Cantatas, choruses, part-songs, solo songs, string and piano quartets, organ sonatas, and a violin sonata.	English.
1855 26 December Ratibor.		**MENDELSSOHN, Arnold (Ph.D.).** Son of a cousin of the great Mendelssohn. Studied law, then music at Berlin. Organist and university teacher at Bonn. Teacher at Cologne Conservatorium in 1885. Improved the music of the Protestant Church. Symphony, violin concerto and sonata, string quartets, piano sonatas, cantatas, madrigals, choruses, songs—about 100 works.	German.
1856 6 January. Capua.	**1909** 1 June. Naples.	**MARTUCCI, Giuseppe.** Pupil of Cesi, C. Costa, Serrao and Rossi at the Naples Conservatorio, where he became professor in 1874 and its director in 1902. Director of the Liceo Musicale at Bologna in '86. Toured as pianist, visiting England in '75. Later became conductor of Prince d'Ardore's orchestra. Symphonies ; piano concertos and solos ; quintets, trios ; sonatas and pieces for organ, violin and 'cello respectively—about 100 works.	Italian.

Born	Died	Name	Nationality
1856 11 January. Kongsberg.		**SINDING, Christian.** The next important Norwegian composer to Grieg. Studied violin at Christiania, and later studied composition, etc., at the Leipsic Conservatorium. Lived in Berlin where he conducted his works. Was in America in 1921 and '22. Lived later at Christiania. Opera, symphonies, symphonic-poems, piano concerto, 2 violin concertos, violin sonatas, suites, quartets, quintet, cantatas, piano pieces and songs—about 80 works.	Norwegian.
1856 18 January. Brooklyn.		**BREWER, John Hyatt (Mus.D.).** Pupil of D. Buck, whom he succeeded as conductor of the Apollo Club in 1903. Organist in various churches. Professor of Music at Adelphi College, Brooklyn, in 1906. Over 200 anthems; 40 cantatas, and songs.	American.
1856 11 February. Rome.		**BOEZI, Ernesto.** Master of the Cappella Giulia at St. Peter's, Rome, in 1905 ; Technical director of the Pontifical School of Sacred Music till 1918. Much sacred music, and operas.	Italian.
1856 5 April. Utrecht.	1914 7 April. Dresden.	**PETRI, Henri Wilhelm.** Violinist ; pupil of Joachim. Concert-meister to the Royal Chapel of Dresden, succeeding Lauterbach. Violin solos, and songs.	Dutch.
1856 19 April. Milan.		**GALLOTTI, Salvatore.** Succeeded Gallignani as director of the choir at Milan Cathedral in 1892. Masses and other sacred music ; symphonic works, and an opera.	Italian.
1856 26 May. New York.		**STRONG, George Templeton.** Studied at Leipzig under R. Hofmann, Jadassohn, and was influenced by Liszt and Raff. Played oboe and viola. Symphony, symphonic-poem, choruses, dramatic cantata, chamber-music, songs, and instrumental solos.	American.
1856 Warsaw.	1912 Lemberg.	**GALL, Jan.** Pupil of Krenn at Vienna ; Rheinberger at Munich ; and later of Lamperti in Italy. Choral conductor and critic at Leipzig, and later at Lemberg. 300 Choral pieces, and 70 songs of national character.	Polish.
1856 23 July. Cambridge (Mass.)		**BIRD, Arthur.** Studied in Berlin under Haupt, Loeschhorn, Rohde and Urban. Worked chiefly in Germany. A symphony, orchestral suites ; piano suites, marches, fugues, variations, etc. ; violin pieces, a comic opera and a ballet.	American.
1856 10 August. Stolp.	1919 3 April. Posen.	**GEISLER, Paul.** Pupil of C. Decker. Conductor at Bremen and Leipzig, and director of the Conservatorium at Posen. 3 Operas, 2 cyclic cantatas, several symphonic-poems, vocal and piano compositions.	German.

Born	Died	Name	Nationality
1856 29 August. Vienna.	**1911** 2 July. Munich.	**MOTTL, Felix.** Pupil of the Vienna Conservatorium. At Carlsruhe was conductor of the Grand Ducal Opera, and director of the Philharmonic Society. Became a director of the Berlin Royal Academy in 1904. Director of the opera at Munich in 1907. 3 Operas, songs, a song cycle, and a string quartet.	Austrian.
1856 22 October. Petrograd.	**1933** August. Meran.	**SCHÜTT, Eduard.** Pupil of Petersen and Stein at Petrograd, and later of the Leipzig Conservatorium. Conductor of the Akademische Wagner-Verein at Vienna. Piano concerto and solos, songs, suite for violin and piano, serenade for strings, etc.	Russian.
1856 6 November Washington, U.S.	**1934**	**SOUSA, John Philip.** Violinist in the orchestra led by Offenbach on his visit to America. Leader of the Marine Corps Band in 1880, and organised his own band in '92. Well-known marches and several operettas.	American.
1856 13 November. Vladimir.	**1915** 5 June. Moscow.	**TANEIEV, Sergius Ivanovich.** Pupil of Rubinstein, Hubert and Tchaikovsky at the Moscow Conservatory, where he succeeded Tchaikovsky as professor of the piano ; and in 1885 succeeded Hubert as its director, until 1889, when he was replaced by Safonov. In early life he toured as an exponent of Tchaikovsky's piano works. 3 Symphonies ; operatic trilogy, " Orestes " ; cantata, choruses, 5 string quartets, and a treatise on counterpoint.	Russian.
1856 2 December. Helsingfors.	**1933** 6 July. Helsingfors.	**KAJANUS, Robert.** Studied at Helsingfors, Leipzig, and at Paris under Svendsen. The *first important representative of Finnish National music.* Conductor and founder of the Helsingfors Municipal Orchestra. Symphony, symphonietta, Finnish Rhapsodies, suite, march, cantatas, choruses, choral works, and songs.	Finnish.
1856 27 December Paris.	**1926** 5 February.	**GÉDALGE, André.** Studied at the Paris Conservatoire under Guiraud, Teacher of Ravel, F. Schmitt, Honegger and Milhaud. 2 Symphonies, suite, quartet, and a comic-opera.	French.
1857 17 January. Waitzen- kirchen.		**KIENZL, Wilhelm.** Pupil of W. Mayer, the Prague Conservatorium, and Rheinberger at Munich. Conductor at Amsterdam, Graz, and Hamburg. Operas, the most successful being " Der Evangelimann " ; 100 songs ; 150 piano solos and duets ; orchestral and chamber music ; choral works ; and musical literature.	Austrian.
1857 30 January. Copenhagen.		**HELSTED, Gustav Carl.** Studied at the Copenhagen Conservatorium, where he became professor of counterpoint. Organist at the Church of Our Lady, Copenhagen. Orchestral works, 'cello and violin concertos, piano and violin sonatas, string quartets, trio, choruses, and songs.	Danish.

Born	Died	Name	Nationality.
1857 3 March. Paris.	**1934** 16 June. Paris.	**BRUNEAU, Louis Charles Bonaventure Alfred.** Pupil of Massenet for composition and Franchomme for 'cello at the Conservatoire. Conductor at the Opéra Comique in 1903. Decorated with the Legion of Honour in 1905. Operas, overtures, choral symphony, Requiem, Mass, songs, " Chansons á dancer," and " Lieds de France."	French.
1857 2 May. Lowmoor, n'r Bradford.		**CLIFFE, Frederic.** Pupil of Sullivan, Stainer, Prout and F. Taylor. Organist at Wyke Parish Church in '56 ; of the Bradford Festival Choral Society from 1873 to '76 ; the Bach Choir from '88 to '94, and the Italian Opera. Toured as a pianist. Professor of the piano at the Royal College in '83 and at the Royal Academy in 1901. Symphonies, orchestral poem, violin concerto, scena for contralto, chorus, songs, and church music.	English.
1857 2 June. Broadheath, Worc.	**1934** 23 February. Worcester.	**ELGAR**, Sir Edward, Bart. The greatest English master since Purcell. Master of the King's Musick in 1924, succeeding Parratt. Received some lessons on the violin from Pollitzer in '77. A member of Stockley's orchestra in Birmingham in '83. Organist at St. George's Church, Worcester, in 1885. Oratorios and cantatas including " Gerontius," " The Light of Life," " Banner of St. George," " King Olaf," " The Black Knight," etc. ; motets, songs, overture, serenade, string quartet ; violin concerto, sonata and pieces ; organ sonatas and voluntaries, piano solos, part-songs, etc.	English.
1857 5 June. Pesth.		**DOPPLER, Arpad.** Son of Karl (1826). Studied at Stuttgart Conservatorium, where afterwards he taught until 1880, when he went as a piano teacher to the Grand Conservatorium, New York. Returned to Stuttgart in 1883, and was chorus-master at the Court Theatre in '89. Overture, suite, scherzo and variations for orchestra, songs, piano music, and an opera.	Hungarian.
1857 Odessa.		**KLENOVSKY, Nicholas Semenovich.** Pupil of the Moscow Conservatoire under Hubert and Tchaikovsky. Conductor of the University orchestra, Moscow ; director of the Music School at Tiflis, in '93; sub-director of the Imperial Chapel in 1902. Was first to organise " Ethnographical Concerts " in Russia. Dramatic music, cantatas, and ballets.	Russian.
1857 4 September Milan.		**MASCHERONI, Edoardo.** Pupil of Boucheron at Milan. Conductor at the Teatro Goldoni, Leghorn, in 1883, and later at the Teatro Apollo, Rome, when he was considered the leading Italian conductor of his time. Operas, Requiem for voices and orchestra, chambermusic, and pianoforte pieces.	Italian.

SIR EDWARD ELGAR.

Born	Died	Name	Nationality
1857 1 October. Perth.		**KENNEDY-FRASER, Marjory.** Pupil of her father ; studied also in Milan and Paris. Singer and collector of folk-songs. Hebridean and many other songs. Hebridean suite for 'cello, suite for piano, etc.	Scottish.
1857 14 November. Cambridge.	**1924** 5 April. London.	**ELLICOTT, Rosalind Frances.** Pupil of T. Wingham at the Royal Academy. Cantatas, " Elysium," " The Birth of Song," etc ; overtures (a Festal, a dramatic, and a concert) ; a fantasia for piano and orchestra ; songs, and chamber-music.	English.
1857 24 November. New Castle, Del.		**JOHNS, Clayton.** Pupil of J. K. Paine and W. H. Sherwood at Boston, and Kiel, Grabow, Raif and Rummel in Berlin. Settled in Boston in 1884. Orchestral, violin and pianoforte pieces, and about 100 songs.	American.
1858 1 January. Botzen.		**LAZZARI, Sylvio.** Pupil of César Franck at the Paris Conservatoire. Symphonic-poem and other orchestral works ; musical dramas, pantomime, pieces for violin and piano with orchestra, sonatas for violin and piano, trios, quartet, octet ; choruses and songs.	Tyrolese. (French school.)
1858 3 January. Cologne.		**FRANCK, Richard.** Studied at Berlin and Leipzig. Teacher at Basle, Berlin, Magdeburg, Cassel, and is now at Heidelberg as Royal Music-director. Overtures, suites, symphonic works ; violin and piano concertos, and sonatas ; over 50 piano pieces, and songs.	German.
1858 20 January. Mantua.		**ROSSI, Cesare.** Various works, the most successful being the opera " Nadeja."	Italian.
1858 17 February. Warminster, Wilts.	**1919** June.	**FORD, Ernest.** Pupil of Sullivan, H. Thomas (piano), Steggall (organ) at the Royal Academy, and of Lalo in Paris. Conductor at various London Theatres. Operas, operettas, ballet music, cantatas, songs, and church services.	English.
1858 17 February. Tramutola.		**FERRONI, Vincenzo.** Succeeded Ponchielli as professor of composition at the Milan Conservatorio. Operas, symphonies, symphonic-poems, violin concerto, a quartet, trios, vocal and piano pieces.	Italian.
1858 8 March. Naples.	**1919** 9 August. Florence.	**LEONCAVALLO, Ruggiero.** Pupil at the Naples Conservatorio under Cesi (piano), Ruta (harmony), and Rossi (composition). Travelled as an accompanist. Wrote libretti to some of his operas and some for other composers' operas. Operas (including " Pagliacci "), operettas, symphonic-poem, and a ballet.	Italian.
1858 18 April. Hohenstein- Ernstthal.	**1908** 18 November. Berka.	**DEGNER, Erich Wolf.** Studied at Weimar and Würzburg. Director of the Ducal Music School, Weimar, in 1902. Symphony and overture for organ and orchestra, oratorio, choruses, organ works, piano pieces, and songs.	German.

Born	Died	Name	Nationality
1858 23 April. London.		**SMYTH, Dame Ethel Mary.** The greatest composer of her sex. Studied for a short time at Leipzig under Heinrich and Herzogenberg. Wrote the libretti of some of her operas. She was a militant suffragist. Operas (including " The Wreckers ") produced at Dresden, Leipzig, New York, Prague, Vienna and London ; overtures, serenades, chamber music, songs, a Solemn Mass, etc.	English.
1858 6 May. Versailles.		**HÜE, Georges Adolph.** Studied under Reber and Paladilhe. Symphony, symphonic-overture, legend, operas, lyric drama, musical drama, pantomime, " Ballade " for violin, choruses and songs.	French.
1858 2 June. New Haven, Conn.		**SHELLEY, Harry Rowe.** Studied under D. Buck and Max Vogrich in New York, and Dvorák in Europe. Organist at Brooklyn, and Fifth Avenue Baptist Church, New York, since 1899. Symphonies, symphonic-poem, violin concerto, lyric-drama, cantatas, choruses, songs, and piano pieces.	American.
1858 22 June. Lucca.	**1924** 29 November. Brussels.	**PUCCINI, Giacomo.** Of musical ancestry. Instructed chiefly by Ponchielli at the Milan Conservatorio. Came to London in 1911. Operas, including " La Tosca," " La Bohème," " Madame Butterfly," etc., & other orchestral music.	Italian.
1858 Petrograd.		**ARTSYBUCHEF, Nicolas Vassilievitch.** Pupil of Rimsky-Korsakov, whom he succeeded as president of the Committee for the encouragement of Russian musicians. Settled in Paris in 1920. Songs and piano pieces.	Russian.
1858 Podolien.	**1922** Warsaw.	**DLUSKI, Erazm.** Pupil of Soloviev and Rimsky-Korsakov. Professor of the opera class at Warsaw Conservatory in 1920. Operas, symphonic works, piano sonatas, 'cello pieces, and many songs.	Polish.
1858 9 August. London.	**1935** 2 September. Paris.	**DE LARA, Isidore.** Studied at Milan under Mizzucati. Settled in London as singer and conductor. A Chevalier of the Legion of Honour. Operas and cantatas (including " The Three Musketeers.")	English.
1858 13 September Christiania.		**ELLING, Catharinus.** Studied in Leipzig and Berlin. Teacher of composition at Lindeman's Conservatorium, Christiania. Collector of Norwegian folk-music. Opera, oratorio, choral works, stage music, symphony, chamber-music, piano and violin pieces, and 200 songs.	Norwegian.

Born	Died	Name	Nationality.
1858 September Pesth.		**HUBAY, Jeno.** Violinist; pupil of his father (Karl), and later of Joachim. Principal professor at the Brussels Conservatoire in '82, and at Budapest in '86. Toured as a soloist and quartet leader. Teacher of Szigeti, Jelly d'Aranji, etc. 2 Operas; songs; concerto, sonata and many pieces for violin.	Hungarian.
1858 November. Bologna.	**1920** 18 September Bologna.	**TORCHI, Luigi.** Studied at Bologna and at the Naples Conservatorio under Serrao. Teacher of history and esthetics at the Liceo, Pesaro (1885), and became professor of composition at the Liceo, Bologna, in 1891. Several operas, symphonic works, and sacred music.	Italian.
1858 November. Waldsee.	**1915** 8 October. Magdeburg.	**KRUG, Joseph.** Studied at the Stuttgart Conservatorium. Conductor at Stuttgart, Hamburg, Augsburg, Nuremburg, and Magdeburg. Royal Prussian Professor in 1913. 4 Operas, symphonic-poem, symphony, overture, choruses, choral works, violin suite, and string quartet.	German.
1859 4 January. Tsarskoe Selo.		**ILYINSKY, Alexander Alexandrovich.** Studied at Berlin under T. Kullak (piano) and Bargiel (theory). Professor of the Music School of the Philharmonic Society at Moscow. 3 Orchestral suites, overture, symphony, and other symphonic pieces; 2 cantatas, an opera, string quartet, songs, piano and violin pieces.	Russian.
1859 February. Dublin.	**1924** 27 May. New York.	**HERBERT, Victor.** Studied at Stuttgart and played the 'cello in the Court orchestra. At New York in 1886 entered the orchestra of the Metropolitan Opera House, and later became solo 'cellist and conductor in the concerts given in New York and Pittsburg, Pa. Concertos, suite and solos for 'cello; symphonic-poem, suites and serenades for orchestra; a dramatic cantata, and many operettas.	Irish.
1859 14 March. Petrograd.	**1922** Petrograd.	**SOKOLOV, Nicholas Alexandrovich.** Pupil of Rimsky-Korsakov at the Petrograd Conservatorium. Incidental music to Shakespeare's " Winter's Tale "; " Elegy "; 3 string quartets, 8 pieces for violin, 6 for 'cello, 11 choruses, and about 80 songs.	Russian.
1859 3 April. Middletown, Conn.	**1920** 16 January. Chicago.	**DE KOVEN, Reginald.** Studied at Stuttgart, Frankfort, Florence, Vienna, and Paris. Critic. Organised an orchestra in Washington. 2 Operas, 20 comic operas, 130 songs, choruses, etc., to opus 411.	American.
1859 11 April. Olveston, Glos.		**HARWOOD, Basil.** Pupil of Dr. Corfe at Oxford, and Reinecke and Jadassohn at Leipzig. Organist at St. Barnabas, Pimlico, in '83; Ely Cathedral in '87, and Christ Church Cathedral, Oxford, in '92. Conductor of the Bach Choir, the Orchestral Association, and the Orpheus Society. Anthems, services; Psalm for soli, chorus, and orchestra; songs, vocal trios, organ sonatas and pieces.	English.

Born	Died	Name	Nationality
1859 27 April. Cologne.		**GOMPERTZ, Richard.** Violinist, pupil of Joachim. Toured as a soloist until 1880, when he took up work as a player and teacher at Cambridge, forming a reputable quartet. In 1899 went to Dresden. Violin concertos, sonatas, studies, and some songs.	German.
1859 1 May. Budapest.		**NACHEZ, Tivadar.** Violinist ; pupil of Joachim and Léonard. Toured as a soloist, and settled in London in 1889. Violin solos, many of Hungarian character.	Hungarian
1859 12 June. Turin.	**1928** 19 November.	**SIMONETTI, Achille.** Violinist ; pupil of Gamba, Sivori, and Dancla, and for composition Pedrotti and Massenet. Lived in London, making frequent visits to the Continent. Violin solos, sonatas for violin and piano, and 2 string quartets.	Italian.
1859 15 June. Ceprano.		**GUGLIELMI, Filippo.** Studied at Naples under D'Arienzo, and in Rome under Terziani. Friend of Liszt. Several symphonic works, and operas.	Italian.
1859 Paris.		**LAMBERT, Lucien.** Pupil of Massenet and Dubois. Toured as a virtuoso pianist on the Continent and in America. Operas, comic operas, scene lyrique, orchestral concert pieces, songs, piano pieces, etc.	French.
1859 15 August. Rotterdam.		**HUTSCHENRUYTER, Wouter.** Conductor at Amsterdam, then of the Symphony Orchestra at Utrecht until 1917, when he became director of the Music School at Rotterdam. Overture, suite, Festive March for wind band, sonatas for 'cello and for violin, piano concerto, duets and pieces.	Dutch.
1859 22 September		**BERGH, Rudolph.** Symphony and other orchestral ; choral works, string quartet, 2 violin sonatas, songs, and piano pieces.	Danish.
1859 24 September Leipzig.		**KLENGEL, Julius.** 'Cellist ; pupil of E. Hegar, and of Jadassohn for composition. Principal 'cellist of the Gewandhaus Orchestra, and teacher at the Leipzig Conservatorium in 1881. Toured as a soloist. 'Cello sonata, 4 concertos, solos ; 2 string quartets ; suites and serenades for string orchestra ; and a piano trio.	German.
1859 14 October. Paris.	**1923** 30 May. Chatou, Paris.	**CHEVILLARD, P. A. Camille.** Pupil at the Paris Conservatoire for piano. At the head of the Société Française de musique de chambre. Symphonic-poem, " Ballade symphonique," " Fantaisie symphonique," etc. ; quintet, quartets, trio, sonatas for violin and 'cello, piano pieces, and songs.	French.
1859 22 October. Reggio Emilia.		**ZUELLI, Guglielmo.** Studied at the Liceo, Bologna, under Busi and Mancinelli. Director at the Parma Conservatorio. Operas, symphonies, quartet, and other vocal and instrumental music.	Italian.

Born	Died	Name	Nationality.
1859 1 November. Lismore.		**FLOOD, William Henry Grattan.** Self-taught. Organist at the Cathedrals of Thurles, Monaghan, and Enniscorthy (1895). Many Masses, motets, songs and part-songs, also much musical literature.	Irish.
1859 7 November. Gatchina.	1935 28 January. Moscow.	**IPPOLITOV-IVANOV, Michael Mikhailovich.** Pupil of Rimsky-Korsakov at the Petrograd Conservatorium. Director of the Music School and conductor of the Symphony Orchestra at Tiflis in '82. Professor at the Moscow Conservatorium in 1893, and conductor of the Private Opera in 1899. Orchestral suite, overture and symphonic scherzo; cantatas, operas, quartets, songs, duets, and choruses.	Russian.
1859 17 November. Kristiansand		**SCHJELDERUP, Gerhard Rosenkrone.** Pupil of Massenet at the Paris Conservatoire. Studied philosophy. Gave concerts in Norway as 'cellist. The most eminent music-dramatist of Norway. 10 Operas to his own words, choral works, symphonic-poem, ballads for chorus and orchestra, and songs.	Norwegian.
1859 18 November. Yaraslav.	1924 11 November Paris.	**LIAPOUNOV, Sergius Mikhailovich.** Pupil of the Moscow Conservatorium. Assistant conductor at the Court Chapel (1894-1902). Symphony, Solemn overture, ballade and polonaise for orchestra, piano concerto, preludes, waltzes, etc., and 35 national songs.	Russian.
1859 21 November. Kempsey, n'r Worcester	1900 4 February London.	**HAYNES, Walter Battison.** Pupil of Taylor and Prout in London, Reinecke and Jadassohn at Leipzig. Organist at St. Philip's, Sydenham, in '84, and the Royal Chapel, Savoy, in '91. Professor of harmony and composition at the Royal Academy in 1890. Symphony, overture; 2 cantatas; sonatas, sketches and Idyll for violin; organ sonata and pieces; a piano trio; lyrics and piano music.	English.
1859 21 November. Cheltenham.		**SPEER, Charlton T.** Student at the Royal Academy under G. and W. Macfarren for composition and piano, and Dr. Steggall for organ. Held several posts as organist. Operas, works for chorus and orchestra, symphonic-poem, songs, piano and church music.	English.
1859 9 December. Durham.		**ASHTON, Algernon Bennet Langton.** Pupil of Heinig, Knorr and Raff, also at Leipzig Conservatorium under Reinecke, Richter and Jadassohn. Professor of the piano at the Royal College in 1885. Symphonies, overtures, suites, concertos (violin and piano), quintets, quartets, trios, songs, piano and organ music—about 200 pieces in all.	English.
1859 27 December Elrington, Glos.		**HADOW, Sir William Henry.** Studied at Darmstadt and under C. H. Lloyd. Lecturer and writer on musical subjects. Cantata, anthem, chorus, lyrics, string quartet, violin sonatas and pieces, piano sonatas, and a viola sonata.	English.

Born	Died	Name	Nationality.
1859 30 December Prague.		**FOERSTER, Josef Bohuslav.** Son of Joseph (1833). Studied at the Organ School, Prague. Professor at the Prague Conservatorium in 1918, and its director in 1922. 6 Operas, 4 symphonies, suites and other symphonic works; melodramas, incidental music, much choral music, Stabat Mater, 3 string quartets, trios, 'cello and violin sonata, ballads and songs.	Bohemian.
1860 8 January. Bristol.	**1924** 21 July. Torquay.	**AMES, John Carlowitz.** Pianist. Studied at Stuttgart and Dresden. Opera, 3 comic operas, 2 piano concertos, Psalm for chorus and orchestra, chamber-music, piano pieces, and songs.	English.
1860 16 January Potsdam.		**LIEPE, Emil.** Studied at the Schwantzer Conservatorium at Berlin, and then at Leipzig and Vienna. Singing-master at the Sondershausen Conservatorium. Symphony, symphonic-poems, overture, opera, songs, and piano pieces.	German.
1860 25 February Copenhagen.		**HANSEN, Robert Emil.** 'Cellist; pupil at the Copenhagen Conservatorium. Director of the Philharmonic Concerts at Aarrhus, Jutland. Symphonic works, 'cello concerto, violin sonata, male choruses; trio for flute, violin and 'cello; songs, and 'cello pieces.	Danish.
1860 5 March. Modica.		**FLORIDIA, Pietro.** Studied at the Liceo, Naples, under Cesi, Serrao and L. Rossi. Professor at the Palermo Conservatorio in 1885; then toured as pianist, settling in America in 1904. Operas, suite and pieces for piano, early Italian songs, etc.	Sicilian.
1860 13 March. Windischgräz	**1903** 22 February. Vienna.	**WOLF, Hugo.** The best-known song writer of his time. Studied at the Vienna Conservatorium. Music critic to the Vienna *Salonblatt* in 1886-'70. Many songs, on the poems of Goethe, Eichendorff, Kleist and Mörike; 2 operas, symphonic-poem, string quartet, and a serenade for string orchestra.	Styrian.
1860 22 March. Scanfs.		**BARBLAN, Otto.** Pupil at Stuttgart Conservatorium under Faisst. Organist of St. Peter's Cathedral, Geneva, 1887, and teacher of composition at the Conservatorium. Choruses, ode, and organ works.	Swiss.
1860 10 May. Burslem, Staffs.		**FORRESTER, James Cliffe.** Studied at the National Training School under O'Leary and F. Bridge. Conductor of Ealing Choral Society for 20 years. Cantatas, choruses, many anthems, part-songs, song-cycles, piano trio, violin and piano pieces.	English.
1860 13 May. Nakskov.		**ENNA, August.** Was self-taught except for a year's study in Germany. In early life was violinist and drummer in Finland, later returning to Copenhagen. Operas, operettas, incidental music, overtures, a symphony suite, piano pieces, and a violin concerto.	Danish.

Born	Died	Name	Nationality
1860 16 May or March. Paris.	**1908** 11 October. Paris.	**MARTY, Eugène Georges.** Pupil of Massenet at the Paris Conservatoire. Chorus-master at the Opéra in '93, and conductor at the Conservatoire from 1901. Symphonic-poem, suite, etc. for orchestra ; operas, cantata, pantomime, songs, and piano pieces.	French.
1860 18 May. Southampton.		**WURM, Marie.** Studied the piano and composition at the Stuttgart Conservatorium under Taylor, Mme. Schumann and Raff. Gave piano recitals in England and Germany. Piano concerto and pieces ; orchestral overture, string quartet, and a 'cello sonata.	English.
1860 28 May. Copenhagen.	**1921** 9 November. Copenhagen.	**GADE, Axel.** Son of Niels, W. (1817). Pupil of Tofte, and Joachim in Berlin. Violin professor at the Copenhagen Conservatorium, and a member of the Royal Chapel. Opera, 3 violin concertos, chamber-music, and songs.	Danish.
1860 10 June. Paris.	**1909** 2 June.	**HILLEMACHER, Lucien.** Worked in collaboration with his brother, Paul (1852)	French.
1860 25 June. Dieuze.		**CHARPENTIER, Gustave.** Pupil of the Conservatoire at Lille, and later of Paris Conservatoire under Massart for violin and Massenet for composition. Succeeded Massenet as a member of the Institut in 1912. Orchestral suites ; choruses ; a symphonic-drama for orchestra, soli and chorus ; operas, the most important being the " Roman musical " of "Louise " set to his own libretto.	French.
1860 27 June. Paris.	**1919** Paris.	**FANELLI, Ernest.** Pupil of Alkan and Delibes at the Conservatoire. Earned his living as an orchestral drummer. Several orchestral suites, string quintet, etc.	French.
1860 Greenock. 3 July.		**WALLACE, William (M.Ch.).** Pupil of the Royal Academy. Son of the Scottish surgeon, James Wallace. Served in the great war as captain in the Medical Corps and ophthalmic specialist. Now lives in London. Several symphonic-poems, choral-symphonies, cantatas, orchestral suites, symphonies, a lyric tragedy, several vocal scenas for voice and orchestra, song-cycles, etc. ; also musical and scientific literature, and translations of German and Finnish text.	Scottish.
1860 7 July. Kalischt.	**1911** 18 May. Vienna.	**MAHLER, Gustav.** Pupil at the Vienna Conservatorium. Chapel-master at Prague ; director of the Opera at Pest in 1888 ; chapel-master at the Stadttheater at Hamburg in '91 ; succeeded Jahns at Vienna in '97, and Richter as conductor of the Philharmonic Concerts. Conducted the German opera at Covent Garden in 1892. 6 Symphonies, " Humoresken " for orchestra, cantata, etc.	Bohemian.
1860 September Turin.		**FRANCHETTI, Alberto.** Studied under Coccon and Magi, then Draeseke at Dresden, and later at the Munich Conservatorium. 5 Operas (" Asrael " being the most successful), operetta, symphonic poem, symphony, overtures, quartet, and smaller works.	Italian.

Born	Died	Name	Nationali*
1860 8 October. Troppau.		**WOYRSCH, Felix.** Self-taught in music. At Altona was conductor of the church choir (1894); of the Academy of Singing (1895); organist of St. John's Church, and conductor of Symphony Concerts. 2 Symphonies, overture, violin concerto, operas, many choruses, oratorio, organ works, piano pieces and songs.	German.
1860 23 October. Strasburg.		**ERB, Joseph Marie.** Pupil at the Niedermeyer School, Paris, and of Widor. Organist of St. Jean's, Strasburg, and professor at the Conservatorium. 4 Operas, symphonic-poems, motets, Masses, and many choral works.	French.
1860 6 November Kurylówka.		**PADEREWSKI, Ignas Jan.** The famous pianist. Pupil of Raguski at Warsaw, Urban and Wüerst at Berlin, and finally of Leschetizky at Vienna. Teacher at the Warsaw Conservatorium, 1879-81, and for a short time at Strasburg. First visited England in 1890. President of Poland in 1919 and '20. Opera; piano concerto and pieces; sonata for violin and piano; songs, etc.	Polish.
1860 17 December Beicha.		**FÄHRMANN, E. Hans.** Pupil of Fischer, Scholtz and J. L. Nicodé at Dresden. Organist and cantor at the Johanniskirche, Dresden, and teacher of the organ at the Conservatorium. Symphony, 11 organ sonatas and a concerto, string quartet, trios, piano sonata, and songs.	German.
1860 28 December Leipzig.		**FIELITZ, Alexander Von.** Pupil of Kretschmer and Schulhoff at Dresden. Professor in the Stern Conservatorium, Berlin, and conductor at the Theater des Westens. 2 Operas, 2 suites for orchestra, piano pieces and songs.	German. (Russian parents)
1861 6 January. Graz.		**NOREN, Heinrich Gottlieb.** Violinist; studied in Paris under Massart for violin, and Gernsheim for composition. Founded a conservatorium at Crefeld, abandoned its directorship, and became teacher at Stern's Conservatorium in 1902. Symphony, orchestral variations, violin concerto, suite and sonata; 'cello sonata and pieces; opera, choruses, songs, and piano pieces.	Styrian.
1861 30 January. Mühlhausen.	**1935** 26 May. Medfield, Mass.	**LOEFFLER, Charles Martin Tornov.** Violinist: pupil of Leonard, Massart and Joachim, and for composition, Guiraud and Kiel. Practised at Paris, Nice, New York and Boston. One of the first "Impressionists." Symphonic-poems, suite for violin and orchestra, a 'cello concerto, octet, sextet, and quartets.	German.
1861 21 February. Bar-le-Duc.		**BREVILLE, Pierre Onfroy de.** Pupil of Dubois and César Franck. A member of the Société Nationale de Musique. Orchestral overtures, works for voice and orchestra, organ pieces, motets and other church music; lyric drama, piano sonata, etc.	French.

Born	Died	Name	Nationality
1861 1 March. Halifax.	**1925** 14 October. London.	**SHARPE, Herbert Francis.** Succeeded Eugene d'Albert as Queen's Scholar at the National Training School. Professor at the Royal College in 1884. A Comic opera, overture ; pieces for flute, violin, and one and two pianos ; songs, part-songs and vocal trios.	English.
1861 15 April. Moscow.		**CATOIRE, George Lvovitch.** Pupil of Klindworth (piano), Rüfer and Liadov (composition). Professor of composition at the Moscow Conservatorium. Symphonies, symphonic-poem, piano concerto, choruses, quintets, quartets, trios, violin sonatas, many songs, and piano pieces.	Russian.
1861 25 April. Salò.	**1925** 24 February. At sea.	**BOSSI, Marco Enrico.** Studied at the Liceo Musicale, Bologna, and at the Milan Conservatorio under Ponchielli for composition and Fumagalli for organ. Organist and chapel-master at Como Cathedral in '81 ; professor at Naples Conservatorio in '91 ; director of the Liceo at Venice in '96 ; and director of the Liceo Musicale, Bologna, in 1902. Oratorio, 3 operas, cantatas, motets, Masses, symphonic-poem, overtures, organ concerto and pieces, violin sonata, piano trios, piano music, and songs—over 100 works.	Italian.
1861 25 April. etrograd.	**1932** April. Berlin.	**MEYER-HELMUND, Erik.** Pupil of Stockhausen for singing and Kiel for composition. Toured as a concert singer. Operas, a burlesque opera ; ballets and songs written to his own words.	Russian.
1861 4 May. Vienna.		**REZNIČEK, Emil Nicholaus von.** Pupil of the Leipzig Conservatorium. Theatre conductor at Graz, Zürich, Stettin and Berlin ; military conductor at Prague. Court chapel-master at Weimar and Mannheim. Teacher at the Scharwenka School at Berlin. Conductor of the Warsaw Philharmonic. Operas, symphonies, symphonic-suite, overtures, serenade, fugue, string quartets, a Requiem, pieces for voice and orchestra, a Mass, songs, etc.	Austrian.
1861 9 May. mprodon.	**1909** 16 June. Cambo-les-Bains.	**ALBÉNIZ, Isaac.** Pupil of Marmontel, Jadassohn, Brassin and Liszt for piano, and of Dupont and Gevaert for composition. He did much to elevate Spanish music. Toured as a pianist. Operas (produced in Barcelona and London), much piano music, and songs.	Spanish.
1861 Paris.	**1918** March.	**D'HARCOURT, Eugène.** Studied at the Paris Conservatoire and at Berlin. 3 Symphonies, opera, ballets, cantatas, quartets, and songs.	French.
1861 9 July. berfeld.	**1908** 28 August. Berlin.	**EYKEN, Heinrich.** Studied at Leipzig and Berlin. Teacher of theory at the Hochschule, Berlin, in 1902. Scenas for voice and orchestra, male choruses, serenade, Psalm, and many choral numbers on which his fame rests.	German.

Born	Died	Name	Nationalit
1861 19 July. Cologne.	**1920** June. Berlin.	**LAZARUS, Gustav.** Pupil of the Cologne Conservatorium under Siess, G. Jensen and Wüllner. Teacher at the Scharwenka Academy, Berlin. About 175 various compositions—many piano pieces.	German.
1861 31 July. Novgorod.	**1906** 26 February. Terioki, Finland.	**ARENSKY, Antony Stepanovich.** Pupil of Zikke, and of Rimsky-Korsakov at the Petrograd Conservatorium. Professor of harmony and counterpoint at the Moscow Conservatorium in '82, and conductor of the Russian Choral Society for 7 years. Director of the Imperial Chapel at Petrograd until 1901, when he was succeeded by Smolensky. 3 Operas, cantatas, songs, vocal duets, church music, 2 symphonies, piano concerto, quintet, trio, 2 string quartets, orchestral ballet and a fantasia, about 100 piano pieces, and theoretical works.	Russian.
1861 8 August. Paris.		**CHAMINADE, Cécile.** Pupil of Le Couppey, Savart, Marsick and Godard. Concert pianist, visiting England regularly since 1892. Several orchestral suites, a " Symphonie lyric," a ballet, comic opera, a concertstück for piano, trios, songs, and attractive piano solos.	French.
1861 9 August. Boston, U.S.A.	**1911** 16 January. Meiningen.	**BERGER, Wilhelm.** Pupil of Kiel at the Hochschule, Berlin. Teacher of the piano in Berlin. Visited England in 1904. 2 Symphonies, several choral works with orchestra, vocal solos, part-songs, chamber-music, and piano pieces—about 100 works.	American (German parents
1861 29 November. Corfu.	**1917** April. Athens.	**SAMARA, Spiro.** Pupil of Stancampiano at Athens and afterwards at the Paris Conservatoire under Delibes. Several operas, the best-known being " La Martire," though none were successful.	**Greek.**
1861 30 November. Bozen.	**1907** 5 February. Munich.	**THUILLE, Ludwig.** Pupil of Pembaur and the Munich Academy, and was later influenced by Ritter. Professor at the Munich School of Music in 1883, and conductor of the " Liederhort "—a male choir. Several operas ; choruses, for male and female choirs ; sextet, quintet, sonata for 'cello, piano works, and songs.	Austrian
1861 17 December Wipperfürth.		**VOLBACH, Fritz.** Pupil of the Royal Institute for Church-music. Music Director at Mainz in 1892, conducting the Oratorio Society and the Handel Society. Professor at Münster University in 1919. Symphonic-poems, choral ballads ; 4 ballads for soli, chorus and orchestra ; a Spring-Poem for orchestra ; a quintet for wind and piano, etc.	German

Born	Died	Name	Nationality.
1861 18 December New York.	**1907** 24 January. New York.	**MacDOWELL, Edward Alexander.** The greatest American-born composer. Studied in America, at the Paris Conservatoire, Stuttgart, and at Wiesbaden under Raff. Chief teacher at the Darmstadt Conservatorium until '87, when he settled at Boston. Filled the chair at the Columbia University, New York, from 1896 to 1904. Symphonic-poems, orchestral suites, etc. ; piano concertos, suites, poems, concert studies, sonatas, etc. ; choruses for male voices ; songs and part-songs—about 70 works.	American.
1862 29 January. Bradford.	**1934** 10 June. Grez-sur-Loing, n'r Paris.	**DELIUS, Frederick.** Studied at the Leipzig Conservatorium under Jadassohn and Reinecke, later being influenced by Grieg. Lived chiefly in France. Sojourn in Florida 1881. Was blind and bedridden for some years before death. The promotion of Delius's music in England is mainly due to the efforts of Sir Thomas Beecham, the great conductor Operas, incidental music, symphonic-poems, choruses, songs, piano concertos, sonatas and solos ; violin concertos, sonatas, and pieces, and all branches of composition. His greatest work, " A Mass of Life," is the most religious work of modern times.	English. (German parents).
1862 30 January. Breslau.		**DAMROSCH, Walter Johannes.** Pupil of his father, Leopold (1832), Rischbieter and Draeseke at Dresden, and Max Pinner at New York. Assisted his father as conductor of the German Opera at New York, and succeeded him as conductor of the Oratorio and Symphony Societies. 2 Operas, a Te Deum, a violin sonata, and several songs.	German.
1862 17 February. Whitchurch, Shropshire.	**1936** 11 November. London.	**GERMAN, Sir Jones Edward.** Student of the Royal Academy under Steggall (organ), Weist-Hill and Burnett (violin). As a composer of light English music he was the successor of Sullivan. Conductor at the Globe Theatre in 1888. A Fellow of the Royal Academy in '95. A member of the Philharmonic Society in 1901, and received the gold medal of that Society in 1934. Operas, operettas, incidental music, symphonic-poem, symphonic suites, symphonies ; music for piano, violin, flute, songs and part-songs.	English.
1862 10 March. Charleroi.		**LE BOME, Fernand.** Pupil of Massenet, Saint-Saëns and César Franck. Critic to the " Petit Parisien." Operas, lyric dramas, symphonic legend ; orchestral suite, symphonic overtures, symphonie-concerto for piano, violin and orchestra ; string quartet, trio, violin sonata ; a Mass, and motets.	Belgian. (French school.)
1862 8 April. Stettin.		**BEHM, Edward.** Pupil at the Leipzig Conservatorium, and of Raif and Kiel at Berlin. Director of the Schwantzer Conservatorium, Berlin. Symphony ; piano concerto ; concerto, sonatas and suite for violin ; quintet and sextet ; 3 operas ; glees, and songs,	German.

Born	Died	Name	Nationality.
1862 21 June. Newark, N.J		**HUSS, Henry Holden.** Studied at Munich under Giehrl and Rheinberger. Concerto and Rhapsody for piano, string quartet, violin sonata, choruses, many piano pieces and songs.	American.
1862 Granada.		**BARRIOS, Angel.** A guitar-player. Founder of the Trio Iberia. Pupil of Segura, Gédalge and C. del Campo. 2 Operas, incidental music, symphonic-poem, etc.	Spanish.
1862 San Juan.		**BERUTTI, Arturo.** Studied under Reinecke and Jadassohn at Leipzig. 7 Operas, and stage works—*the first of National character*—one with own libretto ; violin and piano pieces.	**Argentine.**
1862 Prague.	**1920** Prague.	**KOVAŘOVIC, Karel.** Studied clarinet at the Prague Conservatorium. Chief conductor at the National Theatre, Prague, in 1900. Several operas, melodramas, 7 ballets, symphonic-poem, string quartets, piano concerto, violin sonata, etc.	Bohemian.
1862 Budapest ?		**MOOR, Emanuel.** Studied in Budapest and Vienna. Toured U.S. as Director of Concerts Artistiques, Invented the Duplex-Coupler piano which was demonstrated in London by Tovey. Operas, 7 symphonies, piano concerto, Rhapsody for violin and orchestra, chamber-music, piano pieces, and songs—about 120 works.	Hungarian.
1862 Buenos Ayres.		**WILLIAMS, Alberto.** Studied at Buenos Ayres, and the Paris Conservatoire. Founded the Conservatoire at Buenos Ayres which has about 100 branches throughout Argentine. A notorious poet. 3 Symphonies, 3 suites, overtures, 20 choruses ; many sonatas for violin, 'cello and flute ; 146 piano pieces, and many songs to own words.	Argentine.
1862 3 July. Berlin.		**KOCH, Friedrich E.** 'Cellist of the Royal Court Orchestra, 1883-91. Director of department for theory at the Royal High School, Berlin (1917). 3 Operas, 2 symphonies, symphonic-fugue, suite, violin concerto, chamber-cantata, choruses, string trios, organ works, and songs.	German.
1862 11 July. London.	**1918** 19 September Pinner.	**LEHMANN, Elizabetta (Liza) Nina Mary Fredericka.** Studied singing with her mother and Randegger, and composition with Raunkilde at Rome, and Freudenberg at Wiesbaden. Gave her farewell vocal concert at St. James's Hall on July 14th, 1894. Song-cycles, musical comedy, pianoforte pieces, incidental music, and ballads for voice and orchestra.	English.
1862 10 August. St. Louis, Mo.		**KROEGER, Ernest Richard.** Educated in America only. Organist of Delmar Baptist Church, and conductor of the Morning Choral Club. Orchestral works, choruses, piano sonata, concert studies and many pieces ; violin sonata, and songs.	American.

Born	Died	Name	Nationality
1862 22 August. t. Germain- en-Laye.	**1918** 26 March. Paris.	**DEBUSSY, Claude Achille.** The inventor of " Impressionism " in piano music. The ultra modern tendency of his works aroused much discussion. Pupil of the Paris Conservatoire under Guiraud. Conducted in London in 1909. His "L'Enfant Prodigue" was produced at Sheffield in 1908, and "Pelléas et Mélisande" was given at Paris in 1902, and at Covent Garden in 1909. Lyric drama, cantata, chorus, orchestral suite and 2 other pieces, etc. ; string quartet, lyrics, many songs, piano suites and many solos.	French.
1862 8 September Moscow.	**1933** September. Moscow.	**KONIUS, George Edwardovich.** Harpist. Pupil of his father, and later of the Moscow Conservatory under Taneiev and Arensky. Professor at the Moscow Conservatory from 1891 to 1899, and again from 1918. Professor at the Music School of the Philharmonic Society in 1902. Symphonic-poems, suite, ballet, cantata, 20 piano pieces, and many songs.	Russian.
1862 5 September Insisheim.	**1897** 11 October. Paris.	**BOËLLMANN, Léon.** Pupil of Gigout at the Niedermeyer School in Paris. Organist at the church of St. Vincent de Paul, Paris. A symphony, symphonic-variations for 'cello and orchestra, quartet, trio, sonata for 'cello and piano, suites for organ and organ with orchestra, much church music, songs, and piano pieces.	French.
1862 1 October. Hanover.		**LORENZ, Julius.** Studied at the Leipzig Conservatorium under Reinecke, Paul and Jadassohn. Royal Prussian Music-director in 1903. Opera, cantata, overtures, string quartet, trio, Psalm, songs, and piano pieces.	German.
1862 10 October. Louvain.		**DE GREEF, Arthur.** Pianist. Pupil of Brassin at the Brussels Conservatoire, and of Liszt at Weimar. Professor of the piano and Brussels Conservatoire in 1885. Toured as solo-pianist. Piano concerto, orchestral suite, songs and piano pieces.	Belgian.
1862 15 October. Buchwald.		**ANSORGE, Conrad.** Pupil of the Leipzig Conservatorium and of Liszt. Pianist and teacher. Piano concerto, 3 sonatas, string quartets, sextet, Requiem for male voices and orchestra, orchestral and piano pieces.	German.
1862 November. Utrecht.		**WAGENAAR, Johan (Mus.D.).** Studied under Hol at Utrecht, and Herzogenberg at Berlin. Organist at Utrecht Cathedral in 1888. Director of Music School, Utrecht, in 1904, and of the Royal Academy of Music, The Hague, in 1919. Conductor of several choral societies in Holland. Operas, symphonic-poem, overtures, symphonietta, songs, etc.	Dutch.
1862 5 November. Edgeworth, Penn.	**1901** 17 February. New Haven.	**NEVIN, Ethelbert Woodbridge.** Studied under Lang and Emery at Boston ; Klindworth and Von Bülow at Berlin. Songs, many piano pieces, duets and suites, and a pantomime.	American.

Born	Died	Name	Nationality
1862 29 November. Carlsruhe.		**KLOSE, Friedrich.** Studied under V. Lachner and Ruthardt at Geneva, and Bruckner in Vienna. Succeeded Thuille at the Royal Academy, Munich, until 1920. Living now at Thun in Switzerland. Oratorio, choruses, symphonic-poem and other orchestral pieces; Mass, string quartet, organ fugues, etc.	German.
1863 23 February. Leuben.		**HEYDRICH, R. Bruno.** Studied at the Dresden Conservatorium. Singer and contrabassist. Symphony, other orchestral, choruses with orchestra, string quartets, trio, clarinet sonata, quintet, piano pieces, and operas.	German.
1863 21 March. Berlin.	**1932** 2 April. Berlin.	**KAUN, Hugo.** Studied under Schulz and Kiel. Teacher of composition at the Klindworth-Scharwenka Conservatorium, Berlin. Symphonies, symphonic-poems, overture, suite, piano concerto, 3 operas, choruses, many string quartets, quintets, octets (one for wind), violin sonata, etc.—about 120 works.	German.
1863 7 April. Kherson.		**BLUMENFELD, Felix Michaelovitch.** Pupil of his father and Rimsky-Korsokov. Professor at the Petrograd Conservatory from 1885 till 1918. Symphony; concert-allegro for piano and orchestra; string quartet, *piano pieces*, and songs.	Russian.
1863 21 April. Ghent.	**1920** 4 November. Louvain.	**LEBRUN, Paul Henri Joseph.** Studied at the Ghent Conservatoire, where he became professor in 1890. Symphonic-poem, symphony, opera, lyric-poem, string quartet, etc.	Belgian.
1863 2 May. London.		**BUNNING, Herbert.** Studied in London, Hanover, Harrow, and Milan. Obtained a commission in the 4th Hussars in 1884. Musical director at the Lyric Theatre in '92, and subsequently at the Prince of Wales', '94-6. Operas, overtures, orchestral suites and pieces, scena for baritone and orchestra, and various vocal and instrumental pieces.	English.
1863 5 May. Andover.		**BENNETT, George John.** Studied at the Royal Academy; the Hochschule at Berlin, and at Munich. Organist of Lincoln Cathedral in 1895, and conductor of the Musical and Orchestral Societies and the Musical Festivals in that city. Serenade for orchestra, suite, overture; services, Mass and Hymn with orchestral accompaniment, and a piano trio.	English.
1863 8 May. Maestricht.		**SMULDERS, Carl.** A virtuoso-pianist who demonstrated the Hans keyboard. Studied at the Liège Conservatoire. 3 Symphonic-poems, ballad for orchestra, piano concerto and sonata, cantata, male choruses, songs, and piano pieces.	Dutch. (Naturalised Belgian).

Born	Died	Name	Nationality
1863 12 May. Vouvray-sur-Loire.	**1909** 8 November. Toulon.	**BORDES, Charles.** Pupil of Franck. Chapel-master at Nogent-sur-Marne in '87 and at St. Gervais, Paris, in '90. Founded an association for the study of old church music. Orchestral, chamber, and choral works, also a musical drama.	French.
1863 25 May. Paris.	**1919** 24 April. Paris.	**ERLANGER, Camille.** Studied piano and composition under Mathias, Durand, and Delibes and the Conservatoire, Paris. Operas, Idyl, a dramatic legend, cantata ; serenade and poems for orchestra ; songs and piano pieces.	French.
1863 2 June. Zara. (Dalmatia.)		**WEINGARTNER, Paul Felix.** Studied at Graz with Remy, and at the Leipzig Conservatorium. Chapel-master at Königsberg '84, Danzig in '85, Hamburg '87, Mannheim '89, Berlin in '91, and Vienna, 1907. Visited England first in 1898. Operas, 4 symphonies, quintets, quartets, sonatas, symphonic-poems, many songs, choral and piano works.	Austrian.
1863 5 June. Windermere.		**SOMERVELL, Sir Arthur (Mus.D.).** Studied under Stanford at Cambridge ; Kiel and Bargiel at Berlin ; at the Royal College ; and was a private pupil of Parry. Succeeded Stainer in 1901 as Inspector of Music for England, Wales and Scotland. Sacred and secular choral works, a Mass, songs, orchestral suites and ballad, piano pieces and studies, piano concerto, operettas, violin suites, etc.	English.
1863 13 June. Cattaro.		**WÖSS, Joseph Venantius von.** Studied at the Vienna Conservatorium under Krenn. Editor, teacher and conductor in Vienna. 7 Masses, motets, Requiem, Te Deums for chorus and orchestra, symphonies, overtures, operas, male choruses, and songs.	Austrian.
1863 Norwich.	**1922**	**ARKWRIGHT, Marian Ursula (Mus.D.).** Specialised in rural music. Orchestral suites, Requiem-mass, choruses, operetta and chamber-music for wood wind.	English.
1863 14 July. Volmar.		**WIHTOL or VITOLS, Joseph.** Studied under Johansen and Rimsky-Korsakov at the Petrograd Conservatory, where he was professor in 1886 until the Russian revolution. Director of the Riga Conservatory. Many works founded on Latvian folk-tunes. Symphonic-poem, overtures, choruses, string quartet, piano sonata, songs, etc.	**Latvian.**
1863 16 August. Metz.		**PIERNÉ, Henry Constant Gabriel.** Pupil of the Paris Conservatoire under Marmontel, César Franck and Massenet. Succeeded Franck as organist of St. Clotilde in 1890. Oratorios, operas (grand and comic) ; symphonic-poem ; concertstück for harp and orchestra ; songs ; instrumental pieces ; choral and orchestral works.	French.

Born	Died	Name	Nationality.
1863 27 August. Foggia.		**GIORDANO, Umberto.** Pupil of Serrao at the Naples Conservatorio. Several operas, the most successful being " Andrea Chénier", given in Italy, Berlin and London.	Italian.
1863 15 September Auburndale, Mass.	1919 18 December Cederhurst, N.Y.	**PARKER,** Horatio William (**Mus.D.**). Pupil of his mother, Emery, Orth and Chadwick in U.S., and Rheinberger at Munich. Organist of Holy Trinity Church, Boston, and later at New York. Professor of Music at Yale University in 1894. Oratorio, cantatas, choruses, odes, songs, symphonies, symphonic-poem, overture, organ concerto, quintet, quartets, suite for violin and piano, church services, piano and organ pieces, and operas.	American. (English ancestry).
1863 11 October. Velletri, Paris.	1919 2 February. Paris.	**LEROUX, Xavier Henry Napoleon.** Pupil of the Paris Conservatoire under Massenet. Operas, incidental music, cantata, overture, a lyric scene, motets, Mass with orchestra, and songs.	Italian.
1863 27 October. St. Oswald, Durham.		**DYKES, John St. Oswald.** Son of the Rev. John. Pianist, pupil of Mme. Schumann. Professor of the piano at the Royal College since 1887. Various works.	English.
1863 9 November. London.		**SPEER, William Henry.** Pupil of Dr. Lloyd, and at the Royal College under Parratt and Stanford. Organist at the Parish Church, Bexhill, in 1903. Symphony, overture, rhapsody, quartet, songs, a ballad for chorus and small orchestra, piano and organ sonatas, etc.	English.
1863 7 December. Leghorn.		**MASCAGNI, Pietro.** Pupil of Soffredini, Ponchielli and Saladino. Director of the Conservatorio at Pesaro from 1895 to 1903. Toured much as conductor of opera-companies and orchestras. Operas, including " Cavalleria Rusticana," " Zanetto " and " L'Amico Fritz " ; symphonies, cantatas, odes, and incidental music to Hall Caine's " The Eternal City."	Italian.
1863 25 December Madrid.		**ARBÓS, Enrique Fernandez.** Violinist ; pupil of Monasterio, Vieuxtemps and Joachim. Toured as a soloist and leader. Professor at the Madrid Conservatoire, and later at the Royal College, London. Violin solos with orchestra, a comic opera, 3 trios, orchestral suite, and songs.	Spanish.
1864 26 February. Paris.		**BACHELET, Alfred.** Studied at the Paris Conservatoire. Conductor of the Opéra orchestra during the Great War, and afterwards Principal of the Conservatoire at Nancy. Operas, lyrical dramas, symphonic-poems, songs, etc.	French.

RICHARD STRAUSS.

Born	Died	Name	Nationality.
1864 15 March. Drammen.	**1936** December. Oslo.	**HALVORSEN, Johan.** Studied the violin at the Stockholm Conservatorium and with C. Thomson at Liège. Conductor at the National Theatre in Christiania since 1899, and has toured the capitals. Much theatrical music, arranged also in concert-form ; orchestral works, choruses, violin and viola pieces.	Norwegian.
1864 23 March. Copenhagen.	**1936** February. Copenhagen.	**GLASS, Louis Christian August.** Pupil of his father, N. W. Gade, and Servais at the Brussels Conservatoire. Conductor of the Danish Concert Association. Symphonies, suites, sextets, quartets, trios, violin and piano sonatas, piano pieces and songs.	Danish.
1864 23 March. Christiania.		**BORGSTRÖM, Hjalmar.** Studied under Svendsen, and afterwards at Leipzig, Berlin, London and Paris. Musical-critic. 2 Operas, 5 symphonic-poems, 2 symphonies, piano concerto, quartets, quintets, songs and piano pieces.	Norwegian.
1864 10 April. Glasgow.	**1932** 3 March. Riga.	**ALBERT, Eugène Francis Charles.** Son of C. L. N. (1809). Pupil of Pauer, Prout, Stainer and Sullivan at the National Training School, London ; and of Liszt at Weimar, where he afterwards became chapel-master. 2 Piano concertos, symphony, overtures ; suite and sonata for piano, 2 string quartets, a six-part chorus, 16 operas, and a one-act tragedy.	Scottish.
1864 May. Pennsylvania.	**1894** 29 March. Hampstead.	**PARRY, Joseph Haydn.** Son of Joseph (1841). Professor at the Guildhall School of Music in 1890. Cantata, comic operas, and sonatas for piano.	American. (Welsh descent.)
1864 11 June. Munich.		**STRAUSS, Richard (Dr.).** The greatest living composer (1937). Studied at the Gymnasium at Munich and under F. W. Meyer. Court chapel-master at Munich in 1894 and at Berlin in 1899. Toured as pianist and as conductor. Visited London in '97 as conductor. A "Strauss Festival" was given in St. James' Hall in 1903. His compositions cover several periods, from the classic to the ultra-modern type, the latter exciting controversy among critics. Several operas, tone-poems for orchestra, symphonies symphonic-variations, violin concerto, horn concerto, string quartet, choruses, sonatas, piano works, songs, and part-songs.	German.
1864 15 June. Quingamp.		**ROPARTZ, J. Guy.** Pupil in the Paris Conservatoire under Dubois, Massenet and C. Franck. Director of the Conservatoire at Nancy, and conductor of the symphony concerts there. Director of the Strasburg Conservatoire in 1919. Operas, incidental music, symphony, serenade, suite, march, string quartet, church music, songs, organ and piano music.	French.

Born	Died	Name	Nationality
1864 29 June. Kohlberg.		**BEER-WALBRUNN, Anton.** Pupil of the Academy at Munich ; teacher there in 1901, and professor in 1908. 3 Operas, incidental music, orchestral works, quartets, violin sonatas, and a song cycle of Shakespeare's sonnets.	German.
1864 8 July. Oranienbaum.		**KOCHETOV, Nicholas Razoumnikovich.** Self-taught ; music critic. Opera, symphony, orchestral suite, serenade for strings, many piano pieces and songs.	Russian.
1864 13 October. Moscow.		**GRECHANINOV, Alexander Tikhonovich.** Pupil of Safonov at the Moscow Conservatorium, and of Rimsky-Korsokov at Petrograd. 12 Choruses ; many songs ; a musical picture for bass solo, chorus and orchestra ; string quartets, sacred works, incidental music, 4 symphonies, and operas—about 100 works.	Russian.
1864 25 December Lucerne.		**LAUBER, Joseph.** Studied under Hegar at Zurich, Rheinberger at Munich, and Massenet at Paris. Professor of composition at the Geneva Conservatory, and conductor of the Opera there. 5 Symphonies, symphonic-poems, 2 piano concertos, 2 violin concertos, 2 oratorios, chamber-music, and songs.	Swiss.
1864 26 December Schwerin.		**BERWALD, William Henry.** Studied under Rheinberger and Faisst. Professor of piano and composition at the University of Syracuse, New York. Many anthems, and over 70 piano pieces.	German.
1864 29 December Edenbridge, Kent.		**ALCOCK, Sir Walter Galpin (Mus.D.).** Studied under Sullivan, Stainer and Barnett. Organist of the Chapels Royal 1902-16, and assistant at Westminster Abbey from 1896 to 1916, officiating at the Coronations of Kings Edward and George. Organist of Salisbury Cathedral, 1917. Much church and organ music.	English.
1865 21 January. Shirehampton, Glos.	**1935** 19 July. King's Weston Estate, Glos.	**MILES, Philip Napier, L.L.D.** Studied under Draeseke, Schreyer and Roth in Germany, and Parry and Dannreuther in England. Devoted himself to the encouragement of music, and was responsible for the first performances of many new works at Bristol, Clifton, and at his own estate. 6 Operas (including "Westward Ho !"), lyric overture, orchestral fantasia, choruses with orchestra, part-songs, and songs on words by Masefield, etc.	English.
1865 22 January. Posen.		**ERTEL, J. Paul.** Pupil of Brassin and Liszt. Critic. Operas, symphony, symphonic-poems ; violin concerto, sonata and suites ; quartets ; fugues for organ ; piano pieces, and songs.	German.
1865 5 February. Brooklyn,		**LOOMIS, Harvey Worthington.** Studied composition under Dvořák at the National Conservatory, New York. 5 Operas, several pantomimes, plays ; Hungarian Rhapsody, and other pieces for piano ; songs and part-songs—about 100 works.	American.

Born	Died	Name	Nationality
1865 2 October. Blackburn.	**1931** 23 July. London.	**WOLSTENHOLME, William.** Studied music with Dr. Done at the College for the Blind at Worcester and was aided by Elgar. Organist at King's Weigh-House Chapel, London, in 1902, and at All Saints', Norfolk Square, in 1904. 60 Organ works, piano sonatas and pieces, choral ballad, anthems, songs, part-songs, string quartets, quintets, trios, solos for violin, viola and 'cello, etc.	English.
1865 29 March. Liverpool.		**MACPHERSON, Stewart.** Pupil of G. A. and W. Macfarren at the Royal Academy, where he was appointed professor of harmony and composition in 1887. Conductor of the Westminster Orchestral Society, 1885-1902, and the Streatham Choral Society 1886-1904. Succeeded Corder at the Royal Normal College for the Blind in 1903. Symphony, overtures, violin concerto, Mass, services, songs, piano pieces, and *theoretical works*.	English.
1865 9 May. Merchtem.		**DE BOECK, Auguste.** Pupil of Dupont, Mailly and Kufferath at Brussels Conservatoire, where he became teacher of harmony. Operas and other stage music ; symphonic works, cantatas, choruses, Masses, motets, many songs, and piano pieces.	Belgian.
1865 20 May. Dublin.	**1920** 31 January. Hawarden.	**COLLISSON, Rev. William Alexander Houston (Mus.D.).** Studied at Trinity College, Dublin. Organist in Dublin, and came to London in 1901. Comic operas, cantatas, Irish suite, and songs.	Irish.
1865 9 June. Paris.	**1914** 3 September. Baron, Oise. (killed.)	**MAGNARD, Lucien Denis Gabriel Albéric.** Pupil of Dubois and Massenet at the Conservatoire, and later of d'Indy. Operas (libretti by himself), 4 symphonies, suites, overtures, string quartets, quintets, trios, violin and 'cello sonatas.	French.
1865 9 June. Odense.		**NIELSEN, Carl August.** Studied at the Royal Conservatoire, Copenhagen. Violinist of the Royal Chapel, 1889-1905. Succeeded Neruda as conductor of the Music Society in 1915. 5 Symphonies, overture, 2 operas, 4 string quartets, violin concerto and sonatas, a choral work, songs and ballads.	Danish.
1865 15 June. Brussels.		**GILSON, Paul.** Pupil of Cantillon, Duyck and Gevaert. Professor of harmony at the Conservatoire Royal at Antwerp from 1902. Inspector of musical education in Belgium in 1909. Oratorio, cantatas, choruses, a symphonic work, " La Mer " ; opera, ballet, incidental music, and songs with orchestra ; also educational works.	Belgian.
1865 21 June. Gloucester.	**1928** March.	**BREWER, Alfred Herbert (Dr.).** Pupil of C. H. Lloyd and Parratt. The first of these he succeeded as organist and choirmaster of Gloucester Cathedral in '96, and the latter at St. Giles' Church, Oxford, in 1882. Conducted several societies at Gloucester, and the Musical Festivals of 1898 and 1901. Choruses, odes, services, church music, part-songs, organ music, violin pieces, etc.	English.

Born	Died	Name	Nationalit
1865 Burgo de Osma.	1909 11 February. Madrid.	**OLMEDA DE SAN JOSÉ, Father Federico.** Organist at Tudela Cathedral in 1887, that of Burgos in 1888, and choir-master at the Convent of Descalzas Reales, Madrid, from 1903. Musicologist, historian, etc. 4 Symphonies, symphonic-poem, works for string orchestra, string quartet, piano sonatas, solos, etc.—350 works.	Spanish.
1865 6 July. Vienna.		**JAQUES-DALCROZE, Émile.** Pupil of Fuchs and Bruckner at Vienna, and of Delibes at Paris. Lecturer, critic, and professor of harmony at the Geneva Conservatorio. Operas, lyric comedies, choruses with orchestra, 2 violin concertos and many solos, string quartet, and songs.	Austrian (Swiss descent.
1865 21 July. Mannheim.		**KAHN, Robert.** Studied with Lachner at Mannheim., Kiel at Berlin, and Rheinberger at Munich. Teacher of composition at the Hochschule, Berlin. Chorus with orchestra, string quartets, trios, sonatas for violin and piano, songs, duets and piano solos—about 100 works.	German.
1865 29 July. Petrograd.	1936 23 March. Paris.	**GLAZOUNOV, Alexander Constantinovich.** Pupil of Elenovsky and Rimsky-Korsakov. Professor at the Petrograd Conservatoire in 1900, and its Director in 1906. Conducted at the Paris Exhibition in 1889, and frequently conducted the Russian Symphony Concerts at Petrograd. 7 Symphonies, suites, symphonic-poems, fantasias, serenades, elegy, marches, lyric poem, etc., for orchestra; string quartets, piano sonatas and pieces, instrumental pieces, and songs.	Russian.
1865 9 September. Ventnor, I. of W.	1934 25 September Los Angeles.	**LEMARE, Edwin Henry.** Studied at the Royal Academy. Organist at several London churches, including St. Margaret's, Westminster, and also at Pittsburg, U.S. One of the most brilliant organists of his time. Organ works and arrangements.	English.
1865 11 September Hull.		**HOLLINS, Alfred. (Mus.D.).** Pupil of E. J. Hopkins, Von Bülow and Raff. Blind organist and pianist, in which capacity he toured greatly. Organist at London and Edinburgh, and was professor at the Royal Normal College for the Blind. Organ overtures and pieces, anthems, romance for violin and piano, songs, vocal trios and piano pieces.	English.
1865 1 October. Paris.	1935 May. Paris.	**DUKAS, Paul.** Pupil at the Conservatoire under Guiraud. Critic. Officer of the Legion of Honour, etc. His life was uneventful. Lyric drama, cantatas, choruses, symphony, a symphonic-poem, overtures, piano sonatas, variations, etc.	French.

Born	Died	Name	Nationality
1865 3 December. Tavastehus.		**SIBELIUS, Jean.** The greatest Finnish composer. Pupil of Wegelius at the Helsingfors Conservatorium, of Becker at Berlin, and of Goldmark at Vienna. Principal of the Conservatorium at Helsingfors. His works are of national character and are unique in that respect. Tone poems, including "Finlandia;" 6 symphonies, symphonic-poems, symphony fantasias, suites, overtures, legend, "The Swan of Tuonela"; incidental music, violin concerto, choruses and songs.	Finnish.
1866 1 January. Orel.	**1900** 29 December. Yalta.	**KALINNIKOV, Basil Sergeivich.** Studied at the School of the Philharmonic Society, Moscow, under Ilyinsky and Blaramberg. 2 Symphonies, 2 symphonic sketches, suite, 2 intermezzi, incidental music, string quartet; ballad for solo, chorus and orchestra; songs and piano pieces.	Russian.
1866 9 February. Christine-hamn.		**BECKMAN, Bror.** Pupil of J. Lindegren. Member of the Royal Academy, Stockholm, in 1904, and director of the Royal Conservatorium, Stockholm, in 1910. 3 Symphonic-ballades, symphony, pieces for string band, violin sonata, and piano pieces.	Swedish.
1866 28 March. Berlin.	**1921** 26 January. Berlin.	**DÖBBER, Johannes.** Pupil at Stern's Conservatorium. Critic, teacher of singing and conductor in Darmstadt, Coburg and Berlin. Operas, operettas, ballet, symphonic works, and songs.	German.
1866 1 April. Empoli, n'r Florence.	**1924** 27 July. Berlin.	**BUSONI, Ferruccio Benvenuto.** Pupil of his mother, Hans Schmitt at Graz, and W. A. Remy. Toured as a concert pianist through Europe, America and England. Professor at Helsingfors in '89, in Berlin, 1894 to 1914, Zurich '15 to '19, and returned to Berlin in 1920. Orchestral suite, concertos for violin and piano, string quartets, a concertstück and many piano pieces, operas, symphonic works, and literature.	Italian.
1866 20 April. Leobschütz.		**HOLLÄNDER, Victor.** Brother of Gustave. Pupil of Kullak. Musical director of the Metropol Theater, Berlin. Comic operas, and piano pieces.	German.
1866 13 May. Fehertemp-lom.	**1900** 3 February. New York.	**NOVAČEK, Ottokar.** Violinist; pupil of Dont, Schradieck and Brodsky. 3 String quartets, piano concerto and concerto caprices, Bulgarian dances for violin, pieces, and songs.	Hungarian.
1866 19 May. Krasnoyarsk.	**1920** December. Yalta.	**REBIKOF, Vladimir Ivanovitch.** Studied at the Moscow Conservatory, and later in Berlin under Mühler. *The first to use the "whole tone scale" in practical work.* Taught in Berlin and Vienna. Operas, dramas, sacred works, music with miming, and songs with miming.	Siberian.

Born	Died	Name	Nationalit
1866 15 June. Armagh.	**1926** 12 July. Cambridge.	**WOOD, Charles (Mus.D.).** Pupil of Marks, and at the Royal College under Stanford, Bridge and F. Taylor. Teacher of harmony at the Royal College in 1888 ; conductor of the Cambridge University Musical Society, 1888-94, and was organist-scholar of Gonville and Caius College, '89 to '94. Professor at Cambridge University in '24. Symphonic-variations ; odes for solo, chorus and orchestra ; choruses, songs and folk-songs.	Irish.
1866 Sidney.		**CLUTSUM, George H.** Toured as pianist. Music critic in London. Operas, light operas (including "Lilac-time," arrangement of themes by Schubert) ; piano pieces, and songs.	**Australian**
1866 Sale, Cheshire.	**1920** 26 June. Sale.	**DUNCAN, William Edmonstoune.** Pupil of Parry and Stanford at the Royal College, and later of Macfarren. Critic. Operas, an ode for chorus and orchestra, sonnet for voice and orchestra, overture, trio, etc.	English.
1866 29 July. Palmi.		**CILEA, Francesco.** Studied at the Naples Conservatorio under Cesi (piano) and Serrao (composition). Professor at the Reale Istituto Musicale, Florence, from 1896 to 1904. Director of Palermo Conservatorio, and later of that at Naples. Operas, orchestral suite, trio, 'cello sonata and much piano music.	Italian.
1866 20 September Aigle.		**DORET, Gustave.** Studied at the Paris Conservatoire under Dubois and Massenet (composition) and Marsick (violin). A musical essayist. Operas, incidental music, oratorio, cantata, choruses, and songs.	Swiss.
1866 23 September Aigle.		**COMBE, Edouard.** Pupil of Guilmant in Paris. Initiated the Association of Swiss Musicians. A musicologist. Symphonic-poem, serenade, overture, ode, choruses, and songs.	Swiss.
1866 3 October. Edinburgh.	**1909** 18 June. Edinburgh.	**DRYSDALE, F. Learmont.** Pupil at the Royal Academy. Was an architect. Organist and conductor in London and in Scotland. Overtures, ballad, prelude, opera, musical play, a cantata, songs and piano pieces. 10 Operas are in manuscript.	Scottish.
1866 10 October. Dresden.		**KASKEL, Karl Freiherr, von.** Studied at Leipzig under Reinecke and Jadassohn, and at Cologne under Wüllner. Several operas, operetta, and orchestral ballad.	German.
1866 19 October. Niagara.		**LUCAS, Clarence.** Studied at Montreal, and at Paris under Marty and Dubois. Professor and organist in Canada until he settled in London in 1893, acting as critic, and conductor of the Westminster Choral Society, etc. Operas, oratorios and cantatas ; symphony, symphonic-poems, overtures, 40 piano pieces, organ and string works, and about 100 songs.	**Canadian** (Dutch an Irish extraction)

Born	Died	Name	Nationality
1866 25 October. Königstein.		**SCHUMANN, Georg Alfred (Ph.D.).** Studied at Dresden and at the Leipzig Conservatorium. Conductor of the Dantzig Choral Union in 1890, the Bremen Philharmonic Orchestra in 1896 and the Berlin Academy of Singing in 1900. Chairman of the Advanced School of Composition in 1913, succeeding Max Bruch. Symphonies, symphonic-variations, suite, overtures, choral works with orchestra, quintets, quartets, trios, violin and 'cello sonatas, organ and piano works.	German.
1866 31 October. London.		**PAUER, Max.** Son of Ernst; pupil of V. Lachner. Concert pianist. Professor at Cologne and Stuttgart Conservatoriums. " Kammervirtuos " to the Grand Duke of Hesse. Pianoforte pieces, and arrangements.	English.
1866 9 November. Berlin.		**BAUSSNERN, Waldemar von.** Pupil of the Hochschule, Berlin. Director of the Hoch Conservatorium, Frankfort, from 1916. 6 Operas, 6 symphonies, chamber music, piano pieces and songs.	German.
1866 3 December. Erie, Pa.		**BURLEIGH, Harry Thacker.** Pupil at the National Conservatory under Dvořák. Principal baritone of St. George's Episcopal Church, New York. Over 100 songs and arrangements of Negro spirituals.	American. (Negro.)
1867 19 January. Naples.		**LEVA, Enrico de.** Studied at the Naples Conservatorio under Pannain and Rossomandi for piano, and Puzone and D'Arienzo for composition. A teacher of singing and writer on musical subjects. Over 100 songs, orchestral suites, choruses, violin and piano pieces, and an opera.	Italian.
1867 23 January. London.		**BEDFORD, Herbert.** Husband of Liza Lehmann. Lecturer and painter. The first English composer to receive the Brahms medal (Germany). Opera, symphony, phantasy, suite, overture, string quartet, and songs; also an essay on modern unaccompanied song.	English.
1867 Scarborough. 9 February.	**1934** 7 May. Cambridge.	**NAYLOR, Edward Woodall. M.A. (Mus.D.).** Son of Dr. John (1838) who taught him music. Organist in London and at Emmanuel College, Cambridge. Opera, cantata, chapel services, church works, anthems, part-songs, and a piano trio.	English.
1867 5 February. Hamburg.		**MAUKE, Wilhelm.** Studied at Basle and Munich. Music critic and opera reporter at Munich. Symphonic-poems, symphonies (one with chorus and solo), oratorio, operas, operettas, songs, and hymns—about 80 works.	German.
1867 30 March. Glasgow.		**BRYSON, Robert Ernest.** Opera, symphonies and other orchestral works, string quartet, etc.	Scottish.

Born	Died	Name	Nationality
1867 17 April. London.		**STEGGALL, Reginald.** Son of Dr. Charles. Studied at the Royal Academy where he became organ professor in 1895. Organist at St. Anne's, Soho, in 1866, and succeeded his father in 1905 at Lincoln's Inn Chapel. Symphony, Mass, anthems, church services, scenas, songs, organ pieces, symphonic-poem, overture, 2 suites, quintet, quartet, trio, etc.	English.
1867 24 April. Prague.		**NAVRÁTIL, Carl.** Pupil of Ondricek (violin) and Adler (theory). An honorary member of the Dutch Maatschappij tot Bevordering van Toonkunst. 2 Operas, 5 symphonic-poems, symphony, concertos for violin and piano, trios, quintets, quartets, sonatas, Mass, Psalms, and songs.	Bohemian.
1867 2 May. Turin		**FINO, Giocondo.** A Priest. 3 Operas, sacred cantata, orchestral works, and a string quartet.	Italian.
1867 5 May. Bath.		**NOBLE, Thomas Tertius.** Pupil of the Royal College, where he afterwards became teacher. Organist at York Minster in '92 ; founded the York Symphony Orchestra in '99, and conducted the York Musical Society from 1901. Anthems, church services, cantatas, motets, orchestral and chamber music.	English.
1867 21 May. Liège.		**PAQUE, Marie Joseph Léon Désiré.** Studied at the Liège Conservatoire. Taught piano, organ and composition in Sofia, Athens and Lisbon. Settled in Paris in 1914, devoting himself entirely to composition. Symphonies, overtures, organ concerto, Requiem, lyric drama, quintet, quartet, sonatas for viola, etc.—about 100 works.	Belgian.
1867 25 May. Elberfeld.	1932 3 December. Brussels·	**KREUZ, Emil.** Violinist, violanist and conductor. Pupil of Japha at Cologne, and later at the Royal College, London, under Holmes (violin) and Stanford (composition). Viola concerto, trio, quartet, quintet, songs, and teaching pieces.	German.
1867 27 June. Burscheid		**STRAESSER, Ewald.** Pupil of Wüllner at Cologne Conservatorium. Teacher of composition at the Stuttgart Academy in 1921. 3 Symphonies, symphonic-fantasy, suite, violin concerto, choruses, piano quintet, clarinet quintet, piano suite, violin sonata, and works for piano and strings.	German.
1867 29 July. Lerida.	1916 24 March. English Channel. (Torpedoed.)	**GRANADOS CAMPINA, Enrique.** Studied composition under Pedrell. Virtuoso pianist. Knight of the Spanish Order : Legion of Honour, etc. Operas, zarzuelas, symphonic-poems, suites, madrigal, violin, 'cello and oboe pieces, and all kinds of piano works.	Spanish.

Born	Died	Name	Nationality
1867 5 September. Henniker, N.H.		**BEACH, Mrs. H. H. A. (Amy Marcy Cheney).** Pianist ; pupil of Perabo, Baermann and J. W. Hill at Boston. Self-taught in composition. Played her works in Germany and America. Symphony, piano concerto, cantatas, Mass, male choruses with orchestra, part-songs and piano pieces, string quartet, quintet, church music, and about 100 songs.	American.
1867 25 October. Cannes.		**WEBBER, Amherst.** Pupil of Nicodé at Dresden, and Guiraud at the Paris Conservatoire. Was *maestro al piano* at Covent Garden, and the Metropolitan Opera House, New York. Symphony, comic opera, and songs.	French.
1867 3 November. Schachen, Lindau.		**KALLENBERG, Siegfried Garibaldi.** Studied at Stuttgart and Munich. Director of private conservatoriums at Stettin, Königsberg, Hanover and Munich. His work is tinged with early German Impressionism. 2 Operas, 2 symphonies, many choruses, quintets, quartets and trios, piano sonatas and toccata, and 300 songs.	German.
1867 6 November. Warsaw.		**BRZEZINSKI, Franciszek.** Studied under Kleczynski, then Krehl, Reger and R. Hoffmann at Leipzig. Writer and critic. Violin concerto, piano concerto, fugues, preludes, suite and toccato.	Polish.
1867 7 November. Boston, Mass.		**LANG, Margaret Ruthven.** Pupil of her father J. B. (1837) ; Schmitt at Boston ; Drechsler and Abel at Munich, and Chadwick in America. Overtures, cantata, arias with orchestra, string quartet, songs, and piano pieces.	American.
1867 9 November. Hamburg.		**WEIDIG, Adolf.** Studied at Hamburg under Bargheer and Riemann, and at Munich under Abel and Rheinberger. Settled in America in 1892. Assistant director of Chicago Conservatory. Conducted his works in Chicago, Hamburg, Berlin, and Frankfort. Symphonies, symphonic-poem, suite, overtures, string quartets, quintets; suites for piano, and violin and piano; motet and songs.	German.
1867 9 December Copenhagen.		**HENRIQUES, Fini Valdemar.** Pupil of Tofte, Joachim and Svendsen. Member of the Royal Chapel, Copenhagen, in 1892-6. Operas, symphonies, suite for oboe and orchestra, trio, sonatas for violin and piano, romances, and songs.	Danish.
1868 7 January. Duisburg-o-R		**BISCHOFF, Hermann.** Studied at Leipzig and Munich. Friend of R.Strauss. Symphonies, symphonic-poem, and songs.	German.
1868 28 January. Glasgow.		**LAMOND, Frederick A.** Studied at the Raff Conservatorium under Heermann (violin), Schwarz (piano), and Urspruch (composition), and later under Bülow and Liszt. Concert pianist, specializing on Beethoven. Symphony, overture, trio for piano and strings, piano sonata and pieces.	Scottish.

Born	Died	Name	Nationalit
1868 5 February. Antwerp.		**MORTELMANS, Lodewijk.** Studied at the Ecole de Musique, Antwerp, under Peter Benoit. Professor of counterpoint at the Royal Flemish Conservatoire, Antwerp, from 1902. Symphonies, symphonic-poems, elegies, cantatas, opera, many songs and piano pieces.	Belgian.
1868 17 February. Regensburg.		**RENNER, Joseph.** Pupil of Rheinberger. Organist of Regensburg Cathedral 1896, and teacher of organ at the School for Church music. 10 Masses, 14 Requiems, motets, sacred songs ; organ sonatas, suites, preludes and pieces ; male choruses, a musical comedy, and violin serenades.	German.
1868 22 March. Greenock.	**1916** 2 August. London.	**MACCUNN, Hamish.** Pupil of Sir Hubert Parry at the Royal College. Operatic conductor in London and Edinburgh. Operas, musical comedies, cantatas, ballads, songs, overtures, and pieces for piano, violin and 'cello.	Scottish.
1868 13 April. Hawick.		**MacEWEN, Sir John Blackwood.** Studied at the Royal Academy ; became professor of harmony and composition there in 1898, and succeeded Mackenzie as principal in 1924. Retired in 1936 and was succeeded by Dr. Stanley Marchant. Symphony suite, overtures, viola concerto, string quartets, choral works, Highland dances for strings, piano sonata, and part-songs which are of the ultra-modern school.	Scottish.
1868 19 April. Düren.	**1933** 24 July. Berlin.	**SCHILLINGS, Max von.** Pupil of Brambach and Königslöw at Bonn. Chorusmaster at Bayreuth from 1902. Director of the Prussian State Opera, Berlin, in 1919. Operas, symphonic fantasias, smaller instrumental and vocal works, several books of songs, violin concerto, quintet, quartet, 'cello solos, etc.	German.
1868 29 May. Paris.		**D'ERLANGER, Baron Frédéric.** Studied in Paris under Ehmant. One of the directors of Covent Garden Opera. Resides in London. 4 Operas, including " Tess;" a violin and a piano concerto, quartet, quintet; choral works including a Requiem Mass; violin and piano pieces, and songs.	French.
1868 Manchester.		**BROOME, William Edward, (Mus.D.).** Chorister at Bangor Cathedral. Conductor and organist in Toronto, Canada. Cantatas, motets, anthems and songs—over 70 works.	English.
1868 5 August. Helsingfors.	**1924** 17 February. Helsingfors.	**MERIKANTO, Oskar.** Father of Aarre (1893). Studied at Leipzig and Berlin. Organist of St. John's Church, Helsingfors, from 1892. Conductor of the Finnish Opera, 1911-22. 3 Operas, popular singspiel, organ works, choral works, pieces for violin and piano, and many songs.	Finnish.

Born	Died	Name	Nationality.
1868 7 August. London.		**BANTOCK, Sir Granville.** Pupil of Corder at the Royal Academy. Principal of the Birmingham and Midland Institute from 1900 to 1934. Toured extensively as conductor. Founded the New Brighton Choral Society in 1898, and succeeded H. Wood as conductor of the Wolverhampton Choral Society in 1902. Symphonies, symphonic-poems, tone-poems, overtures, suites, ballet scenas, operas, cantatas, Mass, anthems, many songs, part-songs, sonatas for 'cello and for viola, string quartet, piano pieces, etc.	English.
1868 14 August. Turin.		**SINIGAGLIA, Leone.** Pupil at the Turin Conservatorio, and of Mandyczewski in Vienna. Influenced by Dvorák and Goldmark. String quartets, violin concerto, rhapsody and romance ; variations for oboe and piano, pieces for horn and piano, orchestral dances, choruses, and songs.	Italian.
1868 2 September Zutphen.		**BRANDTS-BUYS, Jan.** Studied at Frankfort. Several operas, 3 piano concertos, chamber music, songs, and piano pieces.	Dutch.
1868 2 September Stratford, Essex.		**IVIMEY, John William (Mus.D.).** Studied at the Guildhall School of music. Director of music at Marlborough College in 1915. Organist at All Souls, Langham Place. Lecturer. A grand opera, 20 light operas, chamber and church music, a symphony and songs.	English.
1868 6 September Somerville, Mass.		**GILBERT, Henry Franklin Belknap.** Pupil of MacDowell. Has made use of " Rag-time " rhythm in art forms. Symphonic-prologue, episodes and American dance for orchestra ; suite, overture, negro dances for piano, and songs.	American.
1868 3 November. Allaman.		**MAURICE, Pierre.** Studied at the Paris Conservatoire under Gédalge, Massenet and Fauré. Lives at his native place. 4 Operas, a Biblical drama, lyric dramas, symphonic-poem, orchestral suite, choruses, songs, and piano fugues.	Swiss.
1868 1 December. Söderhamn.		**ELLBERG, Ernst Henrik.** Studied at the Stockholm Conservatorium, where he became teacher of composition in 1914. Was violinist to the Royal Chapel in 1887 to 1905. Member of the Royal Academy, Stockholm. Operas, ballets, symphony, overtures, fugue for string orchestra, quintet, quartet, male choruses and quartets.	Swedish.
1869 28 January. Aix-la- Chapelle.	**1920** 27 February. Zurich.	**FASSBÄNDER, Peter.** Pupil of the Cologne Conservatorium. Choir-master at Saarbruck 1890 ; town music-director at Lucerne in '95, and conductor of Zurich Choral Society in 1911. 4 Operas, 8 symphonies ; 2 violin, and 3 piano concertos ; a 'cello concerto, choral works, chamber-music, and songs.	German.

Born	Died	Name	Nationality
1869 5 May. Moscow.		**PFITZNER, Hans.** Studied with his father and later with Kwast and Knorr at the Hoch Conservatorium at Frankfort. Teacher at the Stern Conservatorium, Berlin, in '97 and conductor at the Theater des Westens. Music dramas, incidental music; ballads, and scenas for voice, chorus and orchestra; 'cello sonata, chamber music, orchestral, and songs.	Russian. (German parents.)
1869 6 June. Triebschen.		**WAGNER, Helferich Siegfried Richard.** Son of the great Richard Wagner. Pupil of Humperdinck and Kniese, after studying architecture at Charlottenburg. Associate-conductor at Bayreuth Festivals, 1896. Wrote librettos to some operas. Several operas, symphonic-poem, violin concerto, male choruses, etc.	German.
1869 Tourcoing.		**ROUSSEL, Albert.** Devoted himself to music at the age of 25. Formerly a naval officer. Studied under Gigout and d'Indy. A poetic composer. Symphony; opera-ballet, " Padmavati "; choruses with orchestra; " Divertissement " for piano and wind; violin sonata, " Forest Poem " for orchestra, etc.	French.
1869 Melbourne.		**HILL, Alfred.** Professor at the State Conservatory of Music, Sydney, N.S.W. Operas of various types; cantatas; " A Maori " symphony for orchestra; other orchestral; string quintets; quartets; violin sonatas and pieces; piano pieces; many songs, and Maori songs.	**Australian.**
1869 23 July. Lincoln.		**WADDINGTON, Sidney Peine.** Studied at the Royal College, where he became teacher of harmony and counterpoint, and chorus-master of the opera class. *Maestro al pianoforte* at Covent Garden in 1896 to 1906. Choruses, piano concerto, string quartet, trio, quintet, violin and 'cello sonatas, piano solos and duets.	English.
1869 14 August. Viipuri.		**JÄRNEFELT, Edvard Armas.** Studied at Helsingfors, Berlin and Paris. Conductor of the Royal Opera, Stockholm, 1907. Hofkapellmastäre at Stockholm, 1911. Music of national character. Symphonic-poem and fantasy, 2 suites, 2 overtures, choruses with orchestra, male choruses, songs and piano pieces.	Finnish.
1869 20 August. Wegenstedt.		**BÖLSCHE, Franz.** Pupil of the Hochschule, Berlin. Professor at the Cologne Conservatorium. Symphony, overtures, chamber music, choral works and songs.	German.

Born	Died	Name	Nationality
1869 6 September. Oswestry.		**DAVIES, Sir Henry Walford.** Studied at the Royal College under Stanford, Parry and Rockstro. Professor of counterpoint at the Royal College, 1895-1903. Organist of the Temple Church in '98, succeeding Hopkins. Conductor of the Bach Choir, 1903-7, succeeded by Allen. Director of Music in the Universities of Wales in 1919. "Master of the King's Musick" in 1934, succeeding Elgar. Symphonies, string quartets, sonatas (piano, violin, horn, etc.), oratorios, cantatas, anthems, services, choruses, songs, pieces for piano, violin, etc.	Welsh.
1869 15 October. Christiania.		**ANDERSEN WINGAR, Alfred.** Violinist. Pupil of Massenet and Gédalge for composition. 2 Operas, operettas, 2 symphonies, 2 violin concertos, orchestral suites, overtures, rhapsodies and fantasias; songs and piano pieces.	Norwegian.
1869 22 October. Edgbaston.		**DAVIS, John David.** Studied at the Raff Conservatorium, Frankfort, and the Brussels Conservatoire, and later with F. Kufferath. Teacher at the Midland Institute, Birmingham, 1893 to 1904. Symphonic-poem, variations, ballade, suite, Coronation March, etc.; sonatas for violin and piano, string quartet, trio, songs, part-songs, pieces for piano and other instruments, and an opera.	English.
1869 20 November. Beckenham.		**HINTON, Arthur.** Studied at the Royal Academy under Sainton (violin) and Davenport (composition), afterwards at Munich under Rheinberger. Conductor in London theatres. Symphonies, operettas, violin sonata, trios, scenas, piano pieces, and songs.	English.
1870 4 January. London.	**1932** 25 November. London.	**PITT, Percy.** Pupil of Reinecke and Jadassohn at Leipzig, and Rheinberger at Munich. Chorus-master of the Mottl Concerts in 1895; organist of the Queen's Hall in '96; musical adviser and occasional conductor at Covent Garden in 1902. Musical director of the B.B.C. in 1922. Orchestral suites, symphonies, symphonic prelude, overtures, clarinet concerto, rhapsody, ballade for violin and orchestra, poems for voice and orchestra, incidental music, serenades for strings, quintet, trio, etc.	English.
1870 5 January. Liège.		**FOLVILLE, Juliette.** Pupil of Musin and C. Thomson (violin) and Radoux (composition). Pianist and conductor. Teacher of the piano at the Liège Conservatoire, 1898. Settled in England (Bournemouth) in 1914. Opera, symphonic-poem, suites and symphonic-sketches; violin and a piano concertos and suites; piano sonatas, quartet, dramatic pieces, church music, 24 organ pieces, and songs.	Belgian.

Born	Died	Name	Nationality
1870 20 January. Heusy.	1894 21 January. Angers.	**LEKEU, Guillaume.** Pupil at the Verviers Conservatoire and that of Paris under Franck and d'Indy. Etude symphonique, string quartet, adagio for quartet and orchestra, fantaisie for orchestra, violin sonata, etc.	Belgian.
1870 22 January. Bordeaux.		**TOURNEMIRE, Charles Arnould.** Pupil of C. Franck and d'Indy at the Paris Conservatoire. Succeeded Franck and Pierné as organist of St. Clotilde, Paris, in 1898. Has given many organ recitals on the Continent. Lyric-tragedy " Le Sang de la Sirène " for soli, chorus and orchestra ; a symphony, chamber music, and songs.	French.
1870 7 February. Stadskanaal.		**DOPPER, Cornelis.** Studied at the Leipzig Conservatorium. Opera conductor in Canada and at Amsterdam. 4 Operas, 8 symphonies, 2 overtures, 'cello concerto and sonata, violin sonata, string quartet, songs, choral songs, and piano pieces.	Dutch.
1870 13 February. Wilna.		**GODOWSKY, Leopold.** Studied at the Hochschule, Berlin, and under Saint-Saëns at Paris. Toured and established fame as a pianist. Director of the Master piano school at Vienna in 1909 to '12, thence to U.S.A Concert valses, études, concert études, toccata and other piano music, also songs.	Polish. (Russian.)
1870 27 February. Newmark, N.J.	1922 11 September Boston, Mass.	**COERNE, Louis Adolphe (Mus.D.).** Studied under Paine, Kneisel, and Rheinberger in Munich. Organist in Buffalo, 1894, and in Columbus '97. Professor at the Connecticut College for Women, New London, 1915. Opera, cantatas, anthems, choruses, Mass, violin sonata and pieces, piano and organ pieces, etc.	American.
1870 7 April. Bruges.		**RYELANDT, Joseph.** Pupil of Tinel. At first studied philosophy. Oratorios, cantatas, 4 symphonies, symphonic-poem, overtures, church-music, 8 piano sonatas, 5 violin sonatas, 4 string quartets, and many songs.	Belgian.
1870 28 April. Kaiserstuhl.		**SUTER, Hermann.** The most eminent Swiss conductor. Studied organ, piano and composition at Stuttgart and Leipzig. Conductor at Zurich : director of Basle Conservatory, 1918-21. Swiss Symphony, string quartets, sextet, choruses with orchestra and unaccompanied choruses.	Swiss.
1870 30 April. Komarom.		**LEHÁR, Franz.** Studied in Vienna and Prague. Conducted for a short time. One of the most famous operetta writers. 30 Operettas (including " Merry Widow "), also serious operas.	Hungarian.

Born	Died	Name	Nationality
1870 10 May. Edinburgh.	**1927** 28 May. London.	**MACPHERSON, Charles.** Studied organ under Sir George Martin and entered the Royal Academy, where he became teacher of harmony and counterpoint. Sub-organist at St. Paul's in 1895 ; succeeded Martin as organist in 1916. Conductor of the London Church Choirs Association in 1913. Orchestral suites, overture, quartets, sextet, anthems, glees, and church music.	Scottish.
1870 14 May. Strzelce.		**STOJOWSKY, Sigismund Denis Antoine.** Studied at Cracow, the Paris Conservatoire, and later under Paderewski. Toured as a concert pianist. Symphony, suite, symphonic-rhapsody for piano and orchestra, piano concertos, violin concerto, sonatas for violin and 'cello, choruses with orchestra, songs, and piano pieces.	Polish.
1870 Vienna.		**CELANSKY, Ludvik Vitezslav.** Conductor and teacher in Prague. Opera, melodramas, ballad, symphonic-poems, etc.	Austrian.
1870 15 July. Bombay.		**WALKER, Ernest. M.A. (Mus.D).** Mostly self-taught in music. Director of the music at Balliol College, Oxford. Overture, Stabat Mater ; Ode for baritone, chorus and orchestra ; quintets, quartets, trios, sonatas for violin and piano ; songs, and smaller works.	Indo-British.
1870 17 August. Leipzig.		**HERMANN, E. Hans G.** Pupil of Rust, Kretschmer and Herzogenberg. Contrabassist ; teacher at the Klindworth-Scharwenka Academy, Berlin. Symphony, violin sonata, pieces for 'cello, clarinet, and piano ; string quartets, and many songs for which he is noted.	German.
1870 8 October. Poitiers.		**VIERNE, Louis Victor Jules.** Pupil of César Franck and Widor at the Paris Conservatoire. Organist at the Notre-Dame Cathedral, Paris. Played first in England in 1924. Several organ symphonies and 24 pieces ; poems for violin and orchestra, choruses with orchestra, string quartet, violin and a 'cello sonata, piano pieces, etc.	French.
1870 20 November. Pabirze.		**BRAZYS, Theodore.** Organist, then priest at Batstoge. Teacher of singing at Vilna and choir-master of the Cathedral in 1907-17. Cantatas, Masses, much church music, Lithuanian songs, and didactic works.	Lithuanian.
1870 22 November. Brooklyn, N.Y.		**BROCKWAY, Howard A.** Studied under Barth (piano) and Boise (composition) in Berlin. Teacher in New York from 1910. Symphony, suite, choral ballads, violin sonata and other pieces, piano pieces and songs.	American.

Born	Died	Name	Nationality.
1870 5 December Kamenitz.		**NOVÁK, Vítězslav.** Studied at the University and the Conservatorium at Prague under Dvořák. Teacher at Prague and State examiner. His works are entirely programme music, some being based on folk-tunes. Symphonic-poems, suites, overture, serenade, choruses, songs, string quartets ; piano quintets, trios and sonatas, etc.	Bohemian.
1870 6 December. Moscow.		**KORESTCHENKO, Arsène Nicholaevich.** Pupil of Taneiev and Arensky at the Moscow Conservatory, and later became professor of harmony there. Operas, ballet, incidental music ; symphonies, suites and other orchestral works ; cantatas, choruses, string quartets, instrumental solos, songs and piano pieces.	Russian.
1871 15 January. Newton, Mass.		**CONVERSE, Frederick Shepherd.** Studied under Paine at Harvard University, then under Chadwick and Baermann at Boston, and Rheinberger at Munich. Professor of composition at the New England Conservatory. Operas, dramatic poem, symphonic-poems, orchestral works, cantata, choruses, etc.	American.
1871 29 January. Budapest.		**DEMENY, Dezső.** Conductor at St. Stephen's, Budapest. Orchestral and choral works, and over 100 songs.	Hungarian.
1871 7 February. Stockholm.		**STENHAMMAR, K. Wilhelm Eugen.** Pianist and conductor. Studied at Stockholm, Berlin and in Italy. Operas, symphonies, piano concertos, cantatas, 5 string quartets, songs, piano sonata and pieces.	Swedish.
1871 6 March. Liliendorf.		**REUSS, August.** Pupil of Thuille at Munich. Conductor at Augsburg and Magdeburg. Abandoned career through ill-health. Opera, symphonic-poems, quintets, quartets, trios, violin concerto, sonatas, choruses, symphonic prologue, 2 melodramas, octet for wind, songs, and piano pieces.	German.
1871 8 March. Guines.		**BORCH, Gaston.** Pupil of Massenet and Svendsen. 'Cellist. Went to America in 1899. Conductor at the Opera House, Boston, U.S.A. Opera, several symphonies, symphonic-poem, music for piano, violin and 'cello.	French.
1871 22 March. Untermarx- grün.		**GLÄSER, Paul.** Pupil of his father and the Leipzig Conservatorium. Cantor at Grossenhain in Saxony since 1901. A large oratorio, " Jesus " ; motets, choral preludes, and an opera.	German.

Born	Died	Name	Nationality.
1871 25 March. West Ham.		**BUCK, Sir Percy Carter.** Studied at the Guildhall School, and at the Royal College under Parry, Parratt, and C. H. Lloyd. Organist of Worcester College, Oxford, 1891 ; Wells Cathedral '95. Musical director at Harrow 1901 ; Professor at Dublin 1910, and lecturer at Glasgow University, 1923. King Edward Professor, London University. Choral works, organ sonatas, etc., and didactic works.	English.
1871 21 April. Aix-la-Chapelle.		**BLECH, Leo.** Pupil of Bargiel and Rudorff, and later of Humperdinck. Conductor at the Royal Opera House, Berlin, from 1913, and of the Charlottenburg Opera from 1923. Symphonic-poems, choruses, operas, operetta, and a comic opera.	German.
1871 23 May. Drammen.	1904 30 September	**LIE, Sigurd.** Studied at the Leipzig Conservatorium, also at Berlin. Conductor of the " Harmonien " Choral Society, Bergen, and the Central Theatre ; later at Christiania. Symphonies, suites, cantatas, choral works, songs, piano quintet, duets, etc.	Norwegian.
1871 3 July. Madrid.		**ARREGUI GARAY, Vicente.** Studied at the Madrid Conservatory. Operas, lyric-comedies, cantata, symphonic-poem, Mass, motets, string quartet, piano sonata, etc.	Spanish.
1871 8 July. Wimbledon.	1897 23 April. Pentepigadia. (Killed in Battle of.)	**HARRIS, Clement Hugh Gilbert.** Studied at the Frankfort Conservatorium, also under Madame Schumann. Symphonic-poem, songs, concert studies for piano, Romance for violin and piano, and a trio for clarinet, 'cello and piano.	English.
1871 8 August. Ross.		**SQUIRE, William Henry.** 'Cellist, pupil of E. Howell at the Royal College. Principal 'cellist of the Royal Opera in 1895. 'Cello concerto, pieces, etc. ; operettas and songs.	Scottish.
1871 10 August. Berlin.		**FRIED, Oscar.** Pupil of Humperdinck and P. Scharwenka. Director of the Stern Choral Society. Choral pieces, 9 female choruses, double fugues for string orchestra, a piece for 13 wind instruments and 2 harps, etc.	German.
1871 22 September Fort Smith, Ark.		**BOLLINGER, Samuel.** Studied at Leipzig. Fantasie-suite for orchestra, overture, violin sonatas and pieces, songs and piano pieces.	American.
1871 30 September Upsala.		**LILJEFORS, Ruben Mattias.** Studied at Leipzig Conservatorium under Draeseke and Reger. Conductor of the Orchestral Society at Gäfle. Symphony, Festival overture, piano concerto, suite, drama, cantatas, violin sonata, songs, piano pieces, etc.	Swedish.
1871 11 October. Frasnes-l.-G.	1916 4 February. Mont-sur Marchiennes.	**BIARENT, Adolphe.** Studied at Brussels and Ghent. Teacher of harmony and counterpoint at the Academy at Charleroi. Symphonic-poem, suite, legend, rhapsody, quintet, 'cello sonata, piano pieces and songs.	Belgian.

Born	Died	Name	Nationality
1871 30 November. Strasburg.		**HAUG, Gustav.** Studied at the Strasburg Conservatorium. Organist at St. Leonhard's in St. Gollen, and conductor of the Herisau Orchestra since 1904. Many choral works.	German.
1871 20 December Somerville, Mass.		**HADLEY, Henry Kimball.** Studied under Emery and Chadwick at the New England Conservatory, Boston. Organist, choir-master, teacher of the piano and violin at the Cathedral School of St. Paul's, Long Island, 1895 to 1902. Associate conductor of the New York Philharmonic Society since 1920. Symphonies, symphonic-fantasia, tone-poem, overtures, operas, cantatas, choruses, lyric-drama; violin, 'cello and piano solos—over 100 works.	American.
1871 29 December. Moscow.	**1915** 1 April. Moscow.	**SCRIABIN,** Alexander Nicolaevitch. Studied piano and composition at the Moscow Conservatory under Safonof, Taneiev and Arensky. Professor of the piano at the Moscow Conservatory from 1898 to 1904. His works aim at the highest point of musical Art, and have exercised great influence on modern Russian music. Symphonies, poems, piano concerto, sonatas, concert allegro, fantasia, mazurkas, studies, etc.—about 80 works.	Russian.
1872 11 January. Berlin.		**GRAENER, Paul.** Conducted in Königsberg, Berlin and London. Director of the Mozarteum in Salsburg in 1910, and succeeded Reger at the Leipzig Conservatorium in 1920. Operas, symphonies, suites, phantasy, etc. for orchestra; string quartets, violin sonata, piano trio and pieces.	German.
1872 16 January. Toulouse.		**BÜSSER, Paul Henri.** Organist of St. Cloud; chorus-master at the Opéra-Comique, etc., at Paris. Operas, comic-opera, ballet, cantata, etc.	French.
1872 9 March. Moscow.		**JUON, Paul.** Studied at the Moscow Conservatorium under Hrimaly (violin), Taneiev and Arensky (composition); afterwards at the Hochschule, Berlin, under Bargiel. Settled in Berlin as teacher. Professor of composition at the Hochschule in 1906. Symphonies, string quartets, sextet, sonatas for violin and viola, pieces for string band; piano trio, and concert solos—about 100 works.	Russian.
1872 10 March. Burton.		**BOROWSKI, Felix.** Pupil of Rosenthal (violin) and later at the Cologne Conservatorium. Teacher of the violin and composition in America. President of the Chicago Musical College in 1916. Symphonies, symphonic-poem and other orchestral works; piano concerto, organ sonatas, motets, violin and piano pieces, and 20 songs.	English.

Born	Died	Name	Nationality
1872 28 March.		**BORCHMAN, Alexander Adolphovitch.** A Medico. Pupil at Moscow University and later of Gretchaninof and Glière. Symphonic-poem, orchestral variations, string quartet, trio, violin sonata, songs, etc.	Russian.
1872 30 March. London.		**AUSTIN, Frederic.** Brother of Ernest ('74). Studied under his mother, his uncle (Dr. W. H. Hunt), and W. H. Grimshaw for organ. Organist ; oratorio and opera singer. Symphonic-poem, overtures, rhapsody, Festival Prelude for strings and organ, piano trio, church music, songs, and pieces for organ.	English.
1872 23 April. St. Paul, Minn.		**FARWELL, Arthur.** Studied under Norris in Boston, Humperdinck and Pfitzner in Germany, and Guilmant in Paris. Lecturer in America. Studied music of the Indians. Folk-songs of the American Continent, music to masques, choruses, and songs.	American.
1872 29 April. Fredriksstad.	1933 March. Oslo.	**ALNÆS, Eyvind.** Studied at Christiania ; at Leipzig (under Reinecke and Ruthardt), and at Berlin. Organist in Drammen, and at Our Saviour's, Christiania, in 1916. Symphony, symphonic-variations, piano concerto, male chorus, suite for violin and piano, songs, and piano pieces.	Norwegian.
1872 1 May. Stockholm.		**ALFVÉN, Hugo** Studied at the Stockholm Conservatory under Lindegren. Professor of music at Upsala University, and conductor of the Glee Club. 4 Symphonies, rhapsody, symphonic poem, cantata, ballet-pantomime, male chorus, violin sonata, piano pieces, and songs.	Swedish,
1872 20 June. Frankfort-o-M.	1935 January. Frankfort.	**SEKLES, Bernhard.** Studied at Hoch's Conservatorium, where he became teacher of theory in 1896, and its director in 1923. Conductor at theatres in Heidelberg and Mayence. Symphonic-poem, suite, and other orchestral ; opera, burlesque, dance play ; string quartets, 'cello sonata, chamber-music for various instruments ; choruses, songs, and piano pieces.	German.
1872 Litomysl.		**PROKOP, Ladislav.** Pupil of Novák. Practises as a physician in Prague. 3 Symphonic-poems, overture, opera, cantata, piano quintet, string quartet, etc.	Hungarian.
1872 Moscow.		**VASSILENKO, Serge Nikiforovitch.** Pupil of Taneiev and Ippolitov-Ivanov at the Moscow Conservatory. Organiser and conductor of Historic Concerts of the Russian Musical Society. Opera, ballet, music to plays, symphonies, symphonic poem, Epic Poem, violin concerto, quartet, and songs.	Russian.
1872 20 July. Eton.	1936 17 May. London.	**MACLEAN, Alexander Moraven** Studied at Eton. Conductor at Scarborough 1912, and of the Musical Festival in 1920. Operas, comic-operas, incidental music, choruses, orchestral suites, and songs.	English.

Born	Died	Name	Nationality
1872 26 July. Paris.		**BERTELIN, Albert.** Studied at the Conservatoire under Dubois and Widor. 2 Oratorios, lyrical-drama, poems for voice and orchestra, sonatas, quintet, and organ works.	French.
1872 15 August. New York.		**GOLDMARK, Rubin.** Studied under Fuchs in Vienna and Dvořák in New York. Teacher of piano and theory at the National Conservatory, New York. Symphonic-poems, overture, Negro rhapsody, Requiem, quartet, trio, violin sonata, piano pieces, and songs.	American.
1872 4 October. Vienna.		**ZEMLINSKY, Alexander von.** Studied at the Vienna Conservatorium. Conductor at Vienna and Mannheim; now chief conductor of Prague Opera. 3 Symphonies, symphonic-poem, string quartets, and operas.	Austrian.
1872 12 October. Down Ampney, Glos.		# VAUGHAN WILLIAMS, Ralph (Mus.D.). The greatest living English composer. Pupil at the Royal College under Parry, Stanford and Parratt; at Berlin under Max Bruch and Dr. C. Wood; and at Cambridge under Alan Gray. Organist at South Lambert Church, 1896-99, and lectured at Oxford and London Universities. Professor of composition at the Royal College of Music. Orchestral suites, "Impressions," Rhapsodies, fantasias; 4 symphonies; symphony for soli, chorus and orchestra; piano concerto; fantasia for piano and orchestra; choruses, string quartets, quintets, violin solos, and many songs.	English.
1872 16 October. Plymouth.		**LÖHR, Hermann Frederic.** Studied at the Royal Academy. Many popular songs including " My little Grey Home in the West " and " Where my Caravan has rested."	English.
1872 25 October. Manchester.		**LYON, James (Mus.D.).** Almost entirely self-taught. Was music-master at St. Michael's College, Tenbury. Professor of harmony at the Birmingham School of Music until 1933. Toured extensively. Operas, Melomimes, 4 orchestral suites, poems, cantatas, string quartet, trio; sonatas, suites and pieces for organ; violin pieces, songs and piano pieces; also educational works.	English.
1872 4 November. London.		**WALTHEW, Richard Henry.** Studied at the Guildhall School, and at the Royal College under Parry and Stanford. Professor at Queen's College in 1907; conductor at the Guildhall and of the South Place Orchestra, Finsbury, in 1909. Choruses with orchestra, operetta, piano concerto, concertstück for violin and orchestra, quintets, quartets, trios, violin sonata, suites for clarinet and piano, vocal quartets, and about 100 songs.	English.

Born	Died	Name	Nationality.
1872 4 November. Jülich.		**STOCK, Friedrich Wilhelm August.** Violinist and conductor; studied at the Cologne Conservatorium and under Humperdinck, Jensen and Wüllner. A member of the Chicago Symphony Orchestra in 1895, and became conductor in 1905, succeeding Thomas. Symphonic-poems, variations, overtures, string quartets and other chamber music; symphonies, and a violin concerto.	German.
1872 8 December. Söderfors.		**ERIKSSON, Josef.** Studied at the Stockholm Conservatorium, and, later, under Liljefors for composition. Organist and choirmaster at Upsala. Male choruses, string quartet, organ and piano music, and songs.	Swedish.
1872 0 December Tortona.		**PEROSI, Dom Lorenzo.** Studied at Milan Conservatorio and at Ratisbon under Haberl. Choir-master at St. Mark's, Venice, and in 1898 became musical director of the Sistine Chapel in Rome. Improved the music of the Italian Church. Several Oratorios, cantatas, 25 Masses, Stabat Mater, Psalms, etc.; orchestral variations, symphonies, and much organ music.	Italian.
1873 7 January. Helchin.		**RASSE, François.** Began music at the age of 20. Studied under Ysaye (violin) and Huberti (composition) at Brussels Conservatoire, where he became professor of harmony in 1910. Conducted at Amsterdam, Spa and Ghent. Operas, ballet, 3 symphonies, 3 poems, several suites, overture, string quartets, trios, quintet, sonatas for violin, 'cello and piano, and many songs.	Belgian.
1873 February. Olmütz.		**FALL, Leo.** Studied under Fuchs at the Vienna Conservatorium. Conductor at theatres in Berlin, Cologne and Hamburg. Operas and many operettas.	Moravian.
1873 3 February. Taganrog.		**ZOLOTAREF, Vassily Andreievitch.** Pupil of Rimsky-Korsakov at the Petrograd Conservatory. Symphony, overture, overture-fantasy, string quintet, quartets, trio, piano sonata, pieces, and songs.	Russian.
1873 5 February. Sesto Fiorentino.		**BROGI, Renato.** Studied at Florence and Milan. Operas, violin concerto, string quartet, trio, songs, and books of waltzes.	Italian.
1873 19 March. Brand, r Kemnath	1916 11 May. Leipzig.	**REGER, Max.** Pupil of Lindner, and Riemann at Wiesbaden where he became teacher at the Conservatorium. Music-director at Leipzig University, and teacher in the Conservatorium in 1907. Visited England in 1909. Sonatas, suites, etc., for organ, ditto for piano; violin sonatas, choruses, madrigals, many songs and a sinfonietta—about 150 works.	German.

Born	Died	Name	Nationality
1873 19 March. Onega, Novgorod.		**RACHMANINOV, Sergei Vassilievich.** Studied at the Petrograd Conservatory and that of Moscow under Zvierev and Siloti (piano), Taneiev and Arensky (composition). Unique as solo pianist and composer. Toured as solo-pianist and conductor Appeared first in London in 1899. 2 Symphonies, caprice and fantasia for orchestra; piano concertos, suites and pieces (including the " Prelude "); 'cello sonata, violin pieces, trio, cantata, choruses, songs, and an opera.	Russian.
1873 2 May. Petrograd.		**TCHÉREPNIN, Nicolas Nicolaevitch.** Father of Alexander (1899). Studied at the Petrograd Conservatory under Van Arck (piano) and Rimsky-Korsakov (composition). Directed Russian music in Paris. Director of Tiflis Conservatory 1918; settled in Paris 1921. Symphonies, symphonic-poems, piano concerto, string quartet, sketches for orchestra, ballets, dramatic fantasy, Masses, and songs.	Russian.
1873 10 May. Liegnitz.		**WENDLAND, Waldemar.** Studied medicine; later became a pupil of Humperdinck. Husband of Olga Wohlbrück, the authoress. Devotes himself entirely to composition. Operas, pantomimes, songs, etc.	German.
1873 7 June. London.		**RONALD, Sir Landon.** Pupil of Parry, F. Taylor, and Henry Holmes (violin) at the Royal Academy. Conductor. Principal of the Guildhall School of Music in 1910. Orchestral suite, overture, incidental music, Scenas, many songs and piano pieces.	English.
1873 20 July. St. Félix de Caraman.	1921 27 March. Céret.	**SÉVERAC, Joseph Marie Déodat de.** Studied at the Toulouse Conservatoire and later at the *Schola Cantorum*, Paris, under Magnard and d'Indy. Lyric-play, many piano solos, songs, and folk-songs.	French.
1873 20 August. St. Albans.		**BELL, William Henry.** Pupil at the Royal Academy, where he became professor in 1903. Principal of the South African College of Music, Capetown, in 1912. Symphonies, symphonic-poems, symphonic-prelude, and other orchestral; operas, incidental music, ballad for chorus and orchestra, and songs.	English.
1873 26 September Monticelli d'Ongina.		**ZANELLA, Amilcare.** Studied at the Parma Conservatorio, where he became professor. Pianist and conductor. Lived in America for several years. Director of the Liceo at Pesaro in 1905. Opera, symphonies, symphonic-poems, nonet, quintet, quartet, trio; many songs, and piano music.	Italian.
1873 10 October. Paris.		**RABAUD, Henri.** Pupil of Massenet. Director of the Paris Conservatoire in 1919. He is of the modern French school of composition. Symphonic-poems, operas, oratorio, etc.	French.

Born	Died	Name	Nationality
1873 3 October. Madrid.		**VILLA, Ricardo.** Studied at the Madrid Royal Conservatorio. Conductor at the Royal Opera House, Madrid and of his own organised Municipal Band. Zaruela (Spanish operetta), light opera, symphonic-poem, other orchestral, choruses, etc.	Spanish.
1873 November. Brookline, Mass.		**MASON, Daniel Gregory.** Grandson of Lowell Mason. Studied under Paine at Harvard, Chadwick at Boston, and d'Indy in Paris. Delivered over 250 lectures for the Board of Education of New York. Symphony, string quartets, trios, sonatas for various instruments, organ fugue, song-cycles, and much musical literature.	American.
1873 4 December Liège.		**JONGEN, Joseph.** Studied at Liège Conservatoire, where he became professor. Remained in England during the war; and was appointed teacher of counterpoint and fugue at Brussels Conservatoire in 1920. Symphony and other orchestral works; piano quartets, trios and solos; string quartets; violin sonatas; 'cello concerto, sonata and poems; cantatas and songs.	Belgian.
1874 January. Křečovice.	**1935** 29 May. Bedeshof, Prague.	**SUK, Josef.** Studied under Stecker and Dvořák at the Prague Conservatorium, where he became professor at the Master School of Composition in 1922. The joys and sorrows of his life are clearly reflected in his compositions. Son-in-law of Dvořák. Symphony, symphonic-poem, Fantasia for violin and orchestra, many later orchestral works, string quartets, piano-cycles, song-cycles, etc.	Bohemian.
1874 January. Northampton		**WARNER, H. Waldo.** Studied at the Guildhall School of Music under Gibson (violin) and Morgan (composition and piano), becoming professor there until 1920. Viola player in the London String Quartet from 1920. Orchestral suites, 3 fantasies for string quartet, a suite " Pixy-Ring " for string quartet, piano trio, violin sonata, viola sonata, pieces for violin, viola, and 'cello ; piano pieces, and over a 100 songs and part-songs.	English.
1874 February. Resolven, Glam.		**EVANS, David (Mus.D.).** Pupil of Prout. Professor of music at Cardiff University. Overture, suite, cantatas, odes (chorus and orchestra), choruses, anthems, part-songs and church services.	Welsh.
1874 12 March. Vienna.		**EYSLER, Edmund.** Studied at the Vienna Conservatorium for a short time. Operettas.	Austrian.
1874 4 April. Vienna.		**BITTNER, Julius.** Studied under Bruno Walter. A judge for a long time. Operas, dramas and incidental music to his own libretti.	Austrian.

Born	Died	Name	Nationalit
1874 14 June. Moscow.		**IVANOF-BORETSKY, Michael Vladimirovitch.** Pupil of Klenovsky (Moscow), Scontrino and Falconi (Florence) and Rimsky-Korsakov (Petrograd). Professor of musical history at Moscow Conservatory. Operas, string quartet, trio, violin sonata, choruses, songs, and piano pieces.	Russian.
1874 6 July. Schwanen- burg.		**KEUSSLER, Gerhard von.** Studied at Leipzig. Conductor at Prague and Hamburg. Operas, oratorios, symphonic-poems, choral works, and a melodramatic symphony.	German.
1874 9 August. Caracas.		**HAHN, Reynaldo.** Pupil of the Paris Conservatoire under Descombes, Dubois, Lavignac and Massenet. Operas, ballet, symphonic-poem, and many songs.	Venezuele
1874 22 August. Huddersfield		**BAIRSTOW, Sir Edward Cuthbert (Mus.D.).** Pupil of F. Bridge. A great organist and choir trainer. Organist at Wigan in 1899; Leeds, 1906; and York Minster, 1913. Conductor of Leeds Philharmonic Society, York Musical Society and Bradford Festival Choral Society. Anthems, part-songs and organ music.	English.
1874 31 August. Berlin.		**KÄMPF, Karl.** Studied in Berlin. Symphony, suites, symphonic march, etc.; many choruses; sonatas and pieces for violin, 'cello and piano; songs, and pieces for string orchestra.	German.
1874 13 September Sheffield.		**GATTY, Nicholas Comyn (Mus.D.).** Pupil of the Royal College under Stanford. Held musical posts in London, and was critic for the *Pall Mall Gazette* in 1907. Orchestral; operas and other dramatic works; choral and orchestral pieces.	English.
1874 13 September Vienna.		**SCHÖNBERG, Arnold.** Self-taught in composition. A notable painter. *The originator of "Expressionism" in music.* Conducted his works in Amsterdam, Petrograd, Prague and London (1914). Lecturer and teacher of composition in Mödling, n'r Vienna. Orchestral pieces, chamber-symphony, string quartets, septet, piano suite and pieces, opera, dramatic cantata, many songs and song-cycles.	Austrian
1874 21 September Cheltenham.	1934 25 May. London.	**HOLST, Gustav Theodore.** Studied at the Royal College under Stanford and Rockstro. Musical director of various London Colleges. Teacher of composition at the Royal College in 1919. Operas, orchestral suites, scenas and choruses for female choirs; Fugal overture and concerto, choral symphony, etc. "The Planets" and the "Hymn to Jesus" are his best-known works.	English.
1874 23 December Burgos.		**CALLEJA, Gómez Rafael.** Studied at the Madrid Conservatoire. Conductor of theatres in Spain, Portugal and America. 287 Musical comedies; orchestral and vocal pieces.	Spanish

Born	Died	Name	Nationality
1874 7 December Lemberg.		**ETTINGER, Max.** Studied at Berlin and Munich. Operas, choruses, orchestral suite, quintet, violin and 'cello sonatas, etc.	German.
1874 December Kiev.		**GLIÈRE, Reinhold Moritzovich.** Studied under Tanéiev and Hyppolitov-Ivanov at the Moscow Conservatory, where he became professor of composition. He belongs to the " New Russian " school. 3 Symphonies ; octet, sextet, quartets, etc. ; symphonic poems, ballet and many songs.	Russian.
1874 December London.		**AUSTIN, Ernest.** Brother of Frederic (1872). Studied under J. Davenport. Symphonic Idyll, March and Variations for orchestra; piano sonata and various pieces ; trios for various instruments, and about 50 songs.	English.
1875 January. Venice.		**BOGHEN, Felice.** Professor of harmony at the Cherubini Institute at Florence. Opera, piano fugues, and other works.	Italian.
1875 February. Vienna.		**KREISLER, Fritz.** The most famous violinist of the time. Pupil of Hellmesberger and Auer in Vienna, and Massart and Delibes in Paris. Served as captain in the Austrian army during the Great War. Violin pieces and many arrangements, also a string quartet and an operetta.	Austrian.
1875 February. Basle.		**COURVOISIER, Walter.** A medical practitioner until 1902. Studied under Thuille in Munich, and is a representative of the " Munich School." Conductor of the Symphony Concerts in the Kaimsaal, and teacher of composition at the Academy of Music, Munich. Operas, comedy, symphony, funeral service, variations and fugues for piano, and many songs.	Swiss.
1875 February. Iikisalmi.		**MELARTIN, Erkki.** Studied at Helsingfors, Vienna, Rome and Berlin. Has conducted in Stockholm, Copenhagen, Riga, Petrograd, Moscow, etc. His works have Impressionistic and Expressionistic tendencies. Symphonic-poems, 5 symphonies, 3 suites, violin concerto, string quartets, sonatas and pieces for violin and piano, opera, choral works, cantatas, and 200 songs.	Finnish.
1875 February. Gleiwitz.	**1935** 16 January. Erfurt.	**WETZ, Richard.** Studied at the Leipzig Conservatorium, also privately with Apel and R. Hofmann, and later with Thuille at Munich. Conductor at Erfurt and Gotha. Teacher of composition and history at Weimar, 1913 ; professor in 1920. Director of Engelbrecht Madrigal Chorus in 1918. 3 Symphonies, 2 operas, choruses, string quartets, sonatas, etc.	German.

Born	Died	Name	Nationalit
1875 7 March. Ciboure.		**RAVEL, Maurice.** Pupil of the Paris Conservatoire under Fauré (fugue), Pessard (harmony), and C. de Beriot (piano). The most original of French composers of the modern period. Combines the most modern harmony and rhythm to the classical forms. Visited London in 1909 and '21. Formed the friendship of Stravinsky in 1912. Operas; several orchestral works; string quartet and other chamber music; songs; works for voice and orchestra; piano concerto and other piano music. The Russian ballet "Daphnis et Chloé" (choreography by Fokine) is one of his most notable works.	French.
1875 14 March. Kensington.	1934 5 March. London.	**O'NEILL, Norman.** Studied with A. Somervell, and at the Hochschule, Frankfort, under Knorr. Conductor at various theatres. Professor of harmony and composition at the Royal Academy in 1924. Overtures, suite, rhapsody, incidental music, quintet, trio, 'cello sonata, many piano works, and songs.	English.
1875 18 May. Padua.		**FANO, Guido Aberto.** Director of the Parma Conservatorio in 1912 and of that of St. Peter's, Naples, in the same year; later, director of Palermo Conservatorio, and is now at Milan as piano teacher. Symphonic-poems, other orchestral, operas, and piano sonatas, also musical literature.	Italian.
1875 Brignoles.		**BRET, Gustave.** Pupil of Widor and d'Indy. Succeeded Widor as organist of St. Sulpice in 1893-1903. Founded the Bach Society in Paris in 1904. Oratorio, chorus with orchestra, unaccompanied choruses, and songs.	French.
1875 17 July. Eton.		**TOVEY, Sir Donald Francis.** Pupil of Parratt, Higgs and Parry. A remarkable pianist. Played with Joachim, the violinist, in 1894, at Windsor. Professor of music at Edinburgh University in 1914, and conductor of the Reid Orchestra. Piano concerto, quintet, quartets, sonatas for violin, 'cello, and clarinet; suite for wind band, songs, piano pieces, anthems, opera, and a symphony.	English
1875 6 August. Le Vésinet, n'r Paris.		**LABEY, Marcel.** Pupil of d'Indy at the *Schola Cantorum*, where he was professor until 1914. Member of the Société Nationale de Musique. 2 Symphonies, opera, overture, string quartets, sonatas for violin and viola, piano suite, and pieces for flute.	French
1875 15 August. London.	1912 1 September. Croydon.	**COLERIDGE-TAYLOR, Samuel.** Studied violin, and composition under Stanford, at the Royal College. Conductor of the Handel Society in 1904. Oratorios (his last and greatest being "Hiawatha"), cantatas, choruses, incidental music; symphony, string quartet, suites, ballade and dances for orchestra; violin pieces and concerto, piano and organ works, songs and part-songs; to opus 82.	Englis (Africa

Born	Died	Name	Nationality.
1875 18 September Paris.		**RENIÉ, Henriette.** The finest French Harpist since Hasselmans. Soloist to the chief orchestras ; virtuoso and lecturer. Studied at the Paris Conservatoire. Harp concerto, trio for violin, 'cello and harp, sonata for 'cello and piano, " Elegy and Caprice " for harp and orchestra, and characteristic pieces for harp solo.	French.
1875 5 October. Bristol.		**ROOTHAM, Cyril Bradley (Mus.D.).** Studied at the Royal College under Stanford, Parratt and Barton. Succeeded Walford Davies as organist of Christ Church, Hampstead, in 1898 ; became organist of St. Asaph Cathedral in 1901, and in the same year returned to St. John's College, Cambridge. String quartets, organ works, choral works, part-songs ; orchestral suite, overture, a symphony, and an opera.	English.
1876 7 January. London.	**1906** 30 May. London.	**HURLSTONE, William Yeates.** Studied at the Royal College under Stanford (composition), Ashton and Dannreuther (piano). Professor at the R.C.M. in 1905. Orchestral works, piano concerto, suites and pieces ; sonatas for violin and 'cello, suite for clarinet, quintet, string quartet, songs, part-songs, violin and piano pieces.	English.
1876 12 January. Venice.		**WOLF-FERRARI, Ermanno.** Pupil of Rheinberger at Munich. Director of the Liceo Marcello at Venice in 1902 to '12. Operas, oratorio, piano quintet, violin sonata, etc.	Italian.
1876 28 January. West Bromwich.		**HENLEY, William.** Toured throughout the Continent and the British Isles as a virtuoso violinist. Teaches violin, piano and composition in London and Birmingham. 100 Violin solos, 3 concertos, 2 extensive " methods," 7 string quartets, songs, and 4 historical literary works on stringed instruments.	English.
1876 29 January. Nörre Tvede, Zealand.		**NIELSON, Ludolf.** Studied at the Copenhagen Conservatory. Viola-player and conductor. Symphonies, suites, symphonic-poems, overture, string quartets, operas, ballets, piano pieces, and songs.	Danish.
1876 8 February. Kharkof.		**AKIMENKO, Feodor Stepanovich.** Pupil of Balakirev and Rimsky-Korsakov. Professor at Petrograd Conservatory. Opera, ballet, lyric poem and fantasie for orchestra, string quartet, trio, violin and 'cello sonatas, and piano pieces.	Russian.
1876 28 February. Chicago.		**CARPENTER, John Alden (M.A.).** Studied at Harvard University under J. K. Paine. Received French Legion of Honour in 1921. Symphonies, suites, pantomimes, ballets, violin sonata, Chinese songs, etc.	American.

Born	Died	Name	Nationality
1876 8 March. Posillipo.		**ALFANO, Franco.** Studied at Naples and Leipzig. Director and professor of composition at the Liceo, Bologno, and undertook similar posts at the Liceo, Turin, in 1923. Dramatic works, symphony, quartet, orchestral suite, and music for violin and piano.	Italian.
1876 9 March. London.		**SHAW, Martin.** Brother of Geoffrey T. (1879). Pupil of Stanford at the Royal College. Has endeavoured to elevate British music, and to free the English church music of sentimentality. Light operas, music-plays, incidental music, overture, phantasy for piano and orchestra, church-music, songs and part-songs.	English.
1876 13 May. Bordeaux.		**LAPARRA, Raoul.** Makes use of Basque and Spanish folk-lore. Operas, stage-music, orchestral, string quartet, and piano music.	French.
1876 Saragossa.		**AULA GUILLEN, Luis.** Studied at the Royal Conservatoire, Madrid. Professor of the piano at the National School of Music, Saragossa. Symphonic-poem, suite, double quintet, etc.	Spanish.
1876 2 July. Copenhagen		**BÖRRESON, Hakon.** Pupil of Svendsen. 2 Operas, 3 symphonies and other orchestral works; 2 string quartets, sextet, violin concerto, piano pieces and songs.	Danish.
1876 15 July. The Hague		**KOEBERG, F. E. A.** Studied under Viotta ,Scharwenka and Gernsheim. His later works are of Impressionistic tendencies. 3 Symphonies, 7 symphonic-poems, choral works, triple fugue for string quartet, pieces for oboe, violin and piano.	Dutch.
1876 29 July. Frome.		**REED, William Henry.** Violinist, teacher and conductor. Studied at the Royal Academy under Sauret (violin), Prout, Corder and Rose. Leader of the London Symphony Orchestra, the Three Choirs Festivals, etc. Symphonic-poem; Venetian suite, symphony for strings, " Scenes from a ballet "; violin concerto, string quartet, violin pieces, songs and part-songs.	English.
1876 6 August. Chariton, Iowa.		**WILSON, Mortimer.** Studied in Chicago, and later in Leipzig under Sitt and Reger. Conductor in Atlanta and director of the Conservatory, 1913-14; later at New York Malkin School. Symphonic works, violin sonatas, organ sonatas, trios, songs, etc.	American.
1876 12 September Antwerp.		**ALPAERTS, Flor.** Pupil of Benoit and Blockx at the Antwerp Conservatoire, where he became professor in 1903. Manager of the Royal Belgian Opera House in 1922. Opera, symphonic-poems, symphony, cantata, etc.	Belgian.

Born	Died	Name	Nationality
1876 15 September Berlin.		**WALTER, Bruno.** Studied at Stern's Conservatorium, also pupil and friend of Mahler. Conductor at Cologne, Hamburg, Pressburg, Riga, Berlin, Vienna and Munich. Symphonies, choruses with orchestra, quintet, quartet, trio, violin sonata, and songs.	German.
1876 23 November. Cadiz.		**FALLA, Manuel de.** Studied at Madrid and Paris. Religion and patriotism formed the basic element of his musical works. Ballets, concerto for clavicembalo (or piano), works for piano and orchestra, piano and violin pieces, and popular Spanish songs for guitar.	Spanish.
1876 11 December Wiszniewo, Vilna.	**1909** 10 February. Zakopane. (Killed by an avalanche.)	**KARLOWICZ, Mieczyskaw.** Studied at Warsaw and Berlin. Elevated Polish symphonic composition. Symphony, symphonic-poems, violin concerto, serenade for strings, piano sonata, fugue, etc., and songs.	Polish.
1876 24 December Rome.		**BUSTINI, Alessandro.** Pupil of Sgambati. Teacher at the Liceo, Rome. Several operas, chamber music, and concert pieces.	Italian.
1876 25 December		**BOSSI, Constante Adolfo.** Organist of Milan Cathedral in 1907, and professor at the Conservatorio there in 1914. Operas, operetta, Requiem Mass, and many organ pieces.	Italian.
1877 17 January. Zurich.		**JELMOLI, Hans.** Studied at Frankfort under Knorr, Scholz and E. Humperdinck (composition), and Engesser (piano). Opera conductor at Mayence and Würzburg ; now teaches composition at Zurich. Operas, lyric comedy, incidental music, musical comedies, cantata, unaccompanied choruses, and piano pieces.	Swiss.
1877 29 January. Dresden, Staffs.		**BRIAN, William Havergal.** Mostly self-taught. Choral works, tone - poem, suite, overture and variations for orchestra, piano works, songs and part-songs.	English.
1877 1 February. Hampstead, London.		**DUNHILL, Thomas Frederick.** Pupil of F. Taylor (piano) and Stanford (composition) at the Royal College, where he became professor in 1905. Music master at Eton College, 1901-10. Gave a concert of British music in Belgrade in 1922. Operas, symphony, orchestral variations, pieces for organ and strings, quartets, sonatas for violin and piano, songs, etc.	English.
1877 21 February. Moscow.		**GOEDICKE, Alexander Fedorovitch.** Studied under Pabst and Saforof at the Moscow Conservatory, where he became professor of the piano in 1907. 3 Symphonies, overture, opera, piano trio, violin sonata, Russian folk-songs for violin, 'cello and piano ; many piano pieces, songs and various instrumental pieces.	Russian.

Born	Died	Name	Nationality
1877 24 February. Zurich.		**GANZ, Rudolph.** Studied at Zurich, Lausanne, Strasburg and Berlin. Pianist, 'cellist and conductor. At Chicago in 1901. Conductor of St. Louis Symphony Orchestra in 1921. Over 200 songs; symphony, symphonic-variations, and 2 concert pieces for piano.	Swiss.
1877 May. Oxford.		**GARRATT, Percival.** Studied under Rée at Vienna, and Klindworth in Berlin. Toured as pianist. Piano sonata and many pieces; violin solos; many songs; a pantomime, and music to plays.	English
1877 3 June. Vienna.		**SZANTO, Theodor.** Pupil of Dachs and Fuchs in Vienna, Chován and Koessler in Budapest, and Busoni in Berlin. Concert pianist. Played the Delius piano concerto, which is dedicated to him, in England, Germany and Hungary. Orchestral, piano, organ, and violin works.	Austrian.
1877 23 June. Belmont, Mass.		**FAIRCHILD, Blair.** Studied at the Harvard University; at Florence under Bounamici (piano), and at Paris under Widor and Ganaye. Symphonic-poems, other orchestral, Bible Lyrics for chorus and orchestra, ballet-pantomime, string quartets, violin sonata, and chamber pieces for various instruments; to about opus 50.	American.
1877 Chieti.		**FALENI, Arturo.** Studied at Genoa. Founded the Verdi Institute of Music at Buenos Ayres. Overture, fantasia, music-poem, fugue and other orchestral; songs and piano pieces; also didactic works.	Italian.
1877 Lincoln.		**BARRATT, Edgar.** Studied at Leipzig Conservatorium under Schreck. Solo pianist. Much piano and vocal music.	English.
1877 6 July. Toledo, Ohio.		**SMITH, David Stanley.** Studied under Parker at Yale University, Thuille at Munich, and d'Indy in Paris. Professor at Yale in 1916; succeeded Parker as conductor of New Haven Symphony Orchestra in 1919, and was made Dean of the School in 1920. Symphonies, poem, overture, string quartets, choruses, anthems, part-songs, etc.	American.
1877 27 July. Pressburg.		**DOHNANYI, Ernst von.** Studied at the Royal Hungarian Academy at Budapest under Thomán (piano) and Koessler (composition). Toured as pianist, visiting London first in 1898. Piano professor at the Hochschule, Berlin, 1905 to '15; later at Budapest as director of the High School and conductor of the Philharmonic Society. Symphonies, suites, overtures, serenade for strings, quintet, quartet, piano sonatas, rhapsodies, varia- tions, violin concerto and sonata, and songs.	Hungarian.

Born	Died	Name	Nationality.
1877 7 September. Neuchâtel.		**BENNER, Paul.** Pupil of Knorr and Scholz at Frankfort. Organist and conductor of the Oratorio Concerts at Neuchâtel. Choruses, Requiem, chamber music, songs, and piano pieces.	Swiss.
1877 October. Madrid.		**AROCA Y ORTEGA, Jesús.** Studied at the Madrid Conservatory. An authority on the musical history of Spain. Incidental music, comedies, songs, orchestral suite, etc.	Spanish.
1877 1 November Brighton.		**QUILTER, Roger.** Educated at Eton. Studied under Knorr at Frankfort. Songs, the majority being settings of Elizabethan lyrics; orchestral, piano, violin music, and plays.	English.
1877 7 November. London.		**GARDINER, Henry Balfour.** Studied under Knorr at Frankfort. Music master at Winchester College for a short time. Symphonies, overtures, "Fantasy," string quartets, part-songs, etc.	English.
1878 23 January. Aylesbury, Bucks.		**BOUGHTON, Rutland.** Pupil of Stanford at the R.C.M. Teacher at the Birmingham School of Music, 1904-11. Established musico-dramatic festivals at Glastonbury (Som.) in 1914. Operas (including "The Immortal Hour" and "Bethlehem"), choral dramas, ballets, symphonic-poems, choruses, songs, orchestral and chamber music; also literature.	English.
1878 13 February. Frankfort-o-M.		**BÖTTCHER, Lukas J.** Pupil of Humperdinck. Black-and-white artist, and piano teacher at Frankfort; later conductor at Halle and Bad Bruckenau. 2 Operas to own libretti, pantomime, choral works, ballads and songs.	German.
1878 16 February. Pori.		**PALMGREN, Selim.** Studied at the Helsingfors Institute, also in Germany and Italy. Teacher of composition at the Eastman Conservatory, Rochester, New York. Male choruses with orchestra, choral works, opera, orchestral suites; 2 piano concertos, suites and sonatas; songs, etc.	Finnish.
1878 20 February. Ghent.		**HULLEBROECK, Emile.** Studied under Samuel at Ghent Conservatoire. Toured in Europe, Africa and Asia as a singer. Flemish oratorio, symphonic works, choral works, pieces for various instruments and Flemish folk-songs	Belgian.
1878 23 March. Monaco.	**1934** 21 January. Berlin.	**SCHREKER, Franz.** Pupil of Fuchs at Vienna. Founder and conductor of the Philharmonic Choral Society, Vienna, 1911, and teacher of composition at the Imperial Academy. Director of the Academical High School, Berlin, in 1920. Orchestral suite, symphonic-overture, chamber-symphony, operas, opera-poem, choruses, songs poems for violin, etc.	French.

Born	Died	Name	Nationality.
1878 6 April. Dresden.		**EHRENBURG, Carl E. Th.** Studied at the Dresden Conservatorium. Conductor at Würzburg, Augsburg, and of the Berlin State Opera in 1922. Operas, symphonies, suites, overtures, tone-poem, string quartets, violin sonata, trio, piano pieces, songs, and pieces for string band.	German.
1878 6 May. Hohokus, New Jersey.		**FARJEON, Harry.** Came to England in infancy ; studied under Landon Ronald and Storer, and at the Royal Academy under Corder (composition) and Webbe (piano). Professor at the Royal Academy in 1903. Operettas, symphonic poems, suites, string quartets, violin sonata, piano pieces, song cycles, 2 piano concertos, 'cello sonatas, violin and viola pieces, etc.	American. (English parents).
1878 19 May. Newcastle- on-Tyne.		**CARSE, Adam.** Pupil of Corder at the Royal Academy, where he became professor of harmony and counterpoint. Symphonies, symphonic-poem, overtures, a cantata, chamber music, songs, and teaching pieces for piano and violin.	English.
1878 Buenos Ayres.		**GAITO, Constantino.** Studied at Naples Conservatorio under Platania. Director of the Gaito Institute, Buenos Aryes. Operas, overture, suite, piano pieces, and many songs.	Argentine.
1878 6 July. Croydon.		**HOLBROOKE, Josef.** Studied at the Royal Academy under Corder (composition) and Westlake (piano). Conductor and pianist. Symphonic-poems, odes, overtures, variations ; operas, chamber-music, songs and instrumental pieces, of the ultra-modern type.	English.
1878 17 July. Nieuwer- Amstel.		**ZAGWIJN, Henri.** Mostly self-taught. Teacher of composition at the Rotterdam School of Music. 2 Overtures, works for wind instruments, piano trios and pieces, works for recitation and orchestra, many songs and ballads.	Dutch.
1878 18 August. Lucerne.		**BRUN, Fritz.** Studied at Cologne Conservatorium. Conductor of the Symphony Concerts at Berne. 3 Symphonies, symphonic-poem, violin sonata, and many songs.	Swiss.
1879 5 February. Eichwald.		**BRECHER, Gustav.** Studied at Leipzig. Conductor of the Stadttheater, Leipzig ; director of the Royal Opera, Vienna ; at Hamburg in 1903; Cologne, 1911; and Frankfort, 1916. Symphony, symphonic-poem, quintet, piano sonata, and many other works.	Bohemian.
1879 9 February. Stockholm.		**BERG, Natanael.** Studied in Sweden, Germany, France, and Austria. President of the Society of Swedish composers. Operas, pantomime-ballets, symphonic-poems, ballades for voice and orchestra, choruses, string quartet and quintet.	Swedish.

Born	Died	Name	Nationality
1879 11 February Hamburg.		**GILBERT, Jean (Max Winterfeld).** Pupil of X. Scharwenka. Conductor at Hamburg and Berlin. Many operettas and burlesques.	German.
1879 21 February. Palermo.		**DONAUDY, Stefano.** Operas, (including "Sperduti nel buis" and "Ramuntcho"), chamber-pieces, vocal and instrumental music.	Italian.
1879 25 February. Smichow.	1935 20 August. Prague.	**OSTRCIL, Otakar.** Pupil of Fibich. Opera director at Prague, 1920, succeeding Kovařovic. Conducted the Smetana Festival at Prague in 1924. Operas, choral works, melodramas, symphony, 2 orchestral suites, string quartet, songs, etc.	Bohemian.
1879 26 February. Brighton.		**BRIDGE, Frank.** Studied at the Royal College under Stanford. One of the foremost English chamber-music composers. Violanist in string quartets, etc. Conductor in London, and visited U.S.A. in 1923 in that capacity. Symphonic-poems, rhapsody, 'cello concerto, string quartets, trios, piano pieces, songs, etc.	English.
1879 19 March. Maihingen.		**HAAS, Joseph.** Pupil of Max Reger, and of the Leipzig Conservatorium. Teacher of composition at the Stuttgart Conservatorium, 1911, and later at Munich. Symphonic suite, choruses, string quartets, trio, suite for violin and piano; sonatas, suites and pieces for violin, piano and organ; sacred and secular songs.	German.
1879 4 April. Lille.		**GROVLEZ, Gabriel.** Studied at the Paris Conservatoire. Conductor at the Opéra-Comique, and at the Paris Opera since 1914. Symphonic works, comic opera, ballets, lyric drama, sonatas for violin and piano, many piano pieces, and songs.	French.
1879 29 April. Liverpool.		**BEECHAM, Sir Thomas, Bart.** The greatest conductor of the present time. Operatic impresario. Promoter of the great orchestral and operatic works of Delius, Debussy, Richard Strauss, Ethel Smyth, etc. Legion of Honour, 1937. Operas in M.S.	English.
1879 22 May. Brest.	1932 October. Paris.	**CRAS, Jean.** Pupil of Duparc. Lyric drama, symphonic-poem, string quartet, 'cello sonata, piano pieces, etc.	French.
1879 5 June. Langserud.		**WIKLUND, Adolf.** Brother of Victor (1874). Studied at Stockholm, Paris and Berlin. Concert pianist and conductor. 2nd conductor at the Royal Opera, Stockholm, from 1911. A member of the Royal Academy, Stockholm. Symphonic-poem, symphony, overture, piano concerto, string quartet, violin and piano sonatas, and songs.	Swedish.

Born	Died	Name	Nationality
1879 28 June. Ångnö (island).	1919 16 March. Stockholm.	**KOCH, Richert Sigurd Valdemar von.** Studied under Lindegren, and later in Berlin. Orchestral works, sonatas for violin and 'cello, ballad for piano and orchestra, quintet, piano pieces, and songs.	Swedish.
1879 Huelva.		**MORALES, Pedro Garcia.** Studied at the Royal College, London. Critic and poet. Was responsible for the first concerts entirely of Spanish music given in England, at which he appeared as violinist, violanist and conductor. Songs with piano or orchestra, and violin solos.	Spanish.
1879 5 July. Berne.		**ANDREAE, Volkmar.** Studied at Berne, and at Cologne under Wüllner and Staub. Conductor of the symphony concerts at Zurich and visited other countries as conductor. Symphonies, choruses, songs, opera, orchestral suite, string quartet and violin sonata.	Swiss.
1879 9 July. Bologna.	1936 18 April. Rome.	**RESPIGHI, Ottorino.** Studied at the Liceo, Bologna ; in Russia under Rimsky-Korsakov ; and in Berlin under Max Bruch. Director of the Liceo of St. Celilia, Rome, in 1923. Operas, symphonic-poems, dramatic-symphony, violin concerto, sonata, poem, a string quartet, songs, organ pieces, 'cello sonata, etc.	Italian.
1879 13 August. Bowden, Cheshire.		**IRELAND, John.** Studied at the Royal College under Stanford. His violin and piano sonata met with deserved success when, in 1917, it was played by Albert Sammons and William Murdock. Symphonic-rhapsody, Prelude, violin and 'cello sonatas, trios; piano concerto, sonatas and pieces, and songs.	English.
1879 23 August. Cesis.		**KALNINS, Alfreds.** Studied at Petrograd Conservatory under Czerny (piano), Liadov and Soloviev (composition). Symphonic-poem, " Latvia," overture, opera, organ and piano pieces, part-songs and 150 songs with piano.	Latvian.
1879 5 October. Kongsberg.		**CLEVE, Halfdan.** Pupil of O. Raif and Scharwenka at Berlin. Pianist. 5 Piano concertos, 20 piano pieces, songs with orchestra, and a violin sonata.	Norwegian.
1879 18 October. Dinaburg.		**FITELBERG, Grzegorz.** Pupil of Noskowski (composition) and Barcewicz (violin). One of the school called Young Musical Poland. Soloist at Warsaw Philharmonic in 1902, and conductor in 1907. Symphonic-poems, symphony, overtures, violin concerto and sonatas, piano trio and songs.	Polish.
1879 28 October. Madrid.		**CAMPO Y ZABALETA, Conrado del.** Studied at the Real Conservatoire, Madrid. Viola soloist at Madrid Opera House and the symphony orchestra, and teacher of harmony at the Conservatoire. Writer on musical subjects. Several operas ; orchestral suites and pieces, string quartets, Mass for double chorus and orchestra, etc.	Spanish.

Born	Died	Name	Nationality
1879 1 November berndorf-o- N.	**1933** 9 April. Leipzig.	**KARG-ELERT, Sigfrid.** Studied at the Leipzig Conservatorium under Reinecke, Jadassohn, etc. Teacher at the Magdeburg and Leipzig Conservatoriums. Described as a "Tone impressionist." A great amount of organ works, including concertos, sonatas, fugues, etc. ; also sonatas for piano, 'cello and violin ; string quartets, quintets, orchestral and choral works—to Opus 120.	German.
1879 December. illsborough		**HARTY, Sir Herbert Hamilton.** Studied under his father. Organist in Ireland ; came to England in 1900. Conductor of the London Symphony Orchestra and of the Hallé Orchestra, Manchester, in 1920. Symphonies, overtures, violin concerto, quintet, 'cello solos, piano pieces, and an ode for soprano and orchestra.	Irish.
1879 6 December Freiburg.		**WEISMANN, Julius.** Studied under Seyffart, Rheinberger, Herzogenberg and Thuille. Lives at Freiburg as composer. Symphony, 3 fantasies, violin concerto, piano concerto, cantata, choruses, string quartet, violin sonatas, a solo sonata, piano pieces and trio, variations for oboe and piano, many songs, etc.	German.
1880 4 February. London.		**BAINTON, Edgar Leslie.** Studied under Walford Davies, Stanford, and C. Wood. Principal of the Conservatory of Music, Newcastle-on-Tyne, in 1912. Interned in Germany 1914-18. Choruses, symphony, concerto-fantasia for piano and orchestra, viola sonata, piano pieces, songs, etc.	English.
1880 9 February.		**ADAMUS, Henryk.** Studied at Warsaw, and afterwards at Leipzig under Krehl and Klengel ('cello). Solo 'cellist of Warsaw Opera and Philharmonic Orchestras, and later, director of the opera-chorus. 2 Operas, 2 symphonic-poems, overture, and other instrumental pieces.	Polish.
1880 3 February. Mayence.		**ISTEL, Edgar.** Pupil of F. Volbach and Thuille. Lecturer and author. Has lived at Madrid since 1920. Romantic comic operas, burlesque operas, etc. ; choruses, overtures, songs with orchestra, etc.	German.
1880 7 May. Feldkirch.		**BLEYLE, Karl.** Pupil of H. Wehrle, d'Lange, and later of Thuille at Munich. Lives at Canstatt, near Stuttgart. Symphony, overtures, comic opera, violin concerto, male and mixed choruses.	German.
1880 22 May. Higher Runcorn.		**HAZLEHURST, Cecil (Mus.D.).** Studied at Liverpool College of Music. His works are of the Romantic style. Opera, comic opera, operetta, choral ballad, orchestral pieces, piano quintet, string quartets, organ fugue, etc.	English.
1880 Warsaw.		**WERTHEIM, Julius.** Pupil of Moszkowski and Sliwinski for piano and Noskowski for theory. Lives in Berlin as composer. 4 Symphonies ; sonatas, variations and pieces for piano ; many songs, etc.	Polish.

Born	Died	Name	Nationality
1880 24 July. Geneva.		**BLOCH, Ernest.** Studied under Ysaye (violin) and Rasse at the Brussels Conservatoire, and under Knorr at Frankfort, and Thuille at Munich. Went to America in 1915. Director of the Cleveland Institute of Music, Ohio, from 1920. Opera, symphonic-poem and other orchestral music; Hebrew rhapsody for 'cello and orchestra; string quartet, violin sonata, Psalms, piano music, and a sonata.	Swiss (Jew.)
1880 15 September Brussels.		**DELCROIX, Léon.** Pupil of d'Indy and Théo Ysaye. Leader at the Theatre Royal, Ghent. His music is elegant. Symphonic-poems, symphony, suite, quintet, quartets, trio, and sonatas for violin and for 'cello, an opera and a ballet.	Belgian.
1880 17 September Rome.		**TOMMASINI, Vincenzo.** Studied in Rome under Pinelli (violin) and Falchi (composition), and later in Germany under Max Bruch. Several operas, a choreographic comedy, orchestral works, vocal and instrumental chamber music.	Italian.
1880 20 September Parma.		**PIZZETTI, Ildebrando.** Studied at Parma Conservatorio under Tebaldini. Director of the Institute Musicale, Florence, in 1918, and director of Milan Conservatorio in 1924. Writer, lecturer and teacher. Operas, theatrical music, symphonic work, choral music, string quartet, 'cello sonata, and many songs.	Italian.
1880 12 October. Vienna.		**KONTA, Robert.** Pupil of Novák. Teacher of theory at the New Vienna Conservatorium. Several operas to his own libretti, symphony, violin concerto, songs, etc.	Austrian.
1880 2 November Manchester.		**FOULDS, John Herbert.** Conductor of the University of London Musical Society, 1921. *Introduces quarter-tones.* Music-pictures, music poems, etc. for orchestra; suites for small orchestra, stage works, scenas for voice and orchestra, string quartets, 'cello concerto, piano suites, and songs; to opus 80.	English.
1880 3 November. Gualda Tadino.		**CASIMIRI, (Monsignor) Raffaele Casimiro.** Conductor of the choir at St. John's Lateran, Rome. Writer on Roman sacred music. Much sacred music.	Italian.
1880 November. Plzen.		**KAREL, Rudolf.** Dvořák's last pupil in composition. Interned in Russia in 1914; became teacher at the Rostof Conservatory; returned to Bohemia in 1920. Opera, symphonies, symphonic works; string quartet; violin sonata, and concerto; piano sonata, variations, waltzes, etc.	Bohemian.
1880 14 December Fano.		**BARILLI, Bruno.** Critic. Operas, etc.	Italian.
1880 27 December Munich.		**BOEHE, Ernst.** Pupil of R. Louis and Thuille. Conductor in Oldenburg, 1913; director of the Palatinate Orchestra in Ludwigshafen from 1920. 4 Symphonic-poems, overtures, and songs.	German.

Born	Died	Name	Nationality.
1880 8 December Adrianople.		**BINENBAUM, Janks.** Studied at Munich Conservatorium under Gluth and Rheinberger. Original and earnest writings. 3 Symphonies, ballet, quintet, quartets, trio, piano pieces, and songs.	Turk.
1881 10 January. Hanover.		**BECK, Reinhold J.** Composer, and lecturer of science of music at Berlin. Previously was a pharmacist ; then actor. Lyric phantasy, choruses, operettas, chamber concerto for violin, chamber music, and songs.	German.
1881 6 February. Vienna.		**WEIGL, Karl (Mus.D.).** Pupil of Zemlinsky, and at the Vienna Conservatorium under Door and Fuchs. Worked with Mahler as assistant at the Opera House. Teacher at the New Conservatorium, Vienna, since 1918. Symphonies, symphonic-phantasy, symphonic-cantata, string quartets, sextet, many songs, duets, quartets, and choruses.	Austrian.
1881 5 March. Teplitz- Schönau.		**WILLNER, Arthur.** Pupil of Rheinberger and Thuille. Deputy director at Stern's Conservatorium, Berlin. Symphonic-poems, symphony, piano concerto, sonatas, string quartets, violin solo-sonatas, organ voluntaries, piano dances, and songs.	Bohemian.
1881 25 March. Nagyszent- miklós.		**BARTÓK, Béla.** Pupil of Koessler (composition) and Thomán (piano), at the Royal Hungarian High School for Music, Budapest, where he became teacher in 1907. Collector of folk-tunes. Opera, pantomime ; orchestral suites and pieces ; string quartets, violin sonatas, several piano pieces and sonatas, songs, and Hungarian and Roumanian folk-songs for single voices and for chorus.	Hungarian.
1881 8 April. Novogeor- gievsk.		**MIASKOVSKY, Nicolas Jacovlevitch.** Studied at the Petrograd Conservatory. The second living Russian symphonist after Glozounov. Professor of composition at the Moscow Conservatory. Fought on the Austrian front in 1914. 7 Symphonies, symphonic-poem, piano sonatas, 'cello sonata, many songs, and piano pieces.	Russian.
1881 20 April. Amsterdam.		**DRESDEN, Sem.** Studied under Zweers and Pfitzner. Writer, lecturer and conductor. Teacher of composition at Amsterdam Conservatorium in 1919. Orchestral variations ; sextets for wind and for strings ; sonatas for violin, 'cello, harp and flute ; songs, and piano pieces.	Dutch.
1881 11 May. Rotterdam.		**GILSE, Jan van.** Studied under Wüllner at Cologne, and Humperdinck in Berlin. Conductor at Bremen, Amsterdam and Utrecht. 5 Symphonies, cantata, opera, overture, nonet for strings and wind, songs with piano and with orchestra.	Dutch.

Born	Died	Name	Nationality
1881 29 May. Sydney.	1916 13 November Beaucourt. (Killed in action.)	**KELLY, Frederick Septimus.** Studied under C. H. Lloyd at Eton, and Tovey at Oxford; later under Knorr at Frankfort. A memorial concert of his works was given in London in 1919. Rowed in the Eton 8 in 1899; Oxford in 1903, winning the Diamond Sculls 3 times. Serenade for flute, horn, harp and strings; string trio, violin sonata, prelude for organ, and piano works.	Australian
1881 3 June. Paris.		**BACH, Fritz.** Pupil of d'Indy (composition), and Guilmant and Vierne (organ). Teacher and organist at Nyon, Switzerland. Symphony, choruses, piano quintet, and organ pieces.	French.
1881 Lézardieux.		**LE FLEM, Paul.** Studied at the Paris Conservatoire, and later under Lavignac, Roussel and d'Indy at the *Schola Cantorum*, where he is now professor. He uses the popular airs of Brittany. Symphonic-poems, symphony in 4 parts, piano quintet, violin sonata, songs, and piano pieces.	French.
1881 18 August. Frankfort-o-M.		**ZILCHER, Hermann.** Son of Paul (1855). Studied at Hoch's Conservatorium, where he became teacher, then professor of the piano and composition. Director of the Würsburg Conservatorium in 1920. Plays, musical comedy, violin concerto and sonata, 'cello and piano concertos, symphonietta, string quartets, choral works, many songs and song cycles.	German.
1881 28 August. Trondhjem.		**EGGEN, Arne.** Studied at Christiania and Leipzig. Conductor of the Drammen Symphony Orchestra, and organist of the Bragernaes Church. Symphony, incidental music, 2 violin sonatas, chaconne for organ, songs, and a choral work.	Norwegian
1881 29 August. Filipstad.		**KALLSTENIUS, Edvin.** Studied privately. A modern Impressionist. Lives near Stockholm. Piano concerto, orchestral serenade, cantata, string quartets, sonatas for 'cello and violin, organ pastorale and songs.	Swedish.
1881 28 September London.		**GEEHL, Henry Ernest.** Was taught by his father and R. O. Morgan. Concertos for violin and piano, orchestral suites, and much educational piano music.	English.
1881 4 November. Picton, Ontario.		**BRANSCOMBE, Gena** (Mrs. J. F. Tenney). Pupil of Borowski, Tielitz and Humperdinck. Choral works, song cycles, and a fantasy for violin and piano.	Canadian
1881 16 November. Montegiorgio.		**ALALEONA, Domenico** (Dr.). Studied under Renzi (organ) and De Sanctis (composition) at the Liceo of St. Cecilia, Rome, where he now teaches history and esthetics. Lecturer, writer and conductor. Melodrama, intermezzo, many songs, male choruses; Italian canzoni for string quartet and for various other instruments.	Italian.

Born	Died	Name	Nationality
1881 December Johnstown Pa.		**CADMAN, Charles Wakefield.** Studied at Pittsburg. Organist, critic, and lecturer on Indian music. Several operas, cantatas, orchestral and piano suites, string quartets, trio, violin and piano pieces; Indian, Chinese and Japanese song-cycles.	American.
1882 February. Cracow.		**FRIEDMAN, Ignacy.** Pupil of Mme. Grzywinska for piano, and Riemann at Leipzig for composition, also of Leschetizky at Vienna. Pianist. 90 Piano works.	Polish.
1882 18 March. Venice.		**MALIPIERO, Gian Francesco.** Studied at the Liceo, Bologna, and afterwards under Max Bruch in Germany. Teacher of composition at the Parma Conservatorio. Operas, musical comedy, symphonic-drama, works for orchestra and small orchestra; string quartet, 'cello sonata, etc.	Italian.
1882 24 March. Dresden.		**BLUMER, Theodor.** Pupil of his father, and at the Royal Conservatorium, Dresden. Conductor at the Court Theatre, Altenburg, till 1911, when he returned to Dresden. Symphonic-poem, orchestral works, opera, piano quintet, string quartet, violin sonata, quintet and sextet for wind, songs, and piano pieces.	German.
1882 11 May. Graz.		**MARX, Joseph.** Pupil of Degner. Director of the State Academy of Music, Vienna, in 1922, succeeding Löwe. Symphony, piano concerto, trio, violin sonata, 'cello sonata, choruses, and 120 songs.	Styrian.
1882 7 June. anienbaum		**STRAVINSKY, Idor Fedorovitch.** Pupil of Rimsky-Korsakov. Lived in Paris and Switzerland. Original works, aiming at physical appeal. Opera, ballets, a comic-opera; symphonies, suites, etc. for orchestra; string quartets and chamber music for various combinations; a cantata, and songs.	Russian.
1882 Kelc.		**KRICKA, Jaroslav.** Studied at Prague Conservatorium under Stecker. Choirmaster in Prague until 1920, when he became professor at the Conservatorium. Opera, operetta for children, cantata, orchestral pieces, songs and song-cycles.	Moravian.
1882 aithwaite.		**WOOD, Haydn.** Violinist. Studied at the Royal College and at Brussels under César Thomson. Toured for 8 years with the singer Albani. 2 Overtures, 8 suites, piano concerto; "Lochinar" (Scott) for chorus and orchestra; string quartet, many successful songs, violin pieces, and light works for orchestra.	English.

Born	Died	Name	Nationalit
1882 8 July. Brighton, Victoria.		**GRAINGER, George Percy.** Pianist ; pupil of Kwast and Busoni. Came to England in 1900. Migrated to America in 1915. Friend of Grieg. Uses " *beatless* " *bars of irregular measure.* Orchestral, piano, and chamber music, and folk-song arrangements.	Australian
1882 6 September. Edinburgh.		**O'BRIEN, Charles H. F.** Pupil of MacCunn. Singing master and lecturer at the Royal High School, Edinburgh. His work is distinctly Scottish in character. Symphony, overtures, piano sonata, etc.	Scottish
1882 6 September. Richmond, Va.		**POWELL, John.** Studied under his sister, and later under Leschetizky (piano) and Navrátil (composition) in Vienna. Toured as pianist in Germany and England. Overture, Negro Rhapsody ; violin concerto and sonata ; string quartet, piano sonata, suite and pieces ; songs, etc.	American
1882 14 September Upsala.	1919 11 March. Stockholm.	**FRYKLÖF, Harald Leonard.** Studied at the Stockholm Conservatorium under Lindegren (composition) and Anderson (piano). Organist of Nicolai Church, 1908, and professor at Stockholm Conservatorium, 1911. Overture, songs with orchestra, organ and piano pieces and a sonata for violin and piano.	Swedish
1882 15 September Wiese.		**KIESLICH, Leo.** Pupil of Emil Bohn. Choral-conductor and teacher of singing in Neustadt. 3 Oratorios, 3 Masses, singspiels, many choruses, a ballet, orchestral works, piano pieces, and 100 songs.	German
1882 21 September Christiania.		**HURUM, Alf.** Studied in Berlin, Paris and Petrograd. Pianist and conductor. Secretary of the committee of the Norwegian Musicians' Association. Symphonic-poem, suite and smaller orchestral pieces ; màle chorus, 2 violin sonatas, piano suites, and many pieces.	Norwegia
1882 12 October. Göttingen.		**WALTERSHAUSEN, Hermann Wolfgang, Baron.** Pupil of M. J. Erb at Strasburg, and of Thuille at Munich. Established Practical Seminary for advanced music-students in 1917. Director of Munich Academy of Musical Art in 1923. Orchestral, musical comedy, tragedy, songs with orchestra, etc.	German
1882 24 October. Siófok.		**KALMAN, Emerich.** Studied at the High School, Budapest, under Koessler. Many operettas.	Hungari
1882 7 November. Bischheim.		**BECKER, René Louis.** Went to America in 1904. Organist at St. Peter's and St. Paul's, Alton, Ill. Organ, piano and church music.	German

Born	Died	Name	Nationality.
1882 September. Seville.		**TURINA, Joaquín.** Studied in Madrid, and later in Paris under d'Indy (composition) and Moszkowski (piano). Pianist and conductor. Teacher of piano and composition in Madrid. Symphonic-poem and symphonic picture; lyric comedies and stage works; string quartets, piano quintet; "Escena Andaluza" for viola, piano and string quartet; much vocal music, and literature.	Spanish.
1882 6 December Kecskemét.		**KODÁLY, Zoltán.** Studied under Koessler at the High School, Budapest, where he became teacher in 1906. Folk-song collector and critic. Many Hungarian folk-songs, string quartets, 'cello sonata (solo), Psalm, and songs with orchestra.	Hungarian.
1882 December. Frankfort-o-M.		**BRAUNFELS, Walter.** Pupil of Kwast at Frankfort, Leschetizky and Navrátil in Vienna, and Thuille at Munich. Pianist. Operas, choral works; many piano works, some with orchestra, and songs.	German.
1883 1 February. Copenhagen		**KLENAU, Paul von.** Studied under Max Bruch in Berlin, and Thuille at Munich. Was stage-director and conductor for a short time. Now devoted entirely to composition. 3 Symphonies, symphonic-poem, operas, songs with orchestra, string quartet, piano pieces and songs.	Danish.
1883 14 March. Barcelona.		**MANÉN, Juan.** A pianist at 6, a composer at 13, and a master violinist at 20. Travelled as a virtuoso-violinist. Resides in Berlin. Operas (to own libretti), symphony, stage symphony; violin concerto, suite and solos with orchestra.	Spanish.
1883 19 March. Wiener Neustadt.		**HAUER, Josef Matthias.** Theorist. Rejects "modern" composition, basing his music on a system neither consonant or otherwise, and is purely homophonic. Compositions for voice and "tempered" instruments, i.e. piano and harmonium.	Austrian.
1883 20 March. Dohna.		**HASSE, Karl.** Studied at Leipzig and Munich. Founded the High School of Music at Osnabrück. Music-director at Tübingen University. Overture, symphonic variations, choruses, violin sonata; fugues, sonatas and suites for organ and for piano; pieces for string orchestra, and songs.	German.
1883 1 April. Suwalki.		**KENIG, Wlodzimierz.** Pupil of the Warsaw Conservatory, and later studied at Munich. Conductor in Poland and Germany. Symphonies, symphonic-poems, pieces for 'cello and violin, and many songs.	Polish.
1883 9 April. Como.		**BOSSI, Renzo.** Son of Marco E. (1861). Studied at Naples, Venice, and Leipzig. Professor of organ and composition at the Parma Conservatorio in 1913, and of that at Milan in 1916. Conductor and pianist. Symphony, violin concerto, several operatic works, vocal and instrumental chamber-music.	Italian.

Born	Died	Name	Nationalit
1883 28 May. Sacco.		**ZANDONAI, Riccardo.** Pupil of Mascagni at the Liceo, Pesaro. Operas, tragedy, comic operas, Requiem for solo voices, suites of symphonic impressions, violin concerto, and many songs.	Italian.
1883 25 June.		**STEINBERG, Maximilian Osseievitch.** Pupil of Rimsky-Korsakov at the Petrograd Conservatory. Symphonies, dramatic phantasy, cantata, ballet, string quartet, songs, etc.	Russian.
1883 Zurich.		**GLENCK, Hermann von.** Studied at the Hochschule, Berlin, under Kahn. Was opera-conductor at Weimar and Metz. Symphonic-poem, variation-suite, violin concerto, string quartet, pieces for violin and piano, and many songs.	Swiss.
1883 Timoshovka.	**1937** March.	**SZYMANOWSKI, Karol.** The most eminent Polish composer since Chopin. Studied under Noskowski in Warsaw. Symphonies, opera, cantata, violin concerto, sonatas for violin and piano, many songs, violin and piano pieces, choruses, etc.	Polish.
1883 7 July. Vaasa.	**1918** (Murdered.)	**KUULA, Toivo.** Studied at Helsingfors Music Institute ; in Bologna, and also in Paris. 2 East Bothnian Suites for orchestra, vocal works with orchestra, unaccompanied choruses, piano trio, violin sonata, piano pieces, and songs.	Finnish.
1883 20 July. Egremont.		**BRAITHWAITE, Sam Hartley.** Studied at the Royal Academy, under Corder (composition) and Whitemore (piano). Resides at Bournemouth. Military band, orchestral and piano music.	English.
1883 21 July. Hamburg.		**BARTELS, Wolfgang von.** Studied at Munich, and Paris under Gédalge. Lives at Munich. Music to plays, and German songs.	German
1883 25 July. Turin.		**CASELLA, Alfredo.** Studied at the Paris Conservatoire under Diémer (piano) and Fauré (composition). Toured as a pianist. Taught at the Paris Conservatoire and the Liceo, Rome. Founded the Società Nazionale di Musica, Rome, in 1917. Symphonies, suites, quartets, sonatas and other chamber-music, songs, piano solos and duets.	Italian.
1883 29 August. Teutschental		**ANDERS, Erich.** Studied at the Leipzig Conservatorium. Teacher of composition at the Klindworth-Scharwenka Conservatoire, Berlin, in 1922. Operas, choral pieces, chamber music, piano pieces, and many songs.	German
1883 18 September Bridgnorth.		**BERNERS, Lord (Gerald Tyrwhitt).** Entered diplomatic service in 1909. Studied under Stravinsky and Casella. Opera ; " Fantasie " and other pieces for orchestra ; piano pieces, songs and French songs.	English.

Born	Died	Name	Nationality.
1883 6 November. Barnstaple.		**BATH, Hubert.** Studied at the Royal Academy under Beringer (piano) and Corder (composition). Conductor of opera in London. Symphonic-poems, orchestral variations, cantatas, operas, quartets, quintets, and many songs.	English.
1883 8 November. London.		**BAX, Arnold Edward Trevor.** Pupil of Matthay and Corder at the Royal Academy. Husband of Isolde Menges, the violinist. Works of great originality. 6 Symphonies, 4 symphonic-poems, variations; work for chorus and orchestra; octets, septet, quintets, quartets; sonatas for violin and piano, viola and harp, clarinet and piano; songs with Danish and German words.	English.
1883 3 December. Vienna.		**WEBERN, Anton von (Ph.D.).** Studied at the Vienna University. The first disciple of Schönberg. Was conductor at various theatres; now devoted to composition. String quartets, unaccompanied choruses, songs, pieces for orchestra and other smaller instrumental combinations, and pieces for 'cello and piano.	Austrian.
1884 Warsaw.		**RÓŻYCKI, Ludomir.** Studied under his father, then at the Warsaw Conservatory under Noskowski, also at Berlin under Humperdinck. Together with Fitelberg, Szymanowski and Szeluta began the new school called " Young Musical Poland." Several operas, symphonic-poems, piano concerto, quintet, and about 50 songs.	Polish.
1884 22 February. London.		**BOWEN, York.** Studied at the Royal Academy, where he became professor of the piano. Orchestral works; piano concertos and pieces; violin concerto, sonata and pieces for viola; string quartet, and songs.	English.
1884 2 March. Liège.		**JONGEN, Léon.** Brother of Joseph (1873). Studied at the Liège Conservatoire. Served in the Belgian army, 1914-18. Operas, cantatas, string quartet, songs, and many piano pieces.	Belgian.
1884 17 March. Bordeaux.		**BONNET, Joseph Élie Georges Marie.** Pupil of his father, then of Tournemire and Guilmant at the Paris Conservatoire. Organist of Saint-Eustache, Paris, in 1906. Teacher of the organ in the University of Rochester, New York. First visited England in 1910 and America in 1916. Organ works, symphonic pieces, motets, etc.	French.
1884 14 April. Magdeburg.		**PLATEN, Horst.** Pupil of Paul Gilson (composition) and César Thomson (violin). Conductor at the Magdeburg Stadttheater and at the Grand Opera House, Cincinnati. Operas, comic-operas, symphonic-poem, prelude, organ sonata, songs, and piano pieces.	German.

Born	Died	Name	Nationality.
1884 27 April. London.		**WHITE, Felix Harold.** Self-taught except for his mother's early guidance. 250 Songs, some with orchestra, others with violin alone ; many part-songs, and much work in MS. for orchestra and all kinds of orchestral instruments.	English.
1884 19 May. Aerschot.		**MEULEMANS, Arthur.** Pupil of Tinel. Principal of the Limburg Organ and Singing School at Tongres. Opera, oratorios, cantatas, Masses, religious choral works ; symphonic-poem and other orchestral ; sonatas for organ and flute, songs, ' cello and violin pieces.	Belgian.
1884 22 May. Lugo.		**TONI, Alceo.** Pupil of Pratella. Conductor and director of important schools at Bucharest and at the Augusteo, Rome. Operas, sacred works, quintets, quartets, sonatas, and songs.	Italian.
1884 6 September. Cleveland.		**WHITHORNE, Emerson.** Studied in Cleveland, Vienna and Berlin. Teacher and writer in London, 1909-14, then returned to U.S.A. Orchestral, chamber music, songs, etc.	American.
1884 15 October. Belgrade.		**MILOYEVITCH, Miloye.** Studied in Belgrade and Munich. Assistant- professor of musical science at Belgrade University. Symphonic-poem, string quartet, music to drama, chorus with soli and orchestra, pieces for violin and for 'cello, many part-songs, and piano pieces.	**Serbian.**
1884 8 November. Melbourne.		**HAYDON, Claude M.** Resides at Wellington, New Zealand. Opera, incidental music, serenade for piano and string orchestra, string quartets, trio, pieces for 'cello, violin sonata, piano pieces, and songs.	Australian.
1884 13 November. Somfois.		**BLIN, René.** Studied at the *Schola Cantorum*, Paris. Organist of St. Elizabeth's Paris. Symphony, suite for piano and orchestra, organ pieces, and songs.	French.
1884 30 November. Stockholm.		**RANGSTRÖM, Ture.** Studied singing under Julius Hey ; self-taught in composition. A member of the R.A.C., Stockholm. Critic to Stockholm journals. Conductor of the Gothenburg Orchestral Society from 1922. Symphonies, symphonic-poems, suites, operas, string quartet, suites for violin and piano, 2 ballads with orchestra, more than 100 songs, part-songs, etc.	Swedish.
1884 27 December	**1936** 24 April. London.	**DIEREN, Bernard van.** Came to England as music critic in 1909. String quartets, symphony for soli, chorus and orchestra, opera buffa, orchestral works, songs and piano pieces.	Dutch.
1884 30 December. St. Gall.		**DAVID, Karl Heinrich.** Studied at the Conservatorium of Cologne, and at Munich under Thuille. Teacher at Basle Conserva- torium, 1910-14. Opera, choruses, violin concerto, string quartet, etc.	Swiss.

Born	Died	Name	Nationality.
1885 3 January. Warsaw.		**KOCZALSKI, Raoul.** Pupil of his father. Pianist. 2 Operas, and 70 piano works, based mostly on national melodies.	Polish.
1885 27 January. Emmerich-o- Rhine.		**KÜNNEKE, Eduard.** Pupil of Max Bruch at the Hochschule, Berlin. Operas, operettas, music to picture film, orchestral suite, etc.	German.
1885 7 February. Vienna.	**1935** 24 December. Vienna.	**BERG, Alban.** Teacher of composition in Vienna. Was intimate with Schönberg. Opera of a new type, using forms of absolute music ; songs, piano sonata, and clarinet pieces, and a violin concerto composed as a requiem.	Austrian.
1885 26 March. Stourport, Worc.		**HARRISON, Julius.** Studied under Bantock at the Birmingham and Midland Institute. Conducted the Beecham Opera and the Scottish Orchestra. One of the founders of the British National Opera Company. Cantatas, orchestral works, string quartets, quintet for harp and strings, organ and piano pieces, and many songs.	English.
1885 28 March. St. Quentin	**1931** December. Paris.	**DELMAS, Marc.** Pupil of Leroux, Caussade, Lenepveu and Vidal. Symphonic-poems, lyric-legend and lyric-drama, string quartet, trio, and piano pieces.	French.
1885 16 April. Budapest.		**WEINER, Leo.** Pupil of Koessler at the Royal High School, Buda- pest, where he became teacher of harmony in 1907. Overture, string quartets, sonatas for violin and piano, piano pieces, etc.	Hungarian.
1885 Dublin.		**LARCHET, John F.** Pupil of Dr. Kitson. Director of the orchestra at the Abbey Theatre, Dublin, and Professor in the National University. Tone-poem and other orchestral ; choruses, Irish airs for string-orchestra, many songs to words of Longfellow, Shelley and W. B. Yeats.	Irish.
1885 Buenos Ayres.		**SCHLUMA, Alfredo.** Pupil of Romanelo. A concert director. 3 Operas, 5 symphonic-poems, and chamber-music.	Argentine.
1885 Lemberg.		**WALLEK-WALEWSKI, Boleslaw.** Studied at Lemberg, Cracow, and Leipzig under Riemann. Conductor of the Choral Society and the Opera at Cracow, also the Warsaw Opera in 1918. Opera to own libretto, 3 symphonic-poems, choral works, and songs.	Polish.
1885 7 July. Blackheath, London.	**1918** Killed in action.	**FARRAR, Ernest Bristow.** Orchestral suite, rhapsody, symphonic-poem, works for string orchestra, cantata, choruses with orchestra, string quartet, organ pieces, songs, part-songs, and " Celtic Suite " for violin and piano.	English.
1885 12 July. London.	**1916** 5 August. Somme battle.	**BUTTERWORTH, George S. Kaye.** Studied at the Royal Academy for a short time and also privately. Many folk-songs, song cycles, country dance tunes, part-songs, string quartet, and a tone-poem, " Shrop- shire Lad," for orchestra.	English.

Born	Died	Name	Nationality.
1885 17 July. London.		**DALE, Benjamin James.** Studied at the Royal Academy under Lake and Jones for piano, Lemare and Richards for organ, and Corder for composition. Organist in London. Professor of composition at the R.A.M. Symphony, overtures, organ works, a piano sonata, and violin pieces.	English.
1885 17 September Leipzig.		**KIESSIG, Georg.** Studied at the Leipzig Conservatorium under Krehl, Wendling and Hagel. Was conductor in Leipzig, Arnstadt and Rudolstadt. Now devoted entirely to composition. Symphonic-poems, suite, opera, choruses, chamber-music, and piano pieces.	German.
1885 21 October. Vienna.		**WELLESZ, Egon (Mus.D.).** Pupil of Bruno Walter. University lecturer on musical history, etc. Writer of scientific works on various musical subjects. Operas, ballets, symphonic overture, choruses with orchestra, 4 string quartets, many songs, and piano pieces.	Austrian.
1885 22 October. Ampfing.	**1935** 30 May. Mayence.	**WINDSPERGER, Lothar.** Studied under Rheinberger and Louis at Munich. Symphony, symphonic-phantasy, overture, string quartet, violin solo sonata, 'cello solo sonata, violin and organ sonata, 'cello and organ sonata, piano trio and pieces, and songs.	German.
1886 7 January. Dresden.		**STRIEGLER, Kurt.** Studied at Dresden Conservatorium. Teacher of conducting at the High School ; succeeded Draeseke as master of the composition class ; conductor of the Dresden Opera in 1912. Symphonies, chamber symphony ; violin concerto, sonata and variations ; flute sonata, string quartet, operas, choral works, ballads and piano pieces.	German.
1886 12 February. Paris.		**BRUSSELMANS, Michel.** Studied at the Brussels Conservatoire under Paul Gilson, and later became professor of harmony and composition there. Symphonic works, sonatas for violin and for 'cello, songs, and organ pieces.	French. (Belgian parents).
1886 3 March. Glasgow.		**FRISKIN, James.** Studied at the Royal College under Dannreuther and Hartvigson for piano, and Stanford for composition. Teacher at the Institute of Musical Art, New York. Orchestral suite, string quartets, quintets, 'cello pieces, motets, and piano pieces.	Scottish.
1886 13 March. Liège.		**GAGNEBIN, Henri.** Studied in Berlin and Paris. Organist at St. John's, Lausanne, and lecturer at the Conservatoire since 1916. Symphony, symphonic-poem, string quartet ; sonatas for violin, 'cello and piano, respectively.	Belgian.
1886 20 March. Magdeburg.		**BEILSCHMIDT, Kurt.** Studied at the Leipzig Conservatorium. Teacher and author. Orchestral, stage plays, violin and 'cello sonatas, piano suite, choruses, etc.	German.

Born	Died	Name	Nationality.
1886 29 June. Sydney.		**BOYLE, George Frederick.** Pupil of Busoni at Berlin. Toured as a solo-pianist. Went to U.S. in 1910. Symphonic-fantasia ; cantata ; concertos and sonatas for piano and 'cello respectively ; string quartet, and songs.	Australian
1886 4 July. Waldshut.		**KAMINSKI, Heinrich.** Pupil of Wolfrum at Heidelberg, and Klatte, Kaun and Juon in Berlin. Most of his music is in the style of the old contrapuntal school. Concerto grosso and a suite for orchestra ; Psalm and Hymn for soli, chorus and orchestra ; motet, quintets, quartets, etc.	German.
1886 8 August. Amsterdam.		**RUYNEMAN, Daniel.** Pianist. Studied for a short time at the Amsterdam Conservatory. Influenced by the new French School. Symphony for small orchestra ; " Hieroglyphs," for 3 flutes, 2 mandolines, 2 guitars, cup-bells, celesta, harp and piano ; piano sonatina ; pieces for violin and piano, and songs.	Dutch.
1886 August. Alicante.		**ESPLÁ, Oscar.** Devised a scale which he used in expressing music of national character. Opera, symphonic-poems, suites, other symphonic works, choral works, quintet, sonatas for violin and for piano ; also literary works.	Spanish.
1886 23 August. Lindau.		**RÜDINGER, Gottfried.** Studied under Max Reger at the Leipzig Conservatorium, also studied philosophy and theology at Munich. Conductor of the Palestrina Society at Berg-on-Laim, near Munich. Symphony for 'cello and orchestra ; violin concerto ; piano sonatas, pieces and duets ; 'cello solos ; choruses, songs and national songs.	German.
1886 1 September. Brunnen.		**SCHOECK, Othmar.** The best Swiss song writer. Studied at Zurich Conservatory under Niggli and Freund, also at Leipzig under Reger. Conductor of Symphony Concerts at St. Gall since 1917. Operas, comic opera, singspiel, orchestral works, violin concerto, violin sonata, string quartet, choruses, and over 100 songs.	Swiss.
1886 13 September Burgos.		**BLANCO RECIO, José Ramón.** Self-taught in composition. Symphonic works, songs, and pieces for 'cello.	Spanish.
1886 25 September Vittoria.		**GURIDI, Jesús.** Studied under Basabe in Spain, d'Indy in Paris, Jongen at Brussels, and Neitzel at Cologne. Organist at the Basílica del Señor, Santiago ; conductor of the Bilbao Choral Society ; professor of organ and composition at the Vizcaíno Conservatorio. Operas, choruses, many organ works, orchestral works, elegy for violin and orchestra, pieces for piano, and violin and piano.	Spanish.

Born	Died	Name	Nationality.
1886 25 September Sydney.		**CAIROS-REGO, Rex de.** Teacher at Sydney. Ballad for male chorus and orchestra, sonata for 'cello, piano pieces, and songs.	Australian.
1886 26 October. Kamenz.		**UNGER, Hermann.** Studied under Istel and Haas at Munich and under Max Reger at Meiningen. Critic at Cologne. Symphony, symphonic-suite, many other orchestral works ; choruses, songs with chorus and orchestra, string quartet, trios, violin sonata, etc.	German.
1887 4 January. Edgbaston, Birmingham.		**HEATH, John Rippiner.** A medical practitioner. Conductor of the Barmouth Choral Union. Chamber music-drama, string quartets, pieces for string orchestra and timpany, violin pieces, songs, suites, inventions and other pieces for piano.	English.
1887 17 February. Oulu.		**MADETOJA, Leevi.** Studied under Järnefelt and Sibelius at the Music Institute, Helsingfors. Conductor at Helsingfors 1912, and at Viipuri (Viborg) in 1914. Symphonies, symphonic-poems, overtures, cantatas, choruses, piano trio, pieces for violin, 'cello, and piano, etc.	Finnish.
1887 23 February. Gagnef.		**LINDBERG, Oskar Fredrik.** Studied at Stockholm Conservatorium, and later at Sondershausen. Organist at Engelbrekt Church, Stockholm, in 1914, and teacher at the Conservatorium in 1919. Symphonic-poems, symphony, overtures, suites, cantata, Requiem, songs with orchestra, and piano pieces.	Swedish.
1887 31 March. San Sebastian.	**1915** October.	**USANDIZAGA, José Maria.** Studied under Planté (piano) and d'Indy (composition) at the *Schola Cantorum*, Paris. A monument to his memory was erected in the Plaza de Guipúzcoa of his native town. 3 Basque operas, pantomime, chorus with orchestra, symphonic works, string quartet, and piano pieces.	Spanish.
1887 10 April. Königsberg.		**TIESSEN, Heinz.** Pupil of Rüfer and Klatte. Studied law. Now critic and composer in Berlin. Symphonies, other orchestral, septet, quartet, piano sonata and pieces, music to plays, etc.	German.
1887 3 June. Rataje.		**AXMAN, Emil.** Studied under Novák at the Prague University. An official of the National Museum, Prague, in 1913. 2 Symphonic-poems, choral works, 2 piano sonatas, etc.	Moravian.
1887 21 June. Enköping.		**JONSSON, Josef Petrus.** Self-taught ; teacher and critic. Symphony, symphonic-poem, suite, overture, cantatas, scenas for baritone and orchestra, piano quintet and solos, and songs.	Swedish.
1887 Prague.		**BLAHA-MIKEŠ, Záboj.** Pupil of Novák, Spilka and Mikeš. Melodramas, songs, nocturnes, choruses, chamber-music, and piano pieces.	Bohemian.

Born	Died	Name	Nationality.
1887 San Juan.		**BERUTTI, Pablo M.** Studied under Jadassohn at Leipzig. Inspector of the bands of the national army, and director of the Conservatory at Buenos Ayres. Opera, Mass, funeral march, and piano pieces.	Argentine.
1887 21 September Antwerp.		**DE VOCHT, Louis.** Precentor at Antwerp Cathedral; professor of harmony at Antwerp Conservatoire, and conductor of the Nouveaux Concerts, 1921. Symphonic-poems, choruses and songs.	Belgian.
1887 4 November. Kinna.		**HÅKANSON, Knut Algot.** Studied under Lindegren, Liljefors and Bäck. Conductor of Borås Orchestral Society. Overture, marches, ballet, choruses, violin solos with orchestra, chamber-music, and songs.	Swedish.
1887 7 December. Vienna.		**TOCH, Ernst.** Studied medicine and philosophy. Teacher at the High School of Music at Mannheim. Symphony for soli, chorus and orchestra; chamber-symphony; piano concerto and pieces; sonatas for various instruments; 12 string quartets; violin pieces, etc.	Austrian.
1887 11 December Kolsva.		**BROMAN, K. Natanael.** Studied at the Stockholm Conservatorium, and later under Friedman (piano) and Kämpff (composition). Symphonic-poem; ballad, sonata and romance for violin and piano; piano pieces, and songs.	Swedish.
1887 12 December Gothenburg.		**ATTERBERG, Kurt M.** Engineer; music critic. 5 Symphonies, 2 suites, symphonic-poem, cantata, violin and a 'cello concerto, orchestral rhapsodies, overture, string quartet, opera, ballet, music to a Shakespeare play, and a Requiem.	Swedish.
1888 28 January. Normanby, Yorks.		**BESLY, Maurice.** Studied at Leipzig Conservatorium. Organist at the English Church there, 1910-12, and Queen's College, Oxford, in 1919. Incidental music, orchestral suite and "impression"; anthems, motets; organ, violin and piano music, and songs.	English.
1888 12 February. Budapest.		**KOLAR, Victor.** Violinist and conductor. Studied under Dvorák at the Prague Conservatorium. Went to America in 1904. Symphony, poem and suite, rhapsody and other orchestral; songs, and violin pieces.	Hungarian.
1888 13 May. Moscow.		**ALEXANDROF, Anatole Nicolaevitch.** Pupil of Taneiev, Vassilenko, and (for piano) Igumnof at the Moscow Conservatory, where he became professor in 1923. Incidental music, string quartet, piano sonatas and preludes, and songs.	Russian.
1888 29 May. Petrograd.		**SHAPOSHNIKOF, Adrian Gregorievitch.** Pupil of Sokolov and Glazounov at the Petrograd Conservatory. Operas, ballets, symphonic-poem, piano sonatina, and songs.	Russian.

Born	Died	Name	Nationality.
1888 26 August. Munich.		**HARBURGER, Walter.** Writer on music. Lives at Munich. Symphony, string quartets, trio ; sonatas for violin and 'cello ; suites, sonatinas, fugues, etc. for piano ; organ works ; Mass, and a Stabat Mater.	German.
1888 18 September Basle.		**HAY, Frederick Charles.** Pupil of Huber at Basle, Widor and Debussy in Paris, and Fuchs in Vienna. Director of the orchestra and the choral concerts at Geneva University, also lecturer on musical history. Symphonic-poem, piano concerto, string quartet, choruses with orchestra and organ, and songs.	Swiss.
1888 6 October. Berlin.		**BUTTING, Max.** Studied under Dreyer (Berlin), Prill, Klose and Courvoisier (Munich). Songs with orchestra, chamber symphonies, 'cello concerto, quintets, string quartets, trio, solo sonatas for violin, etc.	German.
1888 11 October. Zdunska Wola.		**BOHNKE, Emil.** Pupil of Sitt and Krehl at Leipzig, and Gernsheim at Berlin. Conductor of the Symphony orchestra, Leipzig, 1923, and teacher of the viola at the Hochschule, Berlin. Symphonic-overture, violin concerto, piano sonata, and a trio.	Polish.
1888 8 November. Vefsen.		**JOHANSEN, David Monrad.** Studied at the High School, Berlin, under Kahn and Humperdinck. Solo-pianist and critic. Orchestral suite, male chorus, piano suites and pieces, songs (some on Norwegian folk-poems).	Norwegian.
1888 10 December. London.		**WILLIAMS, Gerrard.** Self-taught ; was an architect until 1920. First recital of own works at Æolian Hall, London, in 1922. Opera, ballad-opera, operettas, orchestral and choral works, string quartets, songs and piano works.	English.
1888 20 December. Kalnukai.		**TALAT-KELPŠA, Juozas.** Studied at Ylakiai, Vilna, Petrograd and Berlin. Director of the Music School of Lithuanian Art Producers. Conductor of the Lithuanian Opera which he helped to initiate. Choruses, orchestral suite, music to plays, collections of songs, etc.	Lithuanian.
1889 14 January. Monaco.		**DAVICO, Vincenzo.** Studied at Turin, and at Leipzig under Reger. Operas, including " Dogaressa " ; symphonies, suites, Requiem, etc.	Italian.
1889 3 March. Berlin.		**BEHREND, Fritz.** Studied under Eyken, Rüfer and Humperdinck. Teacher of composition and piano in Berlin. Opera, symphony, ballad for baritone and orchestra, 2 string quartets, songs, etc.	German.
1889 25 May. Bergen.		**JORDAN, Sverre.** Studied in Berlin. Pianist and critic in Bergen. Orchestral suite, incidental music, violin sonata, violin and piano music, and about 60 songs.	Norwegian.

Born	Died	Name	Nationality.
1889 Lemberg.		**JARECKI, Tadeusz.** Son and pupil of Henryk (1846), who also wrote operas, etc. Director of the Chamber Ensemble, New York. Served in the Polish army in France in 1918. Orchestral preludes and sketches, string quartets, trios, piano sonatas, songs with trio accompaniment.	Polish. (Naturalised American.)
1889 Písek.	**1919** Budéjovice.	**JEREMIÁŠ, Jaroslav.** Studied at the Prague Conservatorium under Stecker, and later under Novák. Pianist, teacher and conductor. Symphonic works, opera, play, oratorio, viola sonata, and songs with orchestra.	Bohemian.
1889 10 August. Great Baddow.		**GIBBS, Cecil Armstrong (Mus.D.).** Studied under Vaughan Williams and Adrian Boult at the Royal College. Incidental music, music to plays, comic opera, symphonic-poem, oboe concerto, phantasy and sonata for violin and piano, string quintets, quartets, trio, choruses, many part-songs, and about 50 songs, on words by W. de la Mare.	English.
1889 23 September Liverpool.		**HENRY, Leigh Vaughan.** Influenced by Bantock. Returned to England after being interned in Germany during the War. Lectured in France, Italy, Germany and Russia. Comedy-ballet, choruses, piano music, pieces for flute, clarinet and bassoon, and much musical literature.	English.
1890 27 February. Riga.		**MEDINS, Janis.** Self-taught. 2 Operas, symphony, 'cello concerto, string quartet, trios, violin and piano works, part-songs, and solo songs.	Latvian.
1890 13 April. Hull.		**LEGINSKA, Ethel (proper name Liggins).** Studied at Hoch's Conservatorium, Frankfort-o-M. under Kwast (piano), Sekles and Ivan Knorr (theory); later under Leschetizky. Has given piano recitals since being the age of 7. Symphonic-poem, poems for string quartet, fantasy for small orchestra, songs, and piano pieces.	English.
1890 Bilbao.		**ISASI, Andrés.** Studied at Berlin under Humperdinck. Symphonic-poem, symphonies, string quartets, violin and piano sonatas, German Lieder, etc.	Spanish.
1890 Geneva.		**MARTIN, Frank.** Studied under Jos. Lauber at Geneva. Orchestral suite, pieces for small orchestra, choral works, piano quintet, violin sonata, and many songs.	Swiss.
1890 Polička.		**MARTINU, Bohuslav.** Studied the violin at the Prague Conservatorium and composition with Suk and later with Roussel in Paris. Orchestral works, operas, ballets, quintet, 3 string quartets, piano trio, etc.	Bohemian.
1890 4 July. Lemberg.		**SOLTYS, Adam (Ph.D.).** Studied under his father, and later in Berlin under G. Schumann, Kahn and K. L. Wolf. Also a musicologist and conductor. Symphonies, overtures, violin sonata, piano sonata and pieces, and many songs.	Polish.

Born	Died	Name	Nationality.
1890 12 July. Namur.		**BARBIER, René Auguste Ernest.** Studied at Namur, and at the Liège Conservatoire under Dupuis. Opera, cantata, Mass, concerto for " Hans " piano, violin sonata, and many songs.	Belgian.
1890 5 August. Brünn.		**GAL, Hans.** Pupil of Robert (piano), and Mandyczewski (composition). Teacher of harmony and counterpoint at the Vienna University. Operas, stage music, overtures, symphonic works, choruses, chamber music, songs, and piano pieces.	Moravian.
1890 9 August. Budapest.		**JEMNITZ, Alexander.** Studied at the Budapest High School under Koessler, and at Leipzig under Reger and Straube. Conductor at Czernowitz Municipal Theatre. Orchestral works, string quartets, trio, violin solo-sonata, piano and violin sonatas, organ quartet, organ fugue, etc., 'cello sonata, male and female choruses, and songs.	Hungarian.
1890 28 August. Gloucester.		**GURNEY, Ivor Bertie.** Studied at the Royal College under Stanford, Sharpe, Alcock and Vaughan Williams. " Gloucester Rhapsody," and " War Elegy " for orchestra; string quartets, preludes for piano, songs and a song-cycle on A. E. Housman's works.	English.
1890 11 September Aalesund.		**ALVESTAD, Marius Moaritz.** Studied in Christiania, Germany, France and Italy. Teaches composition at his own established music academy. Orchestral suites, cantatas, choral work, male choruses, 52 songs and ballads, 110 songs for mixed and male chorus, etc.	Norwegian.
1890 16 November. Montet-Coudrefin.		**FORNEROD, Aloys.** Studied violin and composition at Lausanne and Paris. Teacher of counterpoint in the Montreux Conservatoire and at the Institute, Lausanne. 2 Symphonies, choruses, motets, and interludes for organ.	Swiss.
1890 19 November.		**SHENSHIN, Alexander Alexeievitch.** Pupil of Glière and Javorsky. Professor at the Moscow State Conservatory. Music to children's plays, many songs, and piano pieces.	Russian.
1891 9 January. Weissenfels-o-S.		**HOYER, Karl.** Studied at the Leipzig Conservatorium. Organist at Revel Cathedral in 1911, and chief organist of St. James', Chemnitz. Concertino and chaconne for organ and orchestra ; choral works ; double fugue for 2 pianos ; sonatas for organ, and viola ; and many organ and piano pieces.	German.
1891 9 January. Moscow.		**GOLOVANOF, Nicolas Semenovitch.** Studied at the Moscow Conservatory under Vassilenko. Conductor at the Grand Theatre, Moscow, 1919. Operas, symphonies, etc., cantatas, choruses, church-music, and songs.	Russian.

Born	Died	Name	Nationality
1891 11 April. Solnzevo.		**PROKOVIEV, Serge Sergevitch.** Pupil of the Petrograd Conservatory under Liadov, Wihtol and Rimsky-Korsakov (composition), and Mme. Essipof (piano). Lived in Japan and America, now in Germany. Operas, ballet, symphonietta, 2 tone-poems (one choral), 3 piano concertos, 4 sonatas, violin concertos, instrumental pieces, and songs.	Russian.
1891 15 April. Sortavala.		**RAITIO, Väinö.** Studied at Helsingfors Music Institute, and in Moscow. A modern expressionist. Symphony, tone-poems for orchestra, piano concerto, quintet, quartet, violin sonata, and a poem for 'cello and piano.	Finnish.
1891 23 June. Hamburg.		**MORITZ, Edward.** Violinist; studied composition at Paris, and at Berlin under Juon. Symphony, symphony for voice and orchestra, string quartet, violin sonata, piano and violin works, songs, and a choral suite.	German.
1891 Rome.		**CARABELLA, Ezio.** Symphonic works, operettas, etc.	Italian.
1891 Prague.		**JIRÁK, K. Boleslav.** Studied at Prague University under Novák and Foerster. Conductor at the Hamburg Opera, 1915-18. Professor of composition at the Prague Conservatorium in 1920. Opera, 2 symphonies, overture, string sextet and quartet, sonatas for 'cello and violin, Psalm for chorus and orchestra, and song-cycles.	Bohemian.
1891 London.		**MORRIS, Margaret.** Dancer and musical educationist. Produced songs by Ravel, Debussy and Stravinsky, with dance interpretations, 1915. Ballets and songs.	English.
1891 Sydney.		**WENTZEL, Norbert.** Teaches at Sydney. Orchestral works, cantata, string quartets, viola sonata, songs, and part-songs.	Australian.
1891 2 August. London.		**BLISS, Arthur.** Studied at the Royal College under Stanford and Vaughan Williams. Professor at the Royal College, 1920-23. Symphony, string quartet, songs with various instrumental accompaniments, etc.	English.
1891 8 August. Siegen.		**BUSCH, Adolf.** Brother of Fritz. Pupil at Cologne Conservatorium. Toured as solo-violinist and quartet leader. Succeeded Marteau at the Hochschule, Berlin. Now lives in England. Symphony, overture, choral, violin concerto, sonatas, 'cello sonata, fugues for violin and 'cello, piano variations, organ fantasy, and songs.	German.
1891 13 October. Nuremberg.		**WEBER, Ludwig.** Mostly self-taught. Symphony, chorus with orchestra, unaccompanied choruses, string quartets, quintet, opera, piano pieces, organ pieces and songs.	German.

Born	Died	Name	Nationality
1891 22 October. Josefsthal.		**FINKE, Fidelio.** Pupil of Novák at Prague. Professor at the German Academy of Music and Art at Prague, and director of the School of Composers. Poetic symphony, operatic fragment, suite for string orchestra, orchestral song-cycle, quintet, quartet, 7 trios, and songs.	Bohemian.
1892 4 February. Helsingfors.		**KILPINEN, Yrjö.** Studied in Helsingfors, Vienna and Berlin. Many songs on poems of Finnish, Danish and Swedish writers.	Finnish.
1892 10 March. Le Havre.		**HONEGGER, Arthur.** One of the " Group of Six " French composers. Pupil of Gédalge and Widor in Paris. His works, which are atonal, are constructed contrapuntally. Oratorio, orchestral pieces, incidental music, string quartets ; sonatas for violin, viola and 'cello ; pieces for woodwind, piano music, and songs.	French.
1892 19 March. Zurich.		**DENZLER, Robert F.** Pupil of Andreae. Conductor at Lucerne and Zurich. Symphonic-poems, suite for 2 violins, and songs.	Swiss.
1892 19 April. Pau St.-Maur n'r Paris.		**TAILLEFÈRE, Germaine.** One of the " Group of Six " French composers. Studied at the Paris Conservatoire. Ballets, " Ballade " for piano and orchestra, quartet, violin sonata, etc.	French.
1892 21 April. Fryštát.		**KVAPIL, Jaroslav.** Pupil of Janácek and of Max Reger at Leipzig. Professor of piano and composition at Brno Conservatorium. Conductor of the choir of the Philharmonic Society. 2 Symphonies, orchestral variations, quintets, quartets, sonatas for violin, 'cello and piano, song and piano cycles.	Moravian.
1892 28 April. Liège.	1918 15 November. Bruges.	**ANTOINE, Georges.** Studied at Liège Conservatoire. Served in the Belgian army all through the war. Poem for orchestra, piano concerto, quartets, and songs.	Belgian.
1892 21 June. Bosjökloster.		**ROSENBERG, Hilding C.** Pupil of Anderson (piano), also at Stockholm and Dresden Conservatories. A modern expressionist. Symphony, phantasy-pieces, variations for orchestra, piano concerto, violin solo-sonata, string quartet ; trio for flute, violin and viola ; also songs.	Swedish.
1892 Bergen.		**MORCMAN, Oscar.** Developed his musical gifts unaided. Symphonic overture, and symphonic-poem.	Norwegian.
1892 Moscow.		**OBUKHOF, Nicolas.** *Invented a new system of notation ; abandoning the use of sharps and flats ; ascribing new names for the sounds of the " black " notes.* Studied at the Petrograd Conservatory, and under Ravel in Paris. A vast oratorio in several parts, on texts by Balmont, " The Book of Life."	Russian.

Born	Died	Name	Nationality.
1892 Prague.		**ZITEK, Otakar.** Studied at Prague and Vienna. Operatic producer at National Theatre at Brno, 1921, and teacher at the Conservatorium there. Operas and song collections.	Bohemian.
1892 Aarau.		**WEHRLI, Werner.** Studied at Zurich and Frankfort Conservatories under Kemptner, Hegar and Ivan Knorr. Fantasy for orchestra, comic opera, string quartets, a trio, many songs, etc.	Swiss.
1892 6 July. Oldenburg.		**ROTERS, Ernst.** Pupil of Meyer-Mahr (piano) and Georg Schumann (composition). Conductor at Hamburg Chamber-Plays. An Oratorio, symphony (orchestra, soli and chorus); symphonic-suite for piano and orchestra, chamber-symphony, dance-rhapsody for orchestra, string quartet, trio, piano suite, songs, etc.	German.
1892 26 July. Noisy.		**JARNACH, Philipp.** Studied at Nice and Paris. Teacher at Zurich Conservatorium, 1918, and in Berlin in 1921. Sinfoniettas and other orchestral works, string quartet, ballad and sonata for violin and piano, solo violin sonata, flute sonata, choruses, and songs.	French.
1892 4 September. Aix-en-Provence.		**MILHAUD, Darius.** One of the " Group of Six " French composers. Studied at the Paris Conservatoire under Gédalge. Several lyric dramas, symphonic works, 5 quartets; pieces for violin, piano and for wind instruments; and an opera, " Christopher Columbus."	French.
1892 17 October. Lydney, Glos.		**HOWELLS, Herbert.** Studied under Stanford, Parratt (organ), Parry, Walford Davies, and C. Wood at the Royal College; appointed to the Staff there in 1920. Piano concertos, several string quartets, sonatas for organ, violin and piano; orchestral works, choruses, anthems, part-songs, songs, and other various works.	English.
1893 29 January London.		**CUNDELL, Edric.** Studied at Trinity College; later teacher there. Horn-player and pianist. Conductor of the Westminster Orchestral Society since 1920. Symphonic-poem, suite, sonnet and poem; piano quartet, many songs, and piano pieces.	English.
1893 26 May. London.		**GOOSSENS, Eugène.** Son of namesake (1867). Studied at Bruges, Liverpool, and the Royal College, London, under Stanford, Wood, Rivarde, and Dykes. Conducted the British National and the Carl Rosa Opera Companies, the London Symphony Orchestra, etc. Symphonic music, choruses, piano quintet, quartets, violin sonata; suite for flute, violin and harp; pieces for violin, 'cello and piano; songs, and a ballet.	English.

Born	Died	Name	Nationality.
1893 June. Astizárraga.		**ARMANDOZ, Norberto.** Organist of Seville Cathedral in 1920. Church music, Basque folk-song arrangements, etc.	Spanish.
1893 21 June. Vyzovice.		**HÁBA, Alois.** Studied at the Prague Conservatorium under Novák; later at Vienna and Berlin. Uses quarter-tones melodically and harmonically. Symphonic-music for chamber orchestra, symphonic-phantasy for piano and orchestra, 3 string quartets, violin solo, piano sonata, and pieces in quarter-tones for harmonium.	Moravian.
1893 29 June. Helsingfors.		**MERIKANTO, Aarre.** Son of Oskar (1868). Studied at Leipzig Conservatorium, and later at Moscow. 2 Symphonies, symphonic-poems, piano concerto, etc.	Finnish.
1893 Hastings.		**COLLINS, Anthony Vincett.** Studied at the Royal College. Principal violanist of the London Symphony Orchestra. Operas, ballets, chamber-music, and many songs.	English.
1893 14 August. Bucharest.		**ALESSANDRESCU, Alfred** Studied at the Bucharest Conservatory, and later at Paris. Conductor at Bucharest Opera House from 1921. Symphonic-poem, overture, "songs" for violin and piano.	**Rumanian.**
1893 18 September Sydney.		**BENJAMIN, Arthur.** Studied at the Royal College under Stanford (composition) and Cliffe (piano). Professor of the piano at the State Conservatory, Sydney. Operas, orchestral works, violin concerto, piano concertino and suite, string quartet, violin sonata, songs, etc.	Australian.
1894 13 January. Moscow.		**EVSEIEF, Serge Vassilievitch.** Studied at the Moscow Conservatory, where he became teacher of theory in 1922. Symphony, poem, trio, piano sonata, Russian folk-songs, etc.	Russian.
1894 8 June. Prague.		**SCHULHOFF, Erwin.** Studied in Vienna, Leipzig, Cologne and Berlin. Pianist. His works are expressionistic; resembling Schönberg and Stravinsky. Symphony, overture, suite for chamber orchestra; piano concerto, sonatas, duets, etc.; violin sonata and suite; string quartet, 'cello sonata, songs, etc.	Bohemian.
1894 Toulouse.		**VAURABOURG, Andrée.** Studied at Toulouse, and later at the Paris Conservatoire under Boulanger, Caussade and Widor. One of the modern revolutionary composers. As a pianist she specialises in modern music. Orchestral works, quartet, violin sonata, piano pieces, and songs.	French.
1894 13 July. Mulhouse.	1918 17 December. Tübingen.	**BIENSTOCK, Heinrich.** Pupil of Haeser and Huber at Basle. Operas.	German.

Born.	Died.	Name.	Nationality.
1894 28 July. Barcelona.		**GRANADOS, Eduardo.** Studied at the Academy founded by his father, Enrique (1867), and afterwards under del Campo at Madrid. Director of the Granadas Academy, 1916-19. Several zarzuelas (operettas), incidental music, orchestral works, violin and piano pieces.	Spanish.
1894 8 September. Zeist.		**PIJPER, Willem.** Studied under Mme. Lunteren (piano) and Wagenaar (theory). Critic, and conductor. Teacher of harmony at the Amsterdam School of Music. Symphonies, melodrama, string quartets, trios, septet for wind, violin sonatas, 'cello sonata, songs with orchestra and with piano.	Dutch.
1894 30 October.	**1930** 17 December.	**WARLOCK, Peter (proper name Philip Heseltine).** Studied under C. Taylor at Eton, and later under Delius and van Dieren. Carnegie award 1923. Many excellent songs and song cycles; unaccompanied choruses, serenade for string orchestra; also books — " Delius " and " The English Ayre."	English.
1894 6 November. London.		**ERLEBACH, Rupert.** Studied at the Royal College under Stanford, Vaughan Williams and F. Taylor. Orchestral works, 'cello sonata, string quartet, Legends for violin and piano, folk-song suite, songs, choruses, etc.	English.
1894 31 December. Osterley, n'r London.		**MOERAN, Ernest John.** Studied for a short time at the Royal College. A collector of folk-songs. Rhapsody and a symphonic impression for orchestra, string quartets, trios, violin sonatas, piano pieces and many songs.	English.
1895 3 March. Rotterdam.		**VOORMOLEN, Alex.** Studied under Wagenaar in Holland, and Ravel, Roussel and Rhené-Baton in Paris. Lives at the Hague. His works are influenced by French Impressionism. Many piano works, violin and 'cello sonatas, orchestral works, quartet, trio, 30 songs to French and Dutch words, etc.	Dutch.
1895 3 April. Florence.		**CASTELNUOVO-TEDESCO, Mario.** Studied at the Cherubini Institute, Florence, under Del Valle (piano) and Pizzetti (composition). Orchestral; violin and piano, and violin and orchestral; piano pieces; madrigals, and songs on words by Shakespeare.	Italian.
1895 1 May. Grand Rapids, Mich.		**SOWERBY, Leo.** Studied at the American Conservatory under Lampert and Grainger (piano), and Anderson (theory). Teacher at the American Conservatory, Chicago. Overtures, tone-poem, piano concerto, 'cello concerto, string quartet, violin suite and concerto.	American.

Born.	Died.	Name.	Nationality.
1895 Seville.		**FONT Y DE ANTA, Manuel.** Studied under Turina at Madrid, and Sibelius in America. Toured South America as conductor. Noted for his many numbers of Spanish songs, called *cuplés*. Symphonic-variations, etc.; choral works with orchestra, suite for piano, sonata for violin and piano, light operas, popular songs, marches, etc.	Spanish.
1895 5 July. London.		**JACOB, Gordon (Mus.D.).** Studied at the Royal College, where he became professor of composition, harmony and counterpoint, 1925. Lecturer at Birkbeck College (University of London) 1934. Ballets, symphony, violin concerto, piano concerto, oboe concerto, string quartets, songs, part-songs and didactic works.	English.
1895 14 August. Essex.		**SORABJI, Kaikhosru.** Mostly self-taught. Compositions of great length and difficulty. Piano concertos, sonatas, quintet; symphony for piano and orchestra, chorus and organ; songs to poems by Baudelaire and Verlaine.	English. (Parsi father.)
1895 8 October. Osby.		**DAHL, Viking.** Studied at the Conservatoriums of Malmö and Stockholm, and later in London and Paris under Ravel. Orchestral works, ballet, string quartet, trio, piece for oboe and orchestra, violin suite, songs and piano pieces.	Swedish.
1895 16 November. Hanau.		**HINDEMITH, Paul.** Studied at the Hoch Conservatorium, Frankfort-on-M. Chief conductor at the Opera House, Frankfort, from 1905. 3 Operas; many quintets and quartets for strings, and some for other various instruments; sonatas for violin, viola and 'cello respectively, ballad-cycle, etc.	German.
1895 25 November. Jüterbock.		**KEMPFF, Wilhelm.** Studied under Barth and Kahn at the Hochschule, Berlin. A famous improvisor. Symphony, overture, suite, piano concerto, choruses, violin sonata, piano sonata, variations, etc., and songs.	German.
1895 11 December. Krementchug		**ORNSTEIN, Leo.** Solo-pianist. Visited London in 1914 and New York, 1915. Studied at Petrograd Conservatory, and in 1906 went to New York, studying piano under Mrs. Tapper. Symphonic-poem, suite, piano concerto, violin and a 'cello sonata, songs, and all forms of piano works. About 100 works.	Russian.
1896 5 March. Wenden.		**ERDMANN, Eduard.** Pianist; studied at Riga and Berlin. Symphony, Rondo for orchestra, solo violin sonata, piano pieces, and songs.	German.
1896 16 March. Metz.		**ZOELLNER, Richard.** Son of Heinrich (1854). Studied under Rau and Graener. Orchestral works, chamber-symphony, sacred pieces for string quartet, quintet, and songs.	German.

Born.	Died.	Name.	Nationality.
1896 Prague.		**WEINBERGER, Jaromir.** Pupil of Kricka and Hofmeister. Professor of composition at the Conservatory at Ithaca, U.S.A. Orchestral works, pantomime, piano sonata, and pieces.	Bohemian.
1896 Vals.		**GERHARD, Robert.** Pupil of F. Pedrell. 2 Piano trios, works for voice and piano, piano pieces.	Spanish. (Swiss descent.)
1897 29 May. Brünn.		**KORNGOLD, Erich Wolfgang.** Pupil of Fuchs and Zemlinsky. Conducted many of his own works. Now devoted entirely to composition in Vienna. 3 Operas, symphonic overture, symphonietta, string sextet, quartet, piano sonatas and pieces, quintet, trio, violin sonata, etc.	Moravian.
1898 25 February. Handsworth.		**HOWELL, Dorothy.** Studied under Matthay (piano) and McEwen (composition), at the Royal Academy, there becoming professor of harmony and composition in 1924. Symphonic-poem, orchestral ballet, overture, piano concerto, string quartet, violin sonata, piano solos, and songs.	English.
1898 Paris.		**LAZARUS, Daniel.** Studied at the Paris Conservatoire. Symphonic-poem, fantasy for 'cello and orchestra, violin sonata, piano preludes, and 3 ballets.	French.
1898 12 September Madrid.		**BACARISSE CHINORIA, Salvador.** Studied under Conrado del Campo at the Royal Conservatory, Madrid. Symphonic-poem, 2 nocturnes for violin and orchestra, piano pieces, etc.	Spanish.
1899 7 January. Paris.		**POULENC, Francis.** One of the French " Six " composers. Orchestral and piano music, a ballet, and songs.	French.
1899 8 January. Petrograd.		**TCHEREPNIN, Alexander Nicholaievitch.** Son of Nicolas (1873). Pupil of his father, Liadof and Sokolof (composition), and Mme. Essipof ; later in Paris under Gédalge. Ballet, overture, piano concerto, violin sonata, piano suite, and other pieces.	Russian.
1899 15 February. Lodève.		**AURIC, Georges.** Pupil of Caussade at the Paris Conservatoire, and of d'Indy. One of the French " Six " composers. Theatrical, orchestral, piano works, and songs.	French.
1899 5 March. Cambridge.		**HADLEY, Patrick Arthur Sheldon.** Studied under Wood and Rootham at Cambridge, and Vaughan Williams and Morris at the Royal College, London. Teacher at the Royal College since 1925. " The Trees so High," for full orchestra, chorus and baritone solo ; " La Belle Dame sans Merci " for tenor solo, chorus and orchestra ; songs with chamber orchestra ; string quartet ; etc.	English.
1899 26 March. Horbury, Yorks.	**1922** 6 November. York.	**BAINES, William.** Mostly self-taught. Chamber music, 'cello pieces, many songs, piano pieces and sonata.	English.

Born.	Died.	Name.	Nationality.
1900 Trondhjem.		**KLEVEN, Arvid.** Studied under Lange, and later in Paris. Flautist in the Philharmonic Orchestra, Christiania. Poems for orchestra, and for violin with orchestra.	Norwegian.
1900 Vienna.		**KŘENEK, Arnost (Ernest).** Studied at Berlin and Vienna under F. Schreker. 3 Symphonies, symphonic music for 9 solo instruments, dramatic cantata, 2 string quartets, violin and piano sonatas, ballet, etc.	Austrian.
1901 21 April. Madrid.		**BAUTISTA, Julián.** Pupil of Conrado del Campo. Lyric drama, ballet, orchestral, and violin and piano works.	Spanish.
1902 21 February. Gelsenkirchen		**PETERS, Rudolf.** Pupil of his father, of Grüters at Bonn, and of Pauer and Haas at Stuttgart. Violin sonata, 'cello sonata, string quartet, fantasias and characteristic pieces for piano.	German.
1902 29 March. Oldham.		**WALTON, William Turner.** Studied under Hugh Allen and E. J. Dent. Symphony in 4 movements, overture, string quartets, viola concerto, ballet, toccata for violin and piano, songs, etc., and much music in M.S.	English.
1903 21 February. Manchester.		**FOGG, Eric.** Studied under Granville Bantock. Music-director Empire Service, B.B.C. String quartet, concerto for bassoon, poem and phantasy for 'cello and piano, part-songs, song cycle, piano pieces; works for small orchestra, and chorus and orchestra, etc.	English.
1905 16 January. Madrid.		**HALFTER ESCRICHE, Ernesto.** Pupil of Salazar, Esplá and Falla. Also a brother, Rodolfo, born 1900. Orchestral pieces, string quartet; pieces for violin, 'cello and piano respectively.	Spanish.
1905 London.		**LAMBERT, Constant.** Studied at the Royal College. Conductor of important concerts in London and for the B.B.C. Orchestral works, piano concerto accompanied by 10 instruments, piano sonata, and arrangements of old music.	English.
1905 Northampton		**ALWYN, William.** Studied at the Royal Academy, where he is now professor of composition. Overture, serenade for orchestra, piano concerto, string quartets, oboe sonata, songs for tenor and string quartet, chamber-music, and many piano pieces.	English.
1907 19 March. Hertford- shire.		**MACONCHY, Elizabeth.** Studied under Charles Wood and Vaughan Williams at the Royal College, London, and also in Prague. Orchestral suite " The Land," piano concerto, suite for chamber orchestra, 2 string quartets, quintet for oboe and strings, pieces for 2 violins (unaccompanied) and a viola concerto.	English. (Irish descent.)

Born.	Died.	Name.	Nationality.
1909 11 May. London.		**MURRILL, Herbert Henry John, M.A., Mus.B.** Studied at the Royal Academy, where he became professor of composition in 1933. Organist at Christ Church, Lancaster Gate, 1931, and at St. Thomas's, Regent Street, London, 1932. Opera, ballets, orchestral works, 'cello concerto, piano solos, 'cello solo, clarinet solo, Pastoral and Caprice for piano and string quartet, songs and music to a picture film.	English.
1909 Stoke Newington. London.		**PERKIN, Helen.** Studied at the Royal College under A. Webern. Solo-pianist. "Pastoral Movement for Septet;" Trio for violin, 'cello and piano; "Spring Rhapsody" for violin and piano; and "Preludes" for piano solos.	English.
1912 Le Mans.		**FRANÇAIX, Jean.** Studied at the Paris Conservatoire under Nadia Boulanger. Symphony, piano concertino, suite for violin and piano, and 2 ballets, " Beach " and " School Ballet."	French.
1913 22 November. Lowestoft.		**BRITTEN, Benjamin.** Studied at the Royal College under John Ireland and A. Benjamin. Sinfonietta, Phantasy, Te Deum, Simple Symphony, suite for string quartet, suite for violin and piano, part-songs, etc.	English.

Volume 2.

INDEX

1810 - 1913.

ALPHABETICAL INDEX.

A

B

159

ALPHABETICAL INDEX.—*Continued.*

	Born
Duparc, M. E. H. F. ...	1848
Dupont, A.	1827
Duncan, W. E.	1866
Dunhill, T. F.	1877
Duvernoy, V. A.	1842
Dvorák, A.	1841
Dykes, Rev. J. B.	1823
Dykes, J. St. O.	1863

E

	Born
Eckert, C. A. F.	1820
Eddy, H. C.	1851
Edwards, H. J.	1854
Eeden, J. B. van den ...	1842
Eggen, A.	1881
Ehlert, L.	1825
Ehrenburg, C. E. Th. ...	1878
Eichberg, J.	1824
Elgar, Sir E.	1857
Ellberg, E. H.	1868
Ellicott, R. F.	1857
Elling, C.	1858
Elvey, Sir G. J.	1816
Enna, A.	1860
Erb, J. M.	1860
Erdmann, E.	1896
Eriksson, J.	1872
Erkel, F.	1810
Erlanger, C.	1863
Erlebach, R.	1894
Ernst, H. W.	1814
Ertel, J. P.	1865
Esplá, O.	1886
Esposito, M.	1855
Esser, H.	1818
Ettinger, Max. ...	1874
Evans, D.	1874
Evers, C.	1819
Evseief, S. V.	1894
Eyken, H.	1861
Eysler, E.	1874

F

	Born
Faccio, F.	1840
Fährmann, E. H.	1860
Fairchild, B.	1877
Faisst, I. G. F.	1823
Falchi, S.	1851
Faleni, A.	1877
Fall, L.	1873
Falla, M. de	1876
Faltin, R.	1835
Fanelli, E.	1860
Faning, E.	1850

	Born
Fano, G. A.	1875
Farjeon, H.	1878
Farmer, J.	1836
Farrar, E. B.	1885
Farwell, A.	1872
Fassbänder, P.	1869
Fauré, G. U.	1845
Ferroni, V.	1858
Fesca, A. E.	1820
Fibich, Z.	1850
Fiebach, O.	1851
Fielitz, A. Von	1860
Filippi, F.	1830
Filke, M.	1855
Fink, C.	1831
Finke, F.	1891
Fino, G.	1867
Fitelberg, G.	1879
Fitzwilliam, E. F.	1824
Flood, W. H. G.	1859
Floridia, P.	1860
Flotow, F. F. von	1812
Flowers, G. F.	1811
Foerster, J. B.	1859
Fogg, E.	1903
Folville, J.	1870
Font y de Anta, M.	1895
Foote, A. W.	1853
Ford, E.	1858
Fornerod, A.	1890
Forrester, J. C.	1860
Foster, M. B.	1851
Foster, S. C.	1826
Foulds, J. H.	1880
Françaix, J.	1912
Franchetti, A.	1860
Franck, C.	1822
Franck, R.	1858
Frank, E.	1847
Franz, R.	1815
Fried, O.	1871
Friedman, I.	1882
Friskin, J.	1886
Fryklöf, H. L.	1882
Fuchs, R.	1847
Fumagalli, A.	1828
Fumagalli, L.	1837

G

	Born
Gabriel, M. A. V.	1825
Gade, A.	1860
Gade, N. W.	1817
Gadsby, H.	1842
Gagnebin, H.	1886
Gaito, C.	1878
Gál, H.	1890

160

ALPHABETICAL INDEX.—*Continued.*

	Born
Galitzin, Prince George ...	1823
Gall, J.	1856
Gallignani, G.	1851
Gallotti, S.	1856
Ganz, R.	1877
Gardiner, H. B.	1877
Garratt, P.	1877
Garrett, Dr. G. M.	1834
Gatty, N. C.	1874
Gaul, A. R.	1837
Gédalge, A.	1856
Geehl, H. E.	1881
Geisler, P.	1856
Genée, F. F. R.	1823
Georges, A.	1850
Gerhard, R.	1896
Gericke, W.	1845
German, Sir J. E.	1862
Gernsheim, F.	1839
Gevaërt, F. A.	1828
Gibbs, C. A.	1889
Gigout, E.	1844
Gilbert, H. F. B.	1868
Gilbert J.	1879
Gilse, J. van	1881
Gilson, P.	1865
Giordano, U.	1863
Gladstone, Dr. F. E. ...	1845
Gläser, P.	1871
Glass, L. C. A.	1864
Glazounov, A. C.	1865
Gleason, F. G.	1848
Glenck, H. von	1883
Glière, R. M.	1874
Glover, J. W.	1815
Glover, S. R.	1812
Godard, B. L. P.	1849
Godefroid, D. J. G. F. ...	1818
Godefroid, J. J.	1811
Godowsky, L.	1870
Goedicke, A. F.	1877
Goetz, H.	1840
Goldmark, C.	1830
Goldmark, R.	1872
Goldschmidt, A. von ...	1848
Goldschmidt, O.	1829
Golinelli, S.	1818
Gollmick, A.	1825
Golovanof, N. S.	1891
Goltermann, G. E.	1824
Gomez, A. C.	1839
Gompertz, R.	1859
Goossens, E.	1893
Goovaerts, A. J. M. A. ...	1847
Gottschalk, L. M.	1829
Gounod, C. F.	1818
Gouvy, L. T.	1819
Grädener, C. G. P.	1812

	Born
Grädener, H. T. O.	1844
Graener, P.	1872
Grainger, G. P.	1882
Granados Campina, E. ...	1867
Granados, E.	1894
Gray, A.	1855
Greatheed, Rev. S. S. ...	1813
Grechaninov, A. T.	1864
Gregoir, E. G. J.	1822
Gregoir, J. M. J.	1817
Grieg, E. H.	1843
Grimm, J. O.	1827
Grovlez, G.	1879
Guglielmi, F.	1859
Guilmant, F. A.	1837
Guiraud, E.	1837
Gung'l, J.	1810
Guridi, J.	1886
Gurlitt, C.	1820
Gurney, I. B.	1890
Gutmann, A.	1819

H

	Born
Haarklou, J.	1847
Haas, J.	1879
Hába, A.	1893
Haberbier, E.	1813
Hadley, H. K.	1871
Hadley, P. A. S.	1899
Hadow, Sir W. H.	1859
Hägg, J.	1850
Hahn, R.	1874
Hâkanson, K. A.	1887
Halfter Escriche, E.	1905
Hallén, J. A.	1846
Halvorsen, J.	1864
Hamerik, A.	1843
Hansen, R. E.	1860
Harburger, W.	1888
Harris, C. H. G.	1871
Harrison, J.	1885
Hartmann, E.	1836
Harty, Sir H. H.	1879
Harwood, B.	1859
Hasse, K.	1883
Hauer, J. M.	1883
Haug, G.	1871
Hauser, M.	1820 or 22
Hay, F. C.	1888
Haydon, C. M.	1884
Haynes, W. B.	1859
Hazlehurst, C.	1880
Heap, C. S.	1847
Heath, J. R.	1887
Hecht, E.	1832
Hegar, F.	1841

ALPHABETICAL INDEX.—*Continued.*

ERRATA OF VOLUME I.

Page 31   Tunder,—for Frecobaldi read Frescobaldi.

   „   42   Perti,—for Benidict read Benedict.

   „   61   Gluck,—for Puccinn read Piccinni.

   „   113   for Lindpainter read Linpaintner, also in Alp. Index.

   „   127   Balfe,—for Michaei read Michael.

VOLUME II.

Ashton, A. B. L.	... Died	10 May, 1937.
Cliffe, F. ...	... „	19 November, 1931, London.
Edwards, H. J.	... „	8 April, 1933, Barnstaple.
Gray, Alan	... „	27 September, 1935, Cambridge.
Hadow, W. H.	... „	April, 1937.
Hillemacher, P.	... „	13 August, 1933, Versailles.
Hubay, J.	... „	March, 1937, Budapest.
Mathieu, E.	... „	September, 1932, Ghent.
Mendelssohn, A.	... „	15 March, 1933, Darmstadt.
Nielsen, C. A.	... „	October, 1931, Copenhagen.
Röntgen, J.	... „	13 September, 1932, Utrecht.
Somervell, A.	... „	3 May, 1937.
Widor, C. M.	... „	12 March, 1937, Paris.

444 N

Printed in England
by
The Nutnall Press,
Belbroughton, Worcestershire